We of the
Never-Never

We of the
Never-Never

MRS AENEAS GUNN

HUTCHINSON OF AUSTRALIA

HUTCHINSON GROUP (Australia) Pty Ltd
30–32 Cremorne Street, Richmond, Victoria, 3121

London Melbourne Sydney Auckland
Wellington Johannesburg Cape Town
and agencies throughout the world

First published 1908
Reprinted 1962, 1963, 1964,
1966, 1969, 1971, 1974, 1977, 1979, 1981 (twice), 1982 (twice)

Jacket design by Barbara Beckett
Filmset by T.P. Graphic Arts Services Hong Kong
Printed by Dai Nippon Printing Co. (Hong Kong) Ltd

National Library of Australia Cataloguing in Publication Data

Gunn, Jeannie, 1870–1961.
We of the Never Never.

First published, London 1908.
ISBN 0 09 047093 1.

I. Title.

A823.2

Dedicated to
THE BUSH-FOLK OF
THE NEVER-NEVER

To the Public

It is with the full consent of the bush-folk that this one year of their lives—the year 1902—is given to the world.

"Tell them anything you like," they said, one and all, unconsciously testifying to their single-heartedness. And in the telling I have striven to give that year as I found it.

At every turn the bush-folk have helped me; verifying statements and furnishing details required with minute exactness.

JEANNIE GUNN

Hawthorn
October 1907

Prelude

We—are just some of the bush-folk of the Never-Never. Distinct in the foreground stand:

The Maluka, The Little Missus, The Sanguine Scot, The Head Stockman, The Dandy, The Quiet Stockman, The Fizzer, Mine Host, The Wag, Some of our Guests, A few black "boys" and lubras, A dog or two, Tam-o'-shanter, Happy Dick, Sam Lee, and last, but by no means least, Cheon—the ever-mirthful, ever-helpful, irrepressible Cheon, who was crudely recorded on the station books as cook and gardener.

The background is filled in with an ever-moving company— a strange medley of Whites, Blacks, and Chinese; of travellers, overlanders, and billabongers, who passed in and out of our lives, leaving behind them sometimes bright memories, some-times sad, and sometimes little memory at all.

And All of Us, and many of this company, shared each other's lives for one bright, sunny year, away Behind the Back of Beyond, in the Land of the Never-Never; in that elusive land with an elusive name—a land of dangers and hardships and privations yet loved as few lands are loved—a land that . bewitches her people with strange spells and mysteries, until they call sweet bitter, and bitter sweet. Called the Never-Never, the Maluka loved to say, because they who have lived in it and loved it, Never-Never voluntarily leave it. Sadly enough, there are too many who Never-Never do leave it. Others— the unfitted—will tell you that it is so called because they who succeed in getting out of it swear they will Never-Never return to it. But we who have lived in it, and loved it, and left it, know that our hearts can Never-Never rest away from it.

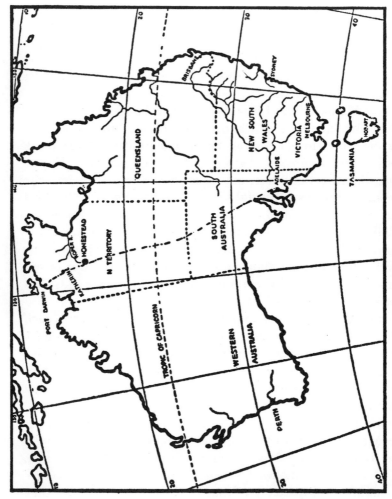

Map showing position of Roper River and the Homestead

I

To begin somewhere near the beginning, the Maluka—better known at that time as the new Boss for the Elsey—and I, his "missus", were at Darwin, in the Northern Territory, waiting for the train that was to take us just as far as it could—one hundred and fifty miles—on our way to the Never-Never. It was out of town just then, up-country somewhere, billabonging in true bush-whacker style, but was expected to return in a day or two, when it would be at our service.

Jack, the Quiet Stockman, was out at the homestead, "seeing to things" there. The Sanguine Scot, the Head Stockman, and the Dandy were in at the Katherine, marking time, as it were, awaiting instructions by wire from the Maluka, while some of the Company "put finishing touches" to their New Year celebrations. And everyone, with, of course, the exception of those in Darwin, was blissfully unconscious of even the existence of the Maluka's missus.

Knowing the Maluka by repute, however, everyone was agreed that the "Elsey had struck it lucky", until the telegraph wire, whispering the gossip of Darwin to the Katherine, whispered that the "new Boss for the Elsey had been and gone and married a missus just before leaving the South, and was bringing her along with him". Then the Sanguine Scot was filled with wrath, the Company with compassion, while the Dandy's consternation found relief in a dismayed "Heavens above!" (The Dandy, by the way, was only a dandy in his love of sweet, clean clothes and orderly surroundings. The

heart of the man had not a touch of dandyism in it.) The Head
Stockman was absent in his camp. Had he been present, much
might have been said on the "advantages of having a woman
about the place". The Wag, however, retained his usual flow
of speech and spirits.

"Buck up, chaps!" he chuckled encouragingly. "They're not
all snorters, you know. You might have the luck to strike one
of the 'ministering angel' variety."

But the Sanguine Scot had been thinking rapidly, and, with
characteristic hopefulness, felt he had the bull by the horns.
"We'll just have to block her, chaps; that's all," he said. "A
wire or two should do it"; and inviting the Dandy "to come
and lend a hand", led the way to the telegraph office; and
presently there quivered into Darwin the first hint that a
missus was not wanted at the Elsey.

"Would advise leaving wife behind till homestead can be
repaired," it said; and, still confident of success, Mac felt that
"ought to do the trick". "If it doesn't," he added, "we'll give
her something stronger."

We in Darwin, having exhausted the sight-seeing resources
of the little town, were wishing "something interesting would
happen", when the message was handed to the Maluka.

"This may do as a stopgap," he said, opening it, adding
as he read it, "It looks brim full of possibilities for interested
onlookers, seeing it advises leaving the wife behind." The
Maluka spoke from experience, having been himself an
interested onlooker "down South", when it had been suggested
there that the wife should be left behind while he spied out
the land; for although the Maluka knew most of the Territory,
he had not yet been to the Elsey Cattle Station.

Preferring to be "the interested onlooker" myself this time,
when we went to the telegraph office it was the Maluka who
wired: "Wife coming, secure buggy"; and in an incredibly
short space of time the answer was back: "No buggy obtainable."

Darwin looked interested. "Mac hasn't wasted much time
in making inquiries," it said.

"Or in apologies or explanations," the Maluka added

shortly, and sent in reply:

"Wife can ride, secure suitable mount."

But the Sanguine Scot's fighting blood was up, and almost immediately the wire rapped out:

"No side-saddle obtainable. Stock horses all flash"; and the onlookers stared in astonishment.

"Mac's in deadly earnest this time," they said, and the Maluka, with a quiet "So am I," went back to the telegraph.

Now, in the Territory everybody knows everybody else, but particularly the telegraph people; and it often happens that when telegrams of general interest are passing through, they are accompanied by confidential asides—little scraps of harmless gossip not intended for the departmental books; therefore it was whispered in the tail of the last message that the Katherine was watching the fight with interest, was inclined to "reckon the missus a goer", and that public sympathy was with the stockman—the Katherine had its women-folk, and was thankful; but the Katherine knew that although a woman in a settlement only rules her husband's home, the wife of a station-manager holds the peace and comfort of the stockmen in the hollow of her hand.

"Stock horses all flash," the Sanguine Scot said, and then went out and apologized to an old bay horse. "We had to settle her hash somehow, Roper, old chap," he said, stroking the beautiful neck, adding tenderly as the grand old head nosed into him: "You silly old fool! You'd carry her like a lamb if I let you."

Then the Maluka's reply came and Mac whistled in amazement. "By George!" he said to those near him, "she *is* a goer, a regular goer"; and after much careful thought wired an inane suggestion about waiting until after the Wet.

Darwin laughed outright, and an emphatic "Wife determined, coming Tuesday's train", from the Maluka, was followed by a complete breakdown at the Katherine.

Then Darwin came in twos and threes to discuss the situation, and while the men offered every form of service and encouragement, the women-folk spoke of a woman "going bush" as "sheer madness". "Besides, no woman travels during the Wet," they said, and the Maluka "hoped she would prove the exception".

"But she'll be bored to death if she does reach the homestead alive," they prophesied; and I told them they were not very complimentary to the Maluka.

"You don't understand," they hastened to explain. "He'll be camping out most of his time, miles away from the homestead," and I said "So will I."

"So you think," they corrected. "But you'll find that a woman alone in a camp of men is decidedly out of place"; and I felt severely snubbed.

The Maluka suggested that he might yet succeed in persuading some suitable woman to come out with us, as maid or companion; but the opposition, wagging wise heads, pursed incredulous lips as it declared that "no one but a fool would go out there for either love or money". A prophecy that came true, for eventually we went "bush" womanless.

The Maluka's eyes twinkled as he listened. "Does the cap fit, little 'un?" he asked; but the women-folk told him that it was not a matter for joking.

"Do you know there is not another white woman within a hundred-mile radius?" they asked; and the Maluka pointed out that it was not all disadvantage for a woman to be alone in a world of men. "The men who form her world are generally better and truer men, because the woman in their midst is dependent on them alone, for companionship, and love and protecting care," he assured them.

"Men are selfish brutes," the opposition declared, rather irrelevantly, looking pointedly at the Maluka.

He smiled with as much deference as he could command. "Also," he said, "a woman alone in a world of men rarely complains of their selfishness"; and I hastened to his assistance. "Particularly when those men are chivalrous bushmen," I began; then hesitated, for, since reading the telegrams, my ideas of bush chivalry needed readjustment.

"Particularly when those men are chivalrous bushmen," the Maluka agreed with the merry twinkle in his eyes; for he perfectly understood the cause of the sudden breakdown. Then he added gravely, "For the average bushman will face fire, and flood, hunger, and even death itself, to help the frail or weak ones who come into his life; although he'll strive to the utmost to keep the Unknown Woman out of his environments, particularly when those environments are a hundred miles from anywhere."

The opposition looked incredulous. "Hunger and death!" it said. "Fiddlesticks!" "It would just serve them right if she went"; and the men-folk pointed out that this was, now, hardly flattering to the missus.

The Maluka passed the interruption by without comment. "The Unknown Woman is brim full of possibilities to a bushman," he went on; "for although she *may* be all womanly strength and tenderness, she may also be anything, from a weak timid fool to a self-righteous shrew, bristling with virtue and indignation. Still," he added earnestly, as the opposition began to murmur, "when a woman does come into our lives, whatever type she may be, she lacks nothing in the way of chivalry, and it rests with herself whether she remains an outsider or becomes just One of Us. Just One of Us," he repeated, unconsciously pleading hard for the bushman and his greatest need—"not a goddess on a pedestal but just a comrade to share our joys and sorrows with."

The opposition wavered. "If it wasn't for those telegrams," it said. But Darwin, seeing the telegrams in a new light, took up the cudgels for the bushmen.

"Poor beggars," it said, "you can't blame them. When you come to think of it, the Unknown Woman *is* brim full of possibilities." Even then at the Katherine the possibilities of the Unknown Woman were being tersely summed up by the Wag.

"You'll sometimes get ten different sorts rolled into one," he said finally, after a long dissertation. "But, generally speaking, there's just three sorts of 'em. There's Snorters— the goers you know—the sort that go rampaging round, looking for insults, and naturally finding them; and then there's fools; and *they're* mostly screeching when they're not smirking—the uncertain-coy-and-hard-to-please variety you know," he chuckled, "and then," he added seriously, "there's the right sort, the sort you tell things to. They're A1 all through the piece."

The Sanguine Scot was confident, though, that they were all alike, and none of 'em were wanted; but one of the Company suggested: "If she was little she'd do. The little 'uns are all right," he said.

But public opinion deciding that "the sort that go messing round where they know they're not wanted are always big and muscular and snorters", the Sanguine Scot was encouraged in his determination to "block her somehow".

"I'll block her yet; see if I don't," he said confidently. "After all these years on their own, the boys don't want a woman messing round the place." And when he set out for the railway along the north track, to face the "escorting trick", he repeated his assurances. "I'll block her, chaps, never fear," he said; and glowering at a "quiet" horse that had been sent by the lady at the Telegraph, added savagely, "and I'll begin by losing that brute first turn out."

2

From sun-up to sun-down on Tuesday the train glided quietly forward on its way towards the Never-Never; and from sun-up to sun-down the Maluka and I experienced the kindly consideration that it always shows to travellers: it boiled a billy for us at its furnace; loitered through the pleasantest valleys; smiled indulgently, and slackened speed whenever we made merry with blacks, by pelting them with chunks of water-melon; and generally waited on us hand and foot, the Man-in-Charge pointing out the beauty spots and places of interest, and making tea for us at frequent intervals.

It was a delightful train—just a simple-hearted, chivalrous, weather-beaten old bush-whacker, at the service of the entire Territory. "There's nothing the least bit officious or stand-offish about it," I was saying, when the Man-in-Charge came in with the first billy of tea.

"Of course not!" he said, unhooking cups from various crooked-up fingers. "It's a Territorian, you see."

"And had all the false veneer of civilization peeled off long ago," the Maluka said, adding, with a sly look at my discarded gloves and gossamer, "It's wonderful how quietly the Territory does its work."

The Man-in-Charge smiled openly as he poured out the tea, proving thereby his kinship with all other Territorians; and as the train came to a standstill, swung off and slipped some letters into a box nailed to an old tree-trunk.

At the far end of the train, away from the engine, the

7

passengers' car had been placed, and as in front of it a long, long line of low-stacked sinuous trucks slipped along in the rear of the engine, all was open view before us; and all day long, as the engine trudged onwards—hands in pockets, so to speak, and whistling merrily as it trudged—I stood beside the Maluka on the little platform in front of the passengers' car, drinking in my first deep, intoxicating draught of the glories of the tropical bush.

There were no fences to shut us in; and as the train zig-zagged through jungle and forest and river-valley—stopping now and then to drink deeply at magnificent rivers ablaze with water-lilies—it almost seemed as though it were some kindly Mammoth creature, wandering at will through the bush.

Here and there, kangaroos and other wild creatures of the bush loped out of our way, and sitting up, looked curiously after us; again and again little groups of blacks hailed us and scrambled after water-melon and tobacco, with shouts of delight, and invariably on nearing the tiny settlements along the railway we drove before us white fleeing flocks of goats.

At every settlement we stopped and passed the time of day and, giving out mail-bags, moved on again into the forest. Now and again, stockmen rode out of the timber and received mail-bags, and once a great burly bushman, a staunch old friend of the Maluka's, boarded the train, and greeted him with a hearty hand-shake.

"Hullo, old chap!" he called in welcome as he mounted the steps of the little platform. "I've come to inspect your latest investment"; but catching sight of the "latest investment" he broke into a deafening roar.

"Good lord!" he shouted, looking down upon me from his great height, "is that all there is of her? They're expecting one of the prize-fighting variety down there," and he jerked his head towards the Never-Never. Then he congratulated the Maluka on the size of his missus.

"Gimme the little 'uns," he said, nearly wringing my hand off in his approval. "You can't beat 'em for pluck. My missus is one of 'em, and *she* went bush with me when I'd nothing but a skeeto net and a quart pot to share with her." Then,

Resting at a water hole.

Jeannie Gunn (Angela Punch McGregor) with her
surrogate Aboriginal daughter, Bett Bett (Sibina
Willi) walking through the Aboriginal camp.

slapping the Maluka vigorously on the back, he told him he'd
got some sense left. "You can't beat the little 'uns," he declared.
"They're just the very thing."

The Maluka agreed with him; and after some comical
quizzing, they decided, to their own complete satisfaction,
that although the bushman's "missus" was the "littlest of all
little 'uns straight up and down", the Maluka's "knocked
spots off her sideways".

But although the Territory train does not need to bend its
neck to the galling yoke of a minute time-table, yet, like all
bush-whackers, it prefers to strike its supper camp before night-
fall, and after allowing us a good ten minutes' chat it blew a
deferential "Ahem" from its engine, as a hint that it would like
to be "getting along". The bushman took the hint, and after
a hearty "Good luck, missus!" and a "Chin, chin, old man,"
left us, with assurances that "her size 'ud do the trick".

Until sun-down we jogged quietly on, meandering through
further pleasant places and meetings; drinking tea and chatting
with the Man-in-Charge between whiles, extracting a maximum of pleasure from a minimum rate of speed: for travelling
in the Territory has not yet passed that ideal stage where the
travelling itself—the actual going—is all pleasantness.

As we approached Pine Creek I confided to the menfolk that
I was feeling a little nervous. "Supposing that telegraphing
bush-whacker decides to shoot me off-hand on my arrival,"
I said; and the Man-in-Charge said amiably, "It'll be brought
in as justifiable homicide; that's all." Then reconnoitring the
enemy from the platform, he "feared" we were "about to be
boycotted".

There certainly were very few men on the station, and the
Man-in-Charge, recognizing one of them as the landlord of the
Playford, assured us there was nothing to fear from the quarter.
"You see, you represent business to him," he explained.

Everyone but the landlord seemed to have urgent business in
the office or at the far end of the platform, but it was quickly
evident that there was nothing to fear from him; for, finding
himself left alone to do the honours of the Creek, he greeted us
with an amused, "She doesn't look up to sample sent by

telegram"; and I felt every meeting would be, at least, unconventional. Then we heard that as Mac had "only just arrived from the Katherine, he couldn't leave his horses until they were fixed up"; but the landlord's eyes having wandered back to the "Goer" he winked deliberately at the Maluka before inviting us to "step across to the Pub".

The Pub seemed utterly deserted, and with another wink the landlord explained the silence by saying that "a cyclone of some sort" had swept most of his "regulars" away; and then he went shouting through the echoing passages for a "boy" to "fetch along tea".

Before the tea appeared, an angry Scotch voice crept to us through thin partitions, saying, "It's not a fit place for a woman, and, besides, nobody wants her!" And in a little while we heard the same voice inquiring for "the Boss".

"The telegraphing bush-whacker," I said, and invited the Maluka to come and see me defy him. But when I found myself face to face with over six feet of brawny, quizzing, wrathful-looking Scotsman, all my courage slipped away, and edging closer to the Maluka, I held out my hand to the bushman, murmuring lamely: "How do you do?"

Instantly a change came over the rugged, bearded face. At the sight of the "Goer" reduced to a meek five feet, all the wrath died out of it, and with twitching lips and twinkling eyes Mac answered mechanically, "Quite well, thank you" and then coughed in embarrassment.

That was all: no fierce blocking, no defying. And with the cough, the absurdity of the whole affair, striking us simultaneously, left us grinning like a trio of Cheshire cats.

It was a most eloquent grinning making all spoken apology or explanation unnecessary; and by the time it had faded away we thoroughly understood each other, being drawn together by a mutual love of the ridiculous. Only a mutual love of the ridiculous, yet not so slender a basis for a lifelong friendship as appears, and by no means an uncommon one "out-bush".

"Does the station pay for the telegrams, or the loser?" the landlord asked in an aside, as we went in to supper; and after supper the preparations began for the morrow's start.

The Sanguine Scot, anxious to make amends for the telegrams, was full of suggestions for smoothing out the difficulties of the road. Like many men of his type, whatever he did he did it with all his heart and soul—hating, loving, avenging, or forgiving with equal energy, and he now applied himself to helping the Maluka "make things easy for her" as zealously as he had striven to "block her somehow".

Sorting out pack-bags, he put one aside, with a "We'll have to spare that for her duds. It won't do for her to be short. She'll have enough to put up with without that." But when I thanked him, and said I could manage nicely with only one, as I would not need much on the road, he and the Maluka sat down and stared at each other in dismay. "That's for everything you'll need till the waggons come," they explained; "your road kit goes in your swag."

The waggons went Inside once a year—"after the Wet", and would arrive at the homestead early in June. As it was then only the middle of January, I too sat down, and stared in dismay from the solitary pack-bag to the great, heaped-up pile that had been sorted out as indispensable.

"You'll have to cull your herd a bit, that's all," Mac said; and needlework was pointed out as a luxury. Then books were "cut out", and after that the house linen was looked to, and as I hesitated over the number of pillow-cases we could manage with, Mac cried triumphantly, "You won't need these anyway, for there's no pillows."

The Maluka thought he had prepared me for everything in the way of roughness; but in a flash we knew that I had yet to learn what a bushman means by rough.

As the pillow-cases fell to the ground Mac was at a loss to account for my consternation. "What's gone wrong?" he exclaimed in concern. Mac was often an unconscious humorist.

But the Maluka came with his ever-ready sympathy. "Poor little coon," he said gently, "there's little else but chivalry and a bite of tucker for a woman out bush."

Then a light broke in on Mac. "Is it only the pillows?" he said. "I thought something had gone wrong." Then his eyes began to twinkle. "There's stacks of pillows in Darwin," he said meaningly.

It was exactly the moral fillip needed, and in another minute we were cheerfully "culling our herd" again.

Exposed to Mac's scorn, the simplest comforts became foolish luxuries. "A couple of changes of everything is stacks," he said encouragingly, clearing a space for packing. "There's heaps of soap and water at the station, and things dry here before you can waltz round twice."

Hopefulness is always infectious and before Mac's cheery optimism the pile of necessities grew rapidly smaller. Indeed, with such visions of soap and water and waltzing washerwomen, a couple of changes of everything appeared absurd luxury. But even optimism can have disadvantages; for in our enthusiasm we forgot that a couple of cambric blouses, a cotton dress or two, and a change of skirts, are hardly equal to the strain of nearly five months' constant wear and washing.

The pillow-cases went in however. Mac settled that difficulty by saying that "all hands could be put on to pluck birds. The place is stiff with 'em," he explained, showing what a simple matter it would be after all. The Maluka, turning out two cushions, a large and a smaller one, simplified matters even more. "A bird in the hand, you know," he said, finding room for them in the swag.

Before all the arrangements were completed, others of the Creek had begun to thaw, and were "lending a hand" here and there. The question of horses coming up I confided in the helpers that I was relieved to hear that the Telegraph had sent a quiet horse. "I am *really* afraid of buck-jumpers, you know," I said, and the Creek looking sideways at Mac, he became incoherent.

"Oh, look here!" he spluttered. "I say! Oh, look here! It really was too bad!" Then after an awkward pause, he blurted out, "I don't know what you'll think, but the brute strayed first camp, and—he's lost, saddle and all."

The Maluka shot him a swift, questioning glance; but poor Mac looked so unhappy that we assured him "we'd manage somehow". Perhaps we could tame one of the flash buck-jumpers, the Maluka suggested. But Mac said it "wouldn't be as bad as that", and, making full confession, placed old Roger at our service.

By morning, however, a magnificent chestnut, "Flash", well-broken into the side-saddle, had been conjured up from somewhere by the Creek. But two of the pack-horses had strayed, and by the time they were found the morning had slipped away, and it was too late to start until after dinner. Then after dinner a terrific thunder-storm broke over the settlement, and as the rain fell in torrents, Mac thought it looked "like a case of tomorrow all right".

Naturally, I felt impatient at the delay, but was told by the Creek that "there was no hurry!" "Tomorrow's still untouched," Mac explained. "This is the Land of Plenty of Time; Plenty of Time and Wait a While. You'll be doing a bit of waiting before you've done with it."

"If this rain goes on, she'll be doing a bit of waiting at the Fergusson; unless she learns the horse's tail trick," the Creek put in. On enquiry, it proved that the "horse's tail trick" meant swimming a horse through the flood, and hanging on to its tail until it fought a way across; and I felt I would prefer "waiting a bit".

The rain did go on, and roaring over the roof made conversation difficult. The bushmen called it a "bit of a storm"; but every square inch of the heavens seemed occupied by lightning and thunderbolts.

"Nothing to what we can do sometimes," everyone agreed. "*We* do things in style up here—often run half a dozen storms at once. You see, when you are weather-bound, you might as well have something worth looking at."

The storm lasted nearly three hours, and when it cleared Mac went over to the Telegraph, where some confidential chatting must have taken place; for when he returned he told us that the Dandy was starting out for the homestead next day to "fix things up a bit". The Head Stockman, however, waited back for orders.

The morning dawned bright and clear, and Mac advised "making a dash for the Fergusson". "We might just get through before this rain comes down the valley," he said.

The Creek was most enthusiastic with its help, bustling about with pack-bags, and surcingles, and generally "mixing things".

When the time came to say good-bye it showed signs of breaking down; but mastering its grief with a mightily audible effort, it wished us "good luck", and stood watching as we rode out of the little settlement.

Every time we looked back it raised its hat; and as we rode at the head of our orderly little cavalcade of pack-horses, with Jackeroo, the black "boy", bringing up the rear, we flattered ourselves on the dignity of our departure. Mac called it "style", and the Maluka was hoping that the Creek was properly impressed, when, Flash unexpectedly heading off for his late home, an exciting scrimmage ensued, and the procession was broken into fragments.

The Creek flew to the rescue, and, when order was finally restored, the woman who had defied the Sanguine Scot and his telegrams, entered the forest that fringes the Never-Never, sitting meekly upon a led horse.

3

Bush chivalry demanding that a woman's discomfiture should be ignored, Mac kept his eye on the horizon for the first quarter of a mile, and talked volubly of the prospects of the Wet and the resources of the Territory; but when Flash was released, and after a short tussle settled down into a free, swinging amble, he offered congratulations in his own whimsical way.

"He's like the rest of us," he said, with a sly, sidelong look at the Maluka, "perfectly reconciled to his fate."

Although it was only sixty-five miles to the Katherine, it took us exactly three days to travel the distance. Mac called it a "tip-top record for the Wet", and the Maluka agreed with him; for in the Territory it is not the number of miles that counts, but what is met with in those miles.

During the first afternoon, we met so many amiable-looking watercourses, that the Sanguine Scot grew more and more hopeful about crossing the Fergusson that night.

"We'll just do it if we push on," he said, after a critical look at the Cullen, then little more than a sweet, shady stream. "Our luck's dead in. She's only just moving. Yesterday's rain hasn't come down the valleys yet."

We pushed on in the moonlight; but when we reached the Fergusson, two hours later, we found our luck was "dead out", for "she" was up and running a banker.

Mac's hopes sank below zero. "Now we've done it," he said ruefully, looking down at the swirling torrent. "It's a case of 'wait-a-while' after all."

15

But the Maluka's hopes always died hard. "There's still the Government yacht," he said, going to a huge iron punt that lay far above high-water mark. Mac called it a forlorn hope, and it looked it, as it lay deeply sunk in the muddy bank.

It was an immense affair, weighing over half a ton, and provided by a thoughtful Government for the transit of travellers "stuck up" by the river when in flood. An army of roughriders might have launched it; but as bushmen generally travel in single file, it lay a silent reproach to the wisdom of Governments.

Some jester had chalked on its sides "H.M.S. *Immovable*"; and after tugging valiantly at it for nearly half an hour, the Maluka and Mac and Jackeroo proved the truth of the bushman's irony.

There was no choice but a camp on the wrong side of the river, and after "dratting things" in general, and the Cullen in particular, Mac bowed to the inevitable and began to unpack the team, stacking pack-bags and saddles up on the rocks off the wet grass.

By the time the billy was boiling he was trying hard to be cheerful, but without much success. "Oh, well," he said, as we settled down round the fire, "this is the Land of Plenty of Time, that's one comfort. Another whole week starts next Sunday"; then relapsing altogether he added gloomily, "We'll be spending it here, too, by the look of things."

"Unless the missus feels equal to the horse's-tail trick," the Maluka suggested.

The missus felt equal to anything *but* the tail trick, and said so; and conversation flagged for a while as each tried to hit upon some way out of the difficulty.

Suddenly Mac gave his thigh a prodigious slap. "I've struck it!" he shouted, and pointing a thick wire rope, just visible in the moonlight as it stretched across the river from flood-bank to flood-bank, added hesitatingly, "We send mail-bags—and—valuables—over on that, when the river's up."

It was impossible to mistake his meaning, or the Maluka's exclamation of relief, or that neither man doubted for a moment that the woman was willing to be flung across a deep, swirling river on a swaying wire; and as many a man has appeared brave because he has lacked the courage to own to his cowardice, so I said airily that "anything was better than going back", and found the men exchanging glances.

"No one's going back," the Maluka said quietly; and then I learned that the Wet does not "do things by half". "Once they began to move the flood waters must have come down the valleys in tidal waves," the Maluka explained. "The Cullen we've just left will probably be a roaring torrent by now."

"We're stuck between two rivers: that's what's happened," Mac added savagely. "Might have guessed that miserable little Cullen was up to her old sneaking ways." And to explain Mac's former "dratting", the Maluka said: "It's a way the rivers have up here. They entice travellers over with smiles and promises, and before they can get back, call down the flood waters and shut them in."

"I am glad I thought of the wire," Mac added cheerfully, and slipped into reminiscences of the Wet, drawing the Maluka also into experiences. And as they drifted from one experience to another, forced camps for days on stony outcrops in the midst of seas of water were touched on lightly as hardly worth mentioning; while "eating yourself out of tucker, and getting down to water-rats and bandicoots", compared favourably with a day or two spent in trees or on stockyard fences. As for crossing a river on a stout wire rope! After the first few reminiscences, and an incident or two in connection with "doing the horse's-tail trick", that appeared an exceedingly safe and pleasant way of overcoming the difficulty, it became very evident why women do not travel "during the Wet".

It was a singularly beautiful night, shimmering with warm tropical moonlight, and hoarse with the shouting of frogs and the roar of the river—a night that demanded attention; and, gradually losing interest in hair-breadth escapes from drowning, Mac joined in the song of the frogs.

"Quar-r-rt! Quar-r-rt pot!" he sang in hoarse strident minims, mimicking to perfection the shouts of the leaders, leaning with them on the "quar-r-rt" in harsh gutturals, and spitting out the "pot" in short, deep staccatos. Quicker and quicker the song ran, as the full chorus of frogs joined in. From minims to crotchets, and from crotchets to quavers it flowed, and Mac, running with it, gurgled with a new refrain at the quavers. "More-water, more-water, hot-water, hot-water," he sang rapidly, in tireless reiteration, until he seemed the leader and the frogs the followers, singing the words he put into their mouths. Lower and lower the chorus sank; but just before it died away, an old bull-frog started everyone afresh with a slow, booming "quar-r-rt pot!" and Mac stopped for breath. "Now you know the song of the frogs," he laughed. "We'll teach you all the songs of the Never-Never in time; listen!" and listening, it was hard to believe that this was our one-time telegraphing bushwhacker. Dropping his voice to a soft, sobbing moan, as a pheasant called from the shadows, he lamented with it for "Puss! Puss! Puss! Puss! Poor Puss! Poor Puss!"

The sound roused a dove in the branches above us, and as she stirred in her sleep and cooed softly, Mac murmured drowsily, "Move-over-dear, Move-over-dear"; and the dove, taking up the refrain, crooned it again and again to its mate.

The words of the songs were not Mac's. They belong to the lore of the bushmen; but he sang or crooned them with such perfect mimicry of tone or cadence, that never again was it possible to hear these songs of the Never-Never without associating the words with the songs.

The night was full of sounds, and one by one Mac caught them up, and the bush appeared to echo him; and leaning, half drowsily, against the pack-saddles and swags, we listened until we slipped into one of those quiet reveries that come so naturally to bush-folk. Shut in on all sides by bush and tall timber, with the rushing river as sentinel, we seemed in a world all our own—a tiny human world, with a camp-fire for its hub; and as we dreamed on, half-conscious of the moonlight and shoutings, the deep inner beauty of the night stole upon us. A mystical, elusive beauty, difficult to define, that lay underneath and around, and within the moonlight—a beauty of deep nestling shadows, crooning whispers, and soft rustling movement.

For a while we dreamed on, and then the Maluka broke the silence. "The wizard of the Never-Never has not forgotten how to weave his spells while I've been South," he said. "It won't be long before he has the missus in his toils. The false veneer of civilization is peeling off at a great rate."

I roused as from a trance; and Mac threw a sharp, searching glance at me, as I sat curled up against a swag. "You're right," he laughed; "there's not a trace of the towney left." And rising to "see about fixing up camp", he added: "You'd better look out, missus! Once caught, you'll never get free again. We're all tethered goats here. Every time we make up our minds to clear out, something pulls us back with a jerk."

"Tethered goats!" Mac called us, and the world must apply the simile as it thinks fit. The wizard of the Never-Never weaves his spells, until hardships, and dangers, and privations, seem all that make life worth living; and then holds us "tethered goats"; and every time the town calls us with promises of gaiety, and comfort, and security, "something pulls us back with a jerk" to our beloved bush.

There was no sign of rain; and as bushmen only pitch a tent when a deluge is expected, our camp was very simple: just camp sleeping mosquito-nets, with calico tops and cheese net for curtains—hanging by cords between stout stakes driven into the ground. "Mosquito pegs" the bushmen call these stakes.

Jackeroo, the unpoetical, was even then sound asleep in his net; and in ten minutes everything was "fixed up". In another ten minutes we had also "turned in", and soon after I was sound asleep, rolled up in a "bluey", and had to be wakened at dawn.

"The river's still rising," Mac announced by way of good morning. We'll have to bustle up and get across, or the water'll be over the wire, and then we'll be done for."

Bustle as we would, however, "getting across" was a tedious business. It took nearly an hour's hustling and urging and galloping before the horses could be persuaded to attempt the swim, and then only after old Roper had been partly dragged and partly hauled through the backwash by the amphibious Jackeroo.

Another half-hour slipped by in sending the horses' hobbles across on the pulley that ran on the wire, and in the hobbling out of the horses. Then, with Jackeroo on one side of the river, and the Maluka and Mac on the other, swags, saddles, pack-bags, and camp baggage went over one by one; and it was well past midday before all was finished.

Then my turn came. A surcingle—one of the long thick straps that keep all firm on a pack-horse—was buckled through the pulley, and the Maluka crossed first, just to test its safety. It was safe enough; but as he was dragged through the water most of the way, the pleasantness of "getting across" on the wire proved a myth.

Mac shortened the strap, and then sat me in it, like a child in a swing. "Your lighter weight will run clear of the water," he said, with his usual optimism. "It's only a matter of holding on and keeping cool"; and as the Maluka began to haul he added final instructions. "Hang on like grim death, and keep cool, whatever happens," he said.

I promised to obey, and all went well until I reached mid-stream. Then, the wire beginning to sag threateningly towards the water, Mac flung his whole weight on to his end of it, and, to his horror, I shot up into the air like a sky-rocket.

"Hang on! Keep cool!" Mac yelled, in a frenzy of apprehension, as he swung on his end of the wire. Jackeroo became convulsed with laughter; but the Maluka pulled hard, and I was soon on the right side of the river, declaring that I preferred experiences when they were over. Later on, Mac accounted for his terror with another unconscious flash of humour. "You never can count on a woman keeping cool when the unexpected happens," he said.

We offered to haul him over. "It's only a matter of holding on and keeping cool," we said; but he preferred to swim.

"It's a pity you didn't think of telegraphing this performance," I shouted across the flood; but, in his relief, Mac was equal to the occasion.

"I'm glad I didn't," he shouted back gallantly, with a sweeping flourish of his hat; "it might have blocked you from coming." The bushman was learning a new accomplishment.

As his clothes were to come across on the wire, I was given a hint to "make myself scarce"; so retired over the bank, and helped Jackeroo with the dinner camp—an arrangement that exactly suited his ideas of the eternal fitness of things.

During the morning he had expressed great disapproval that a woman should be idle, while men dragged heavy weights about. "White fellow, big-fellow-fool all right," he said contemptuously, when Mac explained that it was generally so in the white man's country. A Briton of the Billingsgate type would have appealed to Jackeroo as a man of sound common sense.

By the time the men-folk appeared, he had decided that with a little management I would be quite an ornament to society.

"Missus bin help *me* all right," he told the Sanguine Scot, with comical self-satisfaction.

Mac roared with delight, and the passage of the Fergusson having swept away the last lingering touch of restraint, he called to the Maluka, "Jackeroo reckons he's tamed the shrew for us." Mac had been a reader of Shakespeare in his time.

All afternoon we were supposed to be "making a dash" for the Edith, a river twelve miles farther on; but there was nothing very dashing about our pace. The air was stiflingly, swelteringly hot, and the flies maddening in their persistence. The horses developed puffs, and when we were not being half-drowned in torrents of rain we were being parboiled in steamy atmosphere. The track was as tracks usually are "during the Wet", and for four hours we laboured on, slipping and slithering over the greasy track, varying the monotony now and then with a floundering scramble through a boggy creek crossing. Our appearance was about as dashing as our pace; and draggled, wet through, and perspiring, and out of conceit with primitive travelling—having spent the afternoon combining a minimum rate of travelling with a maximum of discomfort—we arrived at the Edith an hour after sundown to find her a wide eddying stream.

"Won't be more than a ducking," Mac said cheerfully. "Couldn't be much wetter than we are," and the Maluka taking the reins from my hands, we rode into the stream, Mac keeping behind, "to pick her up in case she floats off", he said, thinking he was putting courage into me.

It wasn't as bad as it looked; and after a little stumbling and plunging and drifting the horses were clambering out up the opposite bank, and by next sundown—after scrambling through a few more rivers—we found ourselves looking down at the flooded Katherine, flowing below in the valley of a rocky gorge.

Sixty-five miles in three days, against sixty miles an hour of the express trains of the world. "Speed's the thing," cries the world, and speeds on, gaining little but speed; and we bush-folk travel our sixty miles and gain all that is worth gaining—except speed.

"Hand-over-hand this time," Mac said, looking up at the telegraph wire that stretched far overhead. "There's no pulley here. Hand-over-hand, or the horse's-tail trick."

But Mine Host of the "Pub" had seen us, and running down the opposite side of the gorge, launched a boat at the river's brink; then pulling up-stream for a hundred yards or so in the backwash, faced about, and raced down and across the swift-flowing current with long, sweeping strokes; and as we rode down the steep, winding track to meet him, Mac became jocular, and reminding us that the gauntlet of the Katherine had yet to be run, also reminded us that the sympathies of the Katherine were with the stockmen; adding with a chuckle, as Mine Host bore down upon us: "You don't even represent business here; no woman ever does."

Then the boat grounded, and Mine Host sprang ashore— another burly six-foot bushman—and greeted us with a flashing smile and a laughing "There's not much of her left." And then, stepping with quiet unconcern into over two feet of water, pushed the boat against a jutting ledge for my convenience. "Wet feet don't count," he laughed, with another of his flashing smiles, when remonstrated with, and Mac chuckled in an aside, "Didn't I tell you a woman doesn't represent business here?"

4

The swim being beyond the horses, they were left hobbled out on the north banks, to wait for the river to fall; and after another swift race down and across stream, Mine Host landed everyone safely on the south side of the flood, and soon we were clambering up the steep track that led from the river to the "Pub".

Coming up from the river, the Katherine Settlement appeared to consist solely of the "Pub" and its accompanying store; but beyond the "Pub", which, by the way, seemed to be hanging on to its own verandah posts for support, we found an elongated, three-room building, nestling under deep verandahs, and half-hidden beneath a grove of lofty scarlet flowering poinsettias.

"The Cottage is always set apart for distinguished visitors," Mine Host said, bidding us welcome with another smile, but never a hint that he was placing his own private quarters at our disposal. Like all bushmen, he could be delicately reticent when conferring a favour; but a forgotten razor-strop betrayed him later on.

In the meantime we discovered the remainder of the Settlement from the Cottage verandahs, spying out the Police Station as it lurked in ambush just round the first bend in a winding bush track—apparently keeping one eye on the "Pub"; and then we caught a gleam of white roofs away beyond further bends in the track, where the Overland Telegraph "Department" stood on a little rise, aloof from the "Pub" and the

Police, shut away from the world, yet attending to its affairs, and, incidentally, to those of the bush-folk: a tiny Settlement, with a tiny permanent population of four men and two women—women who found their own homes all-sufficient, and rarely left them, although the men-folk were here, there, and everywhere.

All around and within the Settlement was bush; and beyond the bush, stretching away and away on every side of it, those hundreds of thousands of square miles that constitute the Never-Never—miles sending out and absorbing again from day to day the floating population of the Katherine.

Before supper the Telegraph Department and the Police Station called on the Cottage to present compliments. Then the Wag came with his welcome. "Didn't expect you today," he drawled, with unmistakable double meaning in his drawl. "You've come sooner than we expected. Must have had luck with the rivers"; and Mac became enthusiastic. "Luck!" he cried. "Luck! She's got the luck of the Auld Yin himself—skinned through everything by the skin of our teeth. No one else'll get through those rivers under a week." And they didn't.

Remembering the telegrams, the Wag shot a swift, quizzing glance at him; but it took more than a glance to disconcert Mac once his mind was made up, and he met it unmoved, and entered into a vivid description of the "passage of the Fergusson", which filled in our time until supper.

After supper the Cottage returned the calls, and then, rain coming down in torrents, the Telegraph, the Police, the Cottage, and the "Pub" retired to rest, wondering what the morrow would bring forth.

The morrow brought forth more rain, and the certainty that, as the river was still rising, the swim would be beyond the horses for several days yet; and because of this certainty, the Katherine bestirred itself to honour its tethered guests.

The Telegraph and the Police Station issued invitations for dinner, and the "Pub"—that had already issued a hint that "the boys could refrain from knocking down cheques as long as a woman was staying in the place"—now issued an edict limiting the number of daily drinks per man.

The invitations were accepted with pleasure, and the edict was attended to with a murmur of approval, in which, however, there was one dissenting voice: a little bearded bushman "thought the Katherine was overdoing it a bit", and suggested as an amendment that "drunks could make themselves scarce when she's about". But Mine Host easily silenced him by offering to "see what the missus thought about it".

Then for a day the Katherine "took its bearings", and keen, scrutinizing glances summed up the Unknown Woman, looking her through and through until she was no longer an Unknown Woman, while the Maluka looked on interested. He knew the bush-folk well, and that their instinct would be unerring, and left the missus to slip into whichever niche in their lives they thought fit to place her. And as she slipped into a niche built up of strong, staunch comradeship, the black community considered that they, too, had fathomed the missus; and it became history in the camp that the Maluka had stolen her from a powerful Chief of the Whites, and, deeming it wise to disappear with her until the affair had blown over, had put many flooded rivers between him and his pursuers. "Would any woman have flung herself across rivers on wires, speeding on without rest or pause, unless afraid of pursuit?" the camp asked in committee, and the most sceptical were silenced.

Then followed other days full of pleasant intercourse; for, once sure of its welcome, bushmen are lavish with their friendship. And as we roamed about the tiny Settlement, the Wag and others vied with the Maluka, Mine Host, and Mac in "making things pleasant for the missus"; relating experiences for her entertainment; showing all there was to be shown, and obeying the edict with cheerful, unquestioning chivalry.

Neither the Head Stockman nor the little bushman, however, had made any offers of friendship, Dan having gone out to the station immediately after interviewing the Maluka, while the little bushman spent most of his time getting out of the way of the missus whenever she appeared on his horizon.

"A Tam-o'-Shanter fleeing from the furies of a too fertile imagination," the Maluka laughed after a particularly comical dash to cover.

Poor Tam! Those days must live in his memory like a hideous nightmare! I, of course, knew nothing of the edict at the time—for bushmen do not advertise their chivalry—and wandered round the straggling Settlement, vaguely surprised at its sobriety, and turning up in such unexpected places that the little bushman was constantly on the verge of apoplexy.

But experience teaches quickly. On the first day, after running into me several times, he learned the wisdom of spying out the land before turning a corner. On the second day, after we had come on him while thus engaged several other times, he learned the foolishness of placing too much confidence in corners, and deciding by the law of averages that the bar was the only safe place in the Settlement, availed himself of its sanctuary in times of danger. On the third day he learned that the law of averages is a weak reed to lean on; for on slipping round a corner, and mistaking a warning signal from the Wag, he whisked into the bar, to whisk out again with a clatter of hobnailed boots, for I was in there examining some native curios. "She's in *there* next!" he gasped as he passed the Wag on his way to the cover of the nearest corner.

"Poor Tam!" How he must have hated women as he lurked in the doubtful ambush of that corner!

"*How* did he skoot!" the Wag chuckled later on when recounting with glee, to the Maluka and Mac, the story of Tam's dash for cover.

Pitying Tam, I took his part, and said he seemed a sober, decent little man and couldn't help being shy; then paused, wondering at the queer expression on the men's faces.

Mac coughed in embarrassment, and the Maluka and the Wag seemed preoccupied, and fearing I had been misunderstood, I added hastily, "So is everyone in the Settlement, for that matter," thereby causing further embarrassment.

After a short intense silence, the Wag "thought he'd be getting along", and as he moved off the Maluka laughed. "Oh, missus, missus!" and Mac blurted out the whole tale of the edict—concluding rather ambiguously by saying: "Don't you go thinking it's made any difference to any of us, because it hasn't. We're not saints, but we're not pigs, and, besides, it was a pleasure."

I doubted if it was much pleasure to Tam-o'-Shanter; but forgetting he was sober by compulsion, even he had begun to feel virtuous; and when he heard he had been called a "sober, decent little man", he positively swaggered; and on the fourth morning walked jauntily past the Cottage and ventured a quiet good morning—a simple enough little incident in itself; but it proved Tam's kinship with his fellow-men. For is it not the knowledge that someone thinks well of us that makes us feel at ease in that person's company?

Later in the same day, the flood having fallen, it was decided that it would be well to cross the horses in the rear of a boat, and we were all at the river discussing preparations, when Tam electrified the community by joining the group.

In the awkward pause that followed his arrival he passed a general remark about dogs—there were several with us—and everyone plunged into dog yarns, until Tam, losing his head over the success of his maiden speech, became so communicative on the subject of a dog-fight that he had to be surreptitiously kicked into silence.

"Looks like more rain," Mac said abruptly, hoping to draw public attention from the pantomime. "Ought to get off as soon as possible, or we'll be blocked at the King."

The Katherine seized on the new topic of conversation, and advised "getting out to the five-mile overnight", declaring it would "take all day to get away from the Settlement in the morning". Then came another awkward pause, while everyone kept one eye on Tam, until the Maluka saved the situation by calling for volunteers to help with the horses, and, Tam being pressed into the service, the boat was launched, and he was soon safe over on the far side of the river.

Once among the horses, the little man was transformed. In the quiet, confident horseman that rode down the gorge a few minutes later it would have been difficult to recognize the shy, timid bushman. The saddle had given him backbone, and it soon appeared he was the right-hand man, and, at times, even organizer in the difficult task of crossing horses through a deep, swift-running current.

As the flood was three or four hundred yards wide and many feet deep, a swim was impossible without help, and every horse was to be supported or guided, or dragged over in the rear of the boat, with a halter held by a man in the stern.

It was no child's play. Every inch of the way had its difficulties. The poor brutes knew the swim was beyond them; and as the boat, pulling steadily on, dragged them from the shallows into the deeper water, they plunged and snorted in fear, until they found themselves swimming and were obliged to give all their attention to keeping themselves afloat.

Some required little assistance when once off their feet; just a slow, steady pull from the oars, and a taut enough halter to lean on in the tight places. But others rolled over like logs when the full force of the current struck them, threatening to drag the boat under, as it and the horse raced away downstream with the oarsmen straining their utmost.

It was hard enough work for the oarsmen; but the seat of honour was in the stern of the boat, and no man filled it better than the transformed Tam. Alert and full of resource, with one hand on the tiller, he leaned over the boat, lengthening or shortening rope for the halter, and regulating the speed of the oarsmen with unerring judgment; giving a staunch swimmer time and a short rope to lean on, or literally dragging the faint-hearted across at full speed; careful then only of one thing: to keep the head above water. Never again would I judge a man by *one* of his failings.

There were ten horses in all to cross, and at the end of two hours' hard pulling there was only one left to come—old Roper.

Mac took the halter into his own hands—there was no one else worthy—and, slipping into the stern of the boat, spoke first to the horse and then to the oarsmen; and as the boat glided forward, the noble, trusting old horse—confident that his long-tried human friend would set no impossible task—came quietly through the shallows, sniffing questionings at the half-submerged bushes.

"Give him time!" Mac called. "Let him think it out," as step by step Roper followed, the halter running slack on the water. When almost out of his depth, he paused just a moment, then, obeying the tightening rope, lifted himself to the flood and struck firmly and gravely out.

Staunchly he and Mac dealt with the current: taking time and approaching it quietly, meeting it with taut rope and unflinching nerve, drifting for a few breaths to judge its force; then, nothing daunted, they battled forward, stroke after stroke, and won across without once pulling the boat out of its course.

Only Roper could have done it; and when the splendid neck and shoulders appeared above water as he touched bottom, on the submerged track, he was greeted with a cheer and a hearty, unanimous "Bravo, old chap!" Then Mac returned thanks with a grateful look, and, leaping ashore, looked over the beautiful, wet, shining limbs, declaring he could have "done it on his own" if required.

Once assured that we were anxious for a start, the Katherine set about speeding the parting guests with gifts of farewell. The Wag brought fresh tomatoes and a cucumber; the Telegraph sent eggs; the Police, a freshly baked cake; the Chinese cook baked bread, and Mine Host came with a few potatoes and a flat-iron. To the surprise of the Katherine, I received the potatoes without enthusiasm, not having been long enough in the Territory to know their rare value, and, besides, I was puzzling over the flat-iron.

"What's it for?" I asked, and the Wag shouted in mock amazement: "For! To iron duds with, of course," as Mine Host assured us it was of no use to him beyond keeping a door open.

Still puzzled, I said I thought there would not be any need to iron duds until we reached the homestead, and the Maluka said quietly: "It's *for* the homestead. There will be nothing like that there."

Mac exploded with an impetuous "Good heavens! What *does* she expect? First pillows and now irons!"

Gradually realizing that down South we have little idea of what "rough" means to a bushman, I had from day to day been modifying my ideas of a station home from a mansion to a commodious wooden cottage, plainly but comfortably furnished. The Cottage had confirmed this idea, but Mac soon settled the question beyond all doubt.

"Look here!" he said emphatically. "Before she leaves this place she'll just *have* to grasp things a bit better," and sitting down on a swag he talked rapidly for ten minutes, taking a queer delight in making everything sound as bad as possible, "knocking the stiffening out of the missus", as he phrased it, and certainly bringing the "commodious station home" about her ears, which was just as well, perhaps.

After a few scathing remarks on the homestead in general, which he called "One of those down-at-the-heels, anything-'ll-do sort of places", he described The House. "It's mostly verandahs and promises," he said; "but one room is finished. *We* call it The House, but you'll probably call it a Hut, even though it has got doors and calico windows framed and on hinges."

Then followed an inventory of the furniture. "There's one fairly steady, good-sized table—at least, it doesn't fall over, unless someone leans on it; then there's a bed with a wire mattress, but nothing else on it; and there's a chair or two up to your weight (the Boss'll either have to stand up or lie down), and I don't know that there's much else excepting plenty of cups and plates—they're enamel, fortunately, so you won't have much trouble with the servants breaking things. Of course, there's a Christmas card and a few works of art on the walls for you to look at when you're tired of looking at yourself in the glass. Yes! There's a looking-glass—goodness knows how it got there! You ought to be thankful for that and the wire-mattress. You won't find many of them out bush."

I humbly acknowledged thankfulness, and felt deeply grateful to Mine Host when, with ready thoughtfulness, he brought a couple of china cups and stood them among the baggage—the heart of Mine Host was as warm and sincere as his flashing smile. I learned, in time, to be indifferent to china cups, but that flat-iron became one of my most cherished possessions—how it got to the Katherine is a long, long story, touching on three continents, a man, a woman, and a baby.

The commodious station home destroyed, the Katherine bestirred itself further in the speeding of its guests. The Telegraph came with the offer of their buggy, and then the Police offered theirs; but Mine Host, harnessing two nuggety little horses into his buck-board, drove round to the store, declaring a buck-board was the "only thing for the road". "You won't feel the journey at all in it," he said, and drove us round the Settlement to prove how pleasant and easy travelling could be in the Wet.

"No buggy obtainable," murmured the Maluka, reviewing the three offers. But the Sanguine Scot was quite unabashed, and answered coolly: "You forget those telegrams were sent to that other woman—the Goer, you know—there *was* no buggy obtainable for *her*. By George! Wasn't she a snorter? I knew I'd block her somehow," and then he added with a gallant bow and a flourish, "You can see for yourselves, chaps, that she didn't come."

The Wag mimicked the bow and the flourish, and then suggested accepting all three vehicles and having a procession— "a triumphal exit that'll knock spots off Pine Creek."

"There'd be one apiece," he said, "and with Jackeroo as outrider, and loose horses to fill in with, we could make a real good thing of it if we tried. There's Tam, now; he's had a fair amount of practice lately, dodging round corners, and if he and I stood on opposite sides of the track and dodged around bushes directly the procession passed, coming out farther along, we could line the track for miles with cheering crowds."

The buck-board only being decided on, he expressed himself bitterly disappointed, but promised to do his best with that and the horses; until hearing that Mac was to go out to the "five-mile" overnight with the pack-team and loose horses, leaving us to follow at sun-up, he became disconsolate and refused even to witness the departure.

"I'd 'av willingly bust meself cheering a procession and lining the track with frantic crowds," he said; "but I'm too fat to work up any enthusiasm over two people in a buck-board."

A little before sun-down Mac set out; after instructing the

Katherine to "get the buck-board off early", and just before the Katherine "turned in" for the night, the Maluka went to the office to settle accounts with Mine Host.

In five minutes he was back, standing among the poinsettias, and then after a little while of silence he said gently: "Mac was right. A woman does not represent business here." Mine Host had indignantly refused payment for a woman's board and lodging.

"I had to pay, though," the Maluka laughed, with one of his quick changes of humour. "But, then, I'm only a man."

5

When we arrived at the five-mile in the morning we found Mac
"packed up" and ready for the start, and, passing the reins to
him, the Maluka said, "You know the road best"; and Mac
being what he called a "bit of a Jehu", we set off in great style—
across country apparently—missing trees by a hair's-breadth,
and bumping over the ant-hills, boulders, and broken boughs
that lay half-hidden in the long grass.

After being nearly bumped out of the buck-board several
times, I asked if there wasn't any track anywhere; and Mac
once again exploded with astonishment.

"We're on the track," he shouted. "Good heavens, do you
mean to say you can't see it on ahead there?" and he pointed
towards what looked like thickly timbered country, plentifully
strewn with further boulders and boughs and ant-hills; and
as I shook my head, he shrugged his shoulders hopelessly.
And we're on the main transcontinental route from Adelaide to
Port Darwin," he said.

"Any track anywhere!" he mimicked presently, as we
lurched, and heaved, and bumped along. "What'll she say
when we get into the long-grass country?"

"Long here!" he ejaculated, when I thought the grass we
were driving through was fairly long (it was about three feet).
"Just you wait!"

I waited submissively, if bumping about a buck-board over
thirty miles of obstacles can be called waiting, and next day
we "got into the long-grass country"; miles of grass, waving

33

level with and above our heads—grass ten feet high and more, shutting out everything but grass.

The Maluka was riding a little behind, at the head of the pack-team, to relieve the buck-board horses; but we could see neither him nor the team, and Mac looked triumphantly round as the staunch little horses pushed on through the forest of grass that swirled and bent and swished and reeled all about the buck-board.

"Didn't I tell you?" he said. "This is what we call long grass"; and he asked if I could "see any track now". "It's as plain as a pikestaff," he declared, trying to show what he called a "clear break all the way". "Oh, I'm a dead homer all right," he shouted after further going, as we came out at the "King" crossing.

"Now for it! Hang on!" he warned, and we went down the steep bank at a hand-gallop; and as the horses rushed into the swift-flowing stream, he said, unconcernedly, "I wonder how deep this is," adding, as the buck-board lifted and swerved when the current struck it, "By George! They're off their feet," and leaning over the splashboard, lashed at the undaunted little beasts until they raced up the opposite bank.

"That's the style!" he shouted in triumph, as they drew up,. panting and dripping well over the rise from the crossing. "Close thing, though! Did you get your feet wet?"

"Did you get your feet wet!" That was all, when I was expecting every form of concern imaginable. For a moment I felt indignant at Mac's recklessness and lack of concern, and said severely, "You shouldn't take such risks."

But Mac was blissfully unconscious of the severity. "Risks!" he said. "Why, it wasn't wide enough for anything to happen, bar a ducking. If you rush it, the horses are pushed across before they know they're off their feet."

"Bar a ducking, indeed!" But Mac was out of the buck-board, shouting back: "Hold hard there! It's a swim," and continued shouting directions until the horses were across with comparatively dry pack-bags. Then he and the Maluka shook hands and congratulated each other on being on the right side of everything.

"No more rivers!" the Maluka said.

"Clear run home, bar a deluge," Mac added, gathering up the reins. "We'll strike the front gate tonight."

All afternoon we followed the telegraph line, and there the track was well-defined; then at sun-down Mac drew up, and with a flourish of hats he and the Maluka bade the missus "Welcome Home!" All around and about was bush, and only bush, that, and the telegraph line, and Mac, touching on one of the slender galvanized iron poles, explained the welcome. "This is the front gate!" he said; "another forty-five miles and we'll be knocking at the front door." And they called the Elsey "a nice little place!" Perhaps it was when compared with runs of six million acres.

The camp was pitched just inside the "front gate" near a wide-spreading sheet of water, "Easter's Billabong", and at supper-time the conversation turned on bush cookery.

"Never tasted Johnny cakes!" Mac said. "Your education hasn't begun yet. We'll have some for breakfast; I'm real slap-up at Johnny cakes!" and rummaging in a pack-bag, he produced flour, cream-of-tartar, soda, and a mixing-dish, and set to work at once.

"I'm real slap-up at Johnny cakes! No mistake!" he assured us, as he knelt on the ground, big and burly, in front of the mixing dish, kneading enthusiastically at his mixture. "Look at that!" as air-bubbles appeared all over the light, spongy dough. "Didn't I tell you I knew a thing or two about cooking?" and cutting off nuggety-looking chunks, he buried them in the hot ashes.

When they were cooked, crisp and brown, he displayed them with just pride. "Well!" he said. "Who's slap-up at Johnny cakes?" and standing them on end in the mixing-dish he rigged up tents—a deluge being expected—and carried them into his own for safety.

During the night the deluge came, and the billabong, walking up its flood-banks, ran about the borders of our camp, sending so many exploring little rivulets through Mac's tent that he was obliged to pass most of the night perched on a pyramid of pack-bags and saddles.

Unfortunately, in the confusion and darkness, the dish of Johnny cakes became the base of the pyramid, and was consequently missing at breakfast time. After a long hunt, Mac recovered it and stood looking dejectedly at the ruins of his cookery—a heap of flat, stodgy-looking slabs. "Must have been sitting on 'em all night," he said, "and there's no other bread for breakfast."

There was no doubt that we must eat them or go without bread of any kind; but as we sat tugging at the gluey, gutta-percha-like substance, Mac's sense of humour revived. "Didn't I tell you I was slap-up at Johnny cakes?" he chuckled, adding with further infinitely more humorous chuckles, "You mightn't think it; but I really am." Then he pointed to Jackeroo, who was watching in bewilderment while the Maluka hunted for the crispest crust, not for himself, but the woman. "White fellow big-fellow fool all right, eh, Jackeroo?" he asked, and Jackeroo openly agreed with us.

Finding the black soil flats impassable after the deluge, Mac left the track, having decided to stick to the ridges all day; and all that had gone before was smoothness itself in comparison with what was in store.

All day the buck-board rocked and bumped through the timber, and the Maluka, riding behind, from time to time pointed out the advantages of travelling across country, as we bounced about the buck-board like rubber balls; "There's so little chance of getting stiff with sitting still."

Every time we tried to answer him we bit our tongues as the buck-board leapt over the tussocks of grass. Once we managed to call back, "You won't feel the journey in a buck-board." Then an overhanging bough threatening to wipe us out of our seats, Mac shouted, "Duck!" and as we "ducked" the buck-board skimmed between two trees, with barely an inch to spare.

"I'm a bit of a Jehu all right!" Mac shouted triumphantly. "It takes judgment to do the thing in style"; and the next moment, swinging round a patch of scrub, we flew off at a tangent to avoid a fallen tree, crashing through its branches and grinding over an out-crop of ironstone to miss a big boulder just beyond the tree. It undoubtedly took judgment, this "travelling across country along the ridges"; but the keen, alert bushman never hesitated as he swung in and out and about the timber, only once miscalculating the distance between trees, when he was obliged to back out again. Of course we barked trees constantly, but Mac called that "blazing a track for the next travellers", and everywhere the bush creatures scurried out of our way; and when I expressed fears for the springs, Mac reassured me by saying a buck-board had none, excepting those under the seat.

If Mac was a "bit of a Jehu", he certainly was a "dead homer", for after miles of scrub and grass and timber, we came out at our evening camp at the Bitter Springs, to find the Head Stockman there, with his faithful tawny-coloured shadow, "Old Sool'em", beside him.

Dog and man greeted us sedately, and soon Dan had a billy boiling for us, and a blazing fire, and accepted an invitation to join us at supper and "bring something in the way of bread along with him".

With a commonplace remark about the trip out, he placed a crisp, newly baked damper on the tea-towel that acted as supper-cloth; but when we all agreed that he was "real slap-up at damper-making", he scented a joke and shot a quick, questioning glance around; then deciding that it was wiser not to laugh at all than to laugh in the wrong place, he only said he was "not a bad hand at the damper trick". Dan liked his jokes well labelled when dealing with the Unknown Woman.

He was a bushman of the old type, one of the men of the droving days; full of old theories, old faiths, and old prejudices, and clinging always to old habits and methods. Year by year as the bush had receded and shrunk before the railways, he had receded with it, keeping always just behind the Back of Beyond, droving, bullock-punching, stock-keeping, and unconsciously opening up the way for that very civilization that was driving him farther and farther back. In the forty years since his boyhood, railways had driven him out of Victoria, New South Wales, and Queensland, and were now threatening even the

Never-Never, and Dan was beginning to fear that they would not leave "enough bush to bury a man in".

Enough bush to bury a man in! That is all these men of the droving days have ever asked of their nation; and yet without them the pioneers would have been tied hand and foot, and because of them Australia is what it is.

"Had a good trip out?" Dan asked, feeling safe on that subject, and appeared to listen to the details of the road with interest; but all the time the shrewd hazel eyes were upon me, drawing rapid conclusions, and I began to feel absurdly anxious to know their verdict. That was not to come before bedtime; and only those who knew the life of the stations in the Never-Never know how much was depending on the stockmen's verdict.

Dan had his own methods of dealing with the Unknown Woman. Forty years out-bush had convinced him that "most of 'em were the right sort", but it had also convinced him that "you had to take 'em all differently", and he always felt his way carefully, watching and waiting, ready to open out at the first touch of fellowship and understanding, but just as ready to withdraw into himself at the faintest approach to a snub.

By the time supper was over he had risked a joke or two, and taking heart by their reception, launched boldly into the conversation, chuckling with delight as the Maluka and Mac amused themselves by examining the missus on bushcraft.

"She'll need a deal of educating before we let her out alone," he said, after a particularly bad failure, with the first touch of that air of proprietorship that was to become his favourite attitude towards his missus.

"It's only common sense; you'll soon get used to it," Mac said in encouragement, giving us one of his delightful back-handers. Then in all seriousness, Dan suggested teaching her some of the signs of water at hand, right off, "in case she does get lost any time", and also seriously, the Maluka and Mac "thought it would be as well, perhaps".

Then the townswoman's self-satisfied arrogance came to the surface. "You needn't bother about me," I said, confident

I had as much common sense as any bushman. "If ever I do get lost, I'll just catch a cow and milk it."

Knowing nothing of the wild, scared cattle of the fenceless runs of the Never-Never, I was prepared for anything rather than the roar of delight that greeted that example of town "common sense".

"Missus! Missus!" the Maluka cried, as soon as he could speak, "you'll need a deal of educating"; and while Mac gasped: "Oh, I say! Look here!" Dan, with tears in his eyes, chuckled, "She'll have a drouth on by the time she runs one down"—Dan always called a thirst a drouth. "Oh, lord!" he said, picturing the scene in his mind's eye. " 'I'll catch a cow and milk it,' she says."

Then, dancing with fun, the hazel eyes looked round the company, and as Dan rose, preparatory to turning in, we felt we were about to hear their verdict. When it came it was characteristic of the man in uniqueness of wording.

"She's the dead finish!" he said, wiping his eyes on his shirt-sleeve. "Reckoned she was the minute I heard her talking about slap-up dampers"; and in some indescribable way we knew he had paid the woman who was just entering his life the highest compliment in his power. Then he added, "Told the chaps the little 'uns were generally all right." It is the helplessness of little women that makes them appear "all right" in the eyes of bushmen, helplessness being foreign to snorters.

At breakfast Dan expressed surprise because there was no milk, and the pleasantry being well received, he considered the moment ripe for one of his pet theories.

"She'll do for this place!" he said, wagging his head wisely. "I've been forty years out-bush, and I've known eight or ten women in that time, so I ought to know something about it. Anyway, the ones that could see jokes suited best. There was Mrs Bob out Victoria way. She'd see a joke a mile off; sighted 'em as soon as they got within cooee. Never knew her miss one, and never knew anybody suit the bush like she did." And as we packed up and set out for the last lap of our journey, he was still ambling about his theory. "Yes," he said, "you can dodge most things out-bush; but you can't dodge jokes for long.

They'll run you down sooner or later"; adding with a chuckle: "Never heard of one running Mrs Bob down, though. She always tripped 'em up before they could get to her." Then, finding the missus had thrown away a "good cup of tea just because a few flies had got into it", he became grave. "Never heard of Mrs Bob getting up to those tricks," he said, and doubted whether "the missus'ld do, after all," until reassured by the Maluka that "she'll be fishing them out with the indifference of a Stoic in a week or two"; and I was.

When within a few miles of the homestead, the buck-board took a sharp turn round a patch of scrub, and before anyone realized what was happening, we were in the midst of a mob of pack-horses, and face to face with the Quiet Stockman—a strong, erect young Scot, who carried his six foot two of bone and muscle with the lithe ease of a bushman.

"Hallo!" Mac shouted, pulling up. Then, with the air of a showman introducing some rare exhibit, added, "This is the missus, Jack."

Jack touched his hat and moved uneasily in his saddle, answering Mac's questions in monosyllables. Then the Maluka came up, and Mac, taking pity on the embarrassed bushman, suggested "getting along", and we left him sitting rigidly on his horse, trying to collect his scattered senses.

"That was unrehearsed," Mac chuckled, as we drove on. "He's clearing out! Reckon he didn't set out exactly hoping to meet us, though. Tam's a lady's man in comparison," but loyal to his comrade above his amusement, he added warmly, "You can't beat Jack by much, though, when it comes to sticking to a pal," unconscious that he was prophesying of the years to come, when the missus had become one of those pals.

"There's only the Dandy left now," Mac went on, as we spun along an ever more definite track, "and he'll be all right as soon as he gets used to it. Never knew such a chap for finding something decent in everybody he strikes." Naturally, I hoped he would "find something decent in me," having learned what it meant to the stockmen to have a woman pitchforked into their daily lives, when those lives were to be lived side by side, in camp, or in saddle, or at the homestead.

Aborigines preparing for a Corroboree.

Jeannie Gunn (Angela Punch McGregor) and her
Chinese servant unpack at the homestead, Elsey
Station.

Mac hesitated a moment, and then out flashed one of his happy inspirations. "Don't you bother about the Dandy," he said; "bushmen have a sixth sense, and know a pal when they see one."

Just a bushman's pretty speech aimed straight at the heart of a woman, where all the pretty speeches of the bush-folk *are* aimed; for it is by the heart that they judge us. "Only a pal," they will say, towering strong and protecting; and the woman feels uplifted, even though in the same breath they have honestly agreed with her, after careful scrutiny, that it is not her fault that she was born into the plain sisterhood. Bushmen will risk their lives for a woman—pal or otherwise—but leave her to pick up her own handkerchief.

"Of course," Mac added, as an afterthought, "it's not often they find a pal in a woman"; and I add today that when they do, that woman is to be envied her friends.

"Eyes front!" Mac shouted suddenly, and in a moment the homestead was in sight, and the front gate forty-five miles behind us. "If ever you *do* reach the homestead alive," the Darwin ladies had said; and now *they* were three hundred miles away from us to the north-west.

"Sam's spotted us!" Mac smiled as we skimmed on, and a slim little Chinaman ran across between the buildings. "We'd better do the thing in style," and whipping up the horses, he whirled them through the open slip-rails, past the stockyards, away across the grassy homestead enclosure, and pulled up with a rattle of hoofs and wheels at the head of a little avenue of buildings.

The Dandy, fresh and spotless, appeared in a doorway; black boys sprang up like a crop of mushrooms and took charge of the buck-board; Dan rattled in with the pack-teams, and horses were jangling hobbles and rattling harness all about us, as I found myself standing in the shadow of a queer, unfinished building, with the Maluka and Mac, surrounded by a mob of leaping, bounding dogs, flourishing, as best they could, another "Welcome Home!"

"Well?" Mac asked, beating off dogs at every turn. "Is it a House or a Hut?"

"A Betwixt and Between," we decided; and then the Dandy was presented. And the steady grey eyes apparently finding "something decent" in the missus, with a welcoming smile and ready tact he said:

"I'm sure we're all real glad to see *you*." Just the tiniest emphasis on the word "you"; but that, and the quick, bright look that accompanied the emphasis, told, as nothing else could, that it was "that other woman" that had not been wanted. Unconventional, of course; but when a welcome is conventional out-bush it is unworthy of the name of welcome.

The Maluka knew this well; but before he could speak, Mac had seized a little half-grown dog—the most persistent of all the leaping dogs—by her tightly curled-up tail, and, setting her down at my feet, said, "An' this is Tiddle'ums," adding, with another flourishing bow, "A present from a Brither Scot," while Tiddle'ums in no way resented the indignity. Having a tail that curled tightly over her back like a cup handle, she expected to be lifted up by it.

Then one after the other Mac presented the station dogs: Quart-Pot, Drover, Tuppence, Misery, Buller, and a dozen others; and as I bowed gravely to each in turn, Dan chuckled in appreciation: "She'll do! Told you she was the dead finish."

Then, the introductions over, the Maluka said, "And now I suppose she may consider herself just 'One of Us'."

6

The homestead, standing half-way up the slope that rose from the billabong, had, after all, little of that "down-at-heels, anything'll-do" appearance that Mac had so scathingly described. No one could call it a "commodious station home", and it was even patched up and shabby; but, for all that, neat and cared for. An orderly little array of one-roomed buildings, mostly built of sawn slabs, and ranged round a broad oblong space with a precision that suggested the idea of a section of a street cut out from some neat, compact little village.

The cook's quarters, kitchens, men's quarters, store, meat-house, and waggon house, facing each other on either side of this oblong space, formed a short avenue—the main thorough-fare of the homestead—the centre of which was occupied by an immense wood-heap, the favourite gossiping place of some of the old black fellows, while across the western end of it, and looking down it, but a little aloof from the rest of the build-ings, stood the House, or, rather, as much of it as had been rebuilt after the cyclone of 1897. As befitted their social positions, the forge and black boys' "humpy" kept a respectful distance well round the south-eastern corner of this thorough-fare; but, for some unknown reason, the fowl-roosts had been erected over Sam Lee's sleeping quarters. That comprised this tiny homestead of a million and a quarter acres, with the Katherine Settlement a hundred miles to the north of it, one neighbour ninety miles to the east, another, a hundred and five to the south, and others about two hundred to the west.

Unfortunately, Mac's description of the House had been only too correct. With the exception of the one roughly finished room at its eastern end, it was "mostly verandahs and promises".

After the cyclone had wrecked the building, scattering timber and sheets of iron in all directions, everything had lain exactly where it had fallen for some weeks, at the mercy of the wind and weather. At the end of those weeks a travelling Chinese carpenter arrived at the station with such excellent common-sense ideas of what a bush homestead should be, that he had been engaged to rebuild it.

His plans showed a wide-roofed building, built upon two-foot piles, with two large centre rooms opening into each other, and surrounded by a deep verandah on every side; while two small rooms, a bathroom and an office, were to nestle each under one of the eastern corners of this deep twelve-foot verandah. Without a doubt, excellent common-sense ideas, but, unfortunately, much larger than the supply of timber. Rough-hewn posts for the two-foot piles and verandah supports could be had for the cutting, and therefore did not give out; but the man used joists and uprights with such reckless extravagance that, by the time the skeleton of the building was up, the completion of the contract was impossible. With philosophical indifference, however, he finished one room completely; left a second a mere outline of uprights and tye-beams; apparently forgot all about the bathroom and office; covered the whole roof, including verandahs, with corrugated iron; surveyed his work with a certain amount of stolid satisfaction; then, announcing that "wood bin finissem", applied for his cheque and departed; and from that day nothing further has been done to the House, which stood before us "mostly verandahs and promises".

Although Mac's description of the House had been apt, he had sadly underrated the furniture. There were *four* chairs, all "up" to my weight, while two of them were up to the Maluka's. The cane was all gone, certainly, but had been replaced with green-hide seats (not green in colour, of course, only green in experience, never having seen a tan-pit). In addition to the chairs, the dining-table, the four-poster bed, the wire mattress, and the looking-glass, there was a solid deal side-table, made from the side of a packing-case, with four solid legs and a solid shelf underneath, also a remarkably steady washstand that had no ware of any description, and a remarkably unsteady chest of four drawers, one of which refused to open, while the other three refused to shut. Further, the dining-table was more than "fairly" steady, three of its legs being perfectly sound, and it therefore only *threatened* to fall over when leaned upon. And lastly, although most of the plates and all the cups were enamel ware, there was almost a complete dinner service in china. The teapot, however, was tin, and, as Mac said, as "big as a house".

As for the walls, not only were the "works of art" there, but they themselves were uniquely dotted from ceiling to floor with the muddy imprints of dogs' feet—not left there by a Pegasus breed of winged dogs, but made by the muddy feet of the station dogs, as they pattered over the timber, when it lay awaiting the carpenter, and no one had seen any necessity to remove them. Outside the verandahs, and all around the house, was what was known later as the garden, a grassy stretch of hillocky ground, well scratched and beaten down by dogs, goats, and fowls; fenceless itself, being part of the grassy acres which were themselves fenced round to form the homestead enclosure. Just inside this enclosure, forming, in fact, the south-western barrier of it, stood the "billabong", then a spreading sheet of water; along its banks flourished the vegetable garden; outside the enclosure, towards the south-east, lay a grassy plain a mile across, and to the north-west were the stock-yards and house paddock—a paddock of five square miles, and the only fenced area on the run; while everywhere to the northwards, and all through the paddock, were dotted "white-ant" hills, all shapes and sizes, forming brick-red turrets among the green scrub and timber.

"Well!" Mac said, after we had completed a survey, "I said it wasn't a fit place for a woman, didn't I?"

But the Head Stockman was in one of his argumentative moods. "Any place is a fit place for a woman," he said, "provided the woman is fitted for the place. The right man in the right place, you know. Square people shouldn't try to get into round holes."

"The woman's square enough," the Maluka interrupted; and Mac added, "And so is the *hole*," with a scornful emphasis on the word "hole".

Dan chuckled, and surveyed the queer-looking building with new interest.

"It reminds me of a banyan tree with corrugated-iron foliage," he said, adding as he went into details, "In a dim light the finished room would pass for the trunk of the tree and the uprights for the supports of the branches."

But the Maluka thought it looked more like a section of a mangrove swamp, piles and all.

"It looks very much like a house nearly finished," I said severely; for, because of the verandah and many promises, I was again hopeful for something approaching that commodious station home. "A few able-bodied men could finish the dining-room in a couple of days, and make a mansion of the rest of the building in a week or so."

But the able-bodied men had a different tale to tell.

"Steady! Go slow, missus!" they cried. "It may *look* like a house very nearly finished, but out-bush, we have to catch our hares before we cook them."

"*We* begin at the very beginning of things in the Never-Never," the Maluka explained. "Timber grows in trees in these parts, and has to be coaxed out with a saw."

"It's a bad habit it's got into," Dan chuckled; then pointing vaguely towards the thickly wooded Long Reach, that lay a mile to the south of the homestead, beyond the grassy plain, he "supposed the dining-room was down there just now, with the rest of the House".

With fast-ebbing hopes I looked in dismay at the distant forest undulating along the skyline, and the Maluka said sympathetically, "It's only too true, little 'un."

But Dan disapproved of spoken sympathy under trying circumstances. "It keeps 'em from toeing the line," he believed; and fearing I was on the point of showing the white feather he broke in with, "We'll have to keep her toeing the line, Boss," and then pointed out that "things might be worse". "In some countries there are no trees to cut down," he said.

"That's the style," he added, when I began to laugh in spite of my disappointment. "We'll soon get you educated up to it."

But already the Sanguine Scot had found the bright side of the situation, and reminded us that we were in the Land of Plenty of Time. "There's time enough for everything in the Never-Never," he said. "She'll have many a pleasant ride along the Reach choosing trees for timber. Catching the hare's often the best part of the fun."

Mac's cheery optimism always carried all before it. Pleasant rides through shady forest-ways seemed a fair recompense for a little delay; and my spirits went up with a bound, to be dashed down again the next moment by Dan.

"We haven't got to the beginning of things yet," he interrupted, following up the line of thought the Maluka had at first suggested. "Before any trees are cut down, we'll have to dig a saw-pit and find a pit-sawyer". Dan was not a pessimist; he only liked to dig down to the very root of things, besides objecting to sugar-coated pills as being a hindrance to education.

But the Dandy had joined the group, and being practical, suggested "trying to get hold of Little Johnny", declaring that "he would make things hum in no time".

Mac happened to know that Johnny was Inside somewhere on a job, and it was arranged that Dan should go in to the Katherine at once for nails and "things", and to see if the telegraph people could find out Johnny's whereabouts down the line, and send him along.

But preparations for a week's journey take time, outbush, owing to that necessity of beginning at the beginning of things. Fresh horses were mustered, a mob of bullocks rounded up for a killer, swags and pack-bags packed; and just as all was in readiness for the start, the Quiet Stockman came in, bringing a small mob of colts with him.

"I'm leaving," he announced in the Quarters; then, feeling some explanation was necessary, added, "I *was* thinking of it before this happened." Strictly speaking this may be true, although he omitted to say that he had abandoned the idea for some little time.

No one was surprised, and no one thought of asking *what* had happened, for Jack had always steered clear of women, as he termed it. Not that he feared or disliked them, but because he considered that they had nothing in common with men. "They're such terrors for asking questions," he said once, when pressed for an opinion, adding as an afterthought, "They never seem to learn much either," in his quiet way, summing up the average woman's conversation with a shy bushman: a long string of purposeless questions, followed by inane remarks on the answers.

"I'm leaving!" Jack had said, and later met the Maluka unshaken in his resolve. There was that in the Maluka, however, that Jack had not calculated on—a something that drew all men to him, and made Dan speak of him in after years as "The best boss that ever I struck"; and although the interview only lasted a few minutes, and the Maluka spoke only of the work of the station, yet in those few minutes the Quiet Stockman changed his mind, and the notice was never given.

"I'm staying on," was all he said on returning to the Quarters; and quick decisions being unusual with Jack, everyone felt interested.

"Going to give her a chance?" Dan asked with a grin, and Jack looked uncomfortable.

"I've only seen the Boss," he said.

Dan nodded with approval. "You've got some sense left, then," he said, "if you know a good boss when you see one."

Jack agreed in monosyllables; but when Dan settled down to argue out the advantages of having a woman about the place, he looked doubtful; but having nothing to say on the subject, said nothing; and when Dan left for the Katherine next morning he was still unconvinced.

Dan set out for the north track soon after sun-up, assuring us that he'd get hold of Johnny somehow; and before sundown a traveller crossed the Creek below the billabong at the south track, and turned into the homestead enclosure. We were vaguely chatting on all and sundry matters, as we sat under the verandah that faced the billabong, when the traveller came into sight.

"Horse traveller!" Mac said, lazily shading his eyes, and then sprang to his feet with a yell. "Talk of luck!" he shouted. "You'll do, missus! Here's Johnny himself."

It was Johnny, sure enough; but Johnny had a cheque in his pocket, and was yearning to see the "chaps at the Katherine"; and, after a good look through the House and store, decided that he really would have to go in to the Settlement for—tools and "things".

"I'll be back in a week, missus," he said next morning, as he gathered his reins together before mounting, "and then we shan't be long. Three days in and three out, you know, bar accidents, and a day's spell at the Katherine," he explained glibly. But the "chaps at the Katherine" proved too entertaining for Johnny, and a fortnight passed before we saw him again.

7

The Quiet Stockman was a Scotsman, and, like many Scotsmen, a strange contradiction of shy reserve and quiet, dignified self-assurance. Having made up his mind on women in general, he saw no reason for changing it; and as he went about his work, thoroughly and systematically avoided me. There was no slinking round corners, though; Jack couldn't slink. He had always looked the whole world in the face with his honest blue eyes, and could never do otherwise. He only took care that our paths did not cross more often than was absolutely necessary; but when they did, his Scotch dignity asserted itself, and he said what had to be said with quiet self-possession, although he invariably moved away as soon as possible.

"It's just Jack's way," the Sanguine Scot said, anxious that his fellow Scot should not be misunderstood. "He'll be all there if you ever need him. He only draws the line at conversations."

But when I mounted the stockyard fence one morning, to see the breaking-in of the colts, he looked as though he "drew the line" at that, too.

Fortunately for Jack's peace of mind, horse-breaking was not the only novelty at the homestead. Only a couple of changes of everything, in a tropical climate, meant an unbroken cycle of washing-days, while, apart from that, Sam Lee was full of surprises, and the lubras' methods of house-cleaning were novel in the extreme.

Sam was bland, amiable and inscrutable, and obedient to irritation; and the lubras were apt and merry, and open-hearted and wayward beyond comprehension. Sam did exactly as he was told and the lubras did exactly as they thought fit, and the results were equally disconcerting.

Sam was asked for a glass of milk, and the lubras were told to scrub the floor. Sam brought the milk immediately, and the lubras, after scrubbing two or three isolated patches on the floor, went off on some frolic of their own.

At afternoon tea there was no milk served. There was none, Sam explained blandly. The missus had drunk it all. "Missus bin finissem milk all about," he said. When the lubras were brought back, *they* said *they* had "knocked up longa scrub", and finished, under protest.

The Maluka offered assistance; but I thought I ought to manage them myself, and set the lubras to clean and strip some feathers for a pillow—the Maluka had been busy with a shot-gun—and suggested to Sam that he might spend some of his spare time shooting birds.

Mac had been right when he said the place was stiff with birds. A deep fringe of birds was constantly moving in and about and around the billabong; and the perpetual clatter of the plovers and waders formed an under-current to the life at the homestead.

The lubras worked steadily for a quarter of an hour at the feathers; then a dog-fight demanding all their attention, the feathers were left to the mercy of the winds, and were never gathered together. At sun-down Sam fired into a colony of martins that Mac considered the luck of the homestead. Right into their midst he fired, as they slept in long, graceful garlands —one beside the other along the branches of a gum-tree, each with its head snugly tucked away out of sight.

"Missus want feather!" Sam said, with his unfathomable smile, when Mac flared out at him, and again the missus appeared the culprit.

The Maluka advised making the orders a little clearer, and Sam was told to use more discretion in his obedience, and, smiling and apologetic, promised to obey.

The lubras also promised to be more painstaking, reserving only the right to rest if they should "knock up longa work".

The Maluka, Mac, and the Dandy looked on in amusement while the missus wrestled with the servant question; and even the Quiet Stockman grinned sympathetically at times, unconsciously becoming interested in a woman who was too occupied to ask questions.

For five days I "wrestled"; and the only comfort I had was in Bertie's Nellie, a gentle-faced old lubra—almost sweet-faced. She undoubtedly did her best, and, showing signs of friendship, was invaluable in "rounding up" the other lubras when they show signs of "knocking up".

On the morning of the sixth day Sam surpassed himself in obedience. I had hinted that breakfast should be a little earlier, adding timidly that he might use a little more ingenuity in the breakfast menu, and at the first grey streak of dawn breakfast was announced, and, dressing hurriedly, we sat down to what Sam called "Pump-pce-King pie with raisins and mince". The expression on Sam's face was celestial. No other word could describe it. There was also an underlying expression of triumph which made me suspicious of his apparent ingenuousness, and as the lubras had done little else but make faces at themselves in the looking-glass for two days (I was beginning to hate that looking-glass), I appealed to the Maluka for assistance.

He took Sam in hand, and the triumph slipped away from beneath the stolid face, and a certain amount of discrimination crept into his obedience from henceforth.

Then the Sanguine Scot said that he would "tackle the lubras for her", and in half an hour everywhere was swept and garnished, and the lubras were meek and submissive.

"You need to rule them with a rod of iron," Mac said, secretly pleased with his success. But there was one drawback to his methods, for next day, with the exception of Nellie, there were no lubras to rule with or without a rod of iron.

Jimmy, the water-carrier and general director of the wood-heap gossip, explained that they had gone off with the camp lubras for a day's recreation: "Him knock up longa all about work," he said, with an apologetic smile. Jimmy was either apologetic or condescending.

Nellie rounded them up when they returned, and the Maluka suggested, as a way out of the difficulty, that I should try to make myself more attractive than the camp lubras, which Mac said "shouldn't be difficult", and then coughed, doubtful of the compliment.

I went down to the Creek at once to carry out the Maluka's suggestion, and succeeded so well that I was soon the centre of a delighted dusky group, squatting on its haunches, and deep in the fascinations of teaching an outsider its language. The uncouth mispronunciation tickled the old men beyond description, and they kept me gurgling at difficult gutturals, until, convulsed at the contortion of everyday words and phrases, they echoed Dan's opinion in queer pidgin-English that the "missus needed a deal of education". Jimmy gradually became loftily condescending, and as for old Nellie, she had never enjoyed anything quite so much.

Undoubtedly I made myself attractive to the black-fellow mind; for, besides having proved an unexpected entertainment, I had made everyone feel mightily superior to the missus. That power of inspiring others with a sense of superiority is an excellent trait to possess when dealing with a black fellow, for there were more than enough helpers next day, and the work was done quickly and well, so as to leave plenty of time for merrymaking.

The Maluka and Mac were full of congratulations. "You've got the mob well in hand now," Mac said, unconscious that he was about to throw everything into disorder again.

For six years Mac had been in charge of the station, and when he heard that the Maluka was coming North to represent the owners, he had decided to give bullock-punching a turn as a change from stock-keeping. Sanguine that "there was a good thing in it", he had bought a bullock waggon and team while in at the Katherine, and secured "loading" for Inside. Under these circumstances it was difficult to understand why he had been so determined in his blocking, the only reason he could ever be cajoled into giving being "that he was off the escorting trick, and, besides, the other chaps had to be thought of".

He was now about to go to "see to things", taking Bertie, his right-hand boy, with him, but leaving Nellie with me. Bertie had expressed himself quite agreeable to the arrangement, but at the eleventh hour refused to go without Nellie; and Nellie, preferring the now fascinating homestead to the company of her lord and master, refused to go with him, and Mac was at his wits' end.

It was impossible to carry her off by force, so two days were spent in shrill ear-splitting arguments—the threads of Nellie's argument being that Bertie could easily "catch nuzzer lubra", and that the missus "must have one good fellow lubra on the staff".

Mac, always chivalrous, said he would manage somehow without Bertie, rather than "upset things"; but the Maluka would not agree, and finally Nellie consented to go, on condition that she would be left at the homestead when the waggons went through.

Then Mac came and confessed a long-kept secret. Roper belonged to the station, and he had no claim on him beyond fellowship. "I've ridden him ever since I came here, that's all," he said, his arm thrown across the old horse. "I'd have stuck to him somehow, fair means or foul, if I hadn't seen you know how to treat a good horse."

The Maluka instantly offered fair means, but Mac shook his head. "Let the missus have him," he said, "and they'll both have a good time. But—I'm first offer when it comes to selling." So the grand old horse was passed over to me to be numbered among the staunchest and truest of friends.

"Oh, well," Mac said in good-bye. "All's well that end's well," and he pointed to Nellie, safely stowed away in a grove of dogs that half-filled the back of the buck-board.

But all had not ended for us. So many lubras put themselves on the homestead staff to fill the place left vacant by Nellie, that the one room was filled to overflowing while the work was being done, and the Maluka was obliged to come to the rescue once more. He reduced the house staff to two, allowing a shadow or two extra in the persons of a few old black fellows and a piccaninny or two, sending the rejected to camp.

In the morning there was a free fight in camp between the

Staff and some of the camp lubras; the Rejected, led by Jimmy's lubra—another Nellie—declaring the Maluka had meant two different lubras each day.

Again there was much ear-splitting argument, but finally a compromise was agreed on. Two lubras were to sit down permanently, while as many as wished might help with the washing and watering. Then the Staff and the shadows settled down on the verandahs beside me to watch while I evolved dresses for two lubras out of next to nothing in the way of material, and as I sewed, the Maluka, with some travellers who were In to help him, set to work to evolve a garden also out of next to nothing in the way of material.

Hopeless as it looked, oblong beds were soon marked out at each of the four corners of the verandah, and beyond the beds a broad path was made to run right round the House. "The wilderness shall blossom like the rose," the Maluka said, planting seeds of a vigorous-growing flowering bean at one of the corner-posts.

The travellers were deeply interested in the servant wrestle, and when the Staff was eventually clothed, and the Rejected green with envy, decided that the "whole difficulty was solved, bar Sam".

Sam, however, was about to solve his part of the difficulty to everyone's satisfaction. A master as particular over the men's table as his own was not a master after Sam's heart, so he came to the Maluka, and announced, in the peculiar manner of Chinese cooks, that he was about to write for a new cook for the station, who would probably arrive within six weeks, when Sam, having installed him to our satisfaction, would, with our permission, leave our service.

The permission was graciously given, and as Sam retired we longed to tell him to engage someone renowned for his disobedience. We fancied later that our willingness piqued Sam, for after giving notice he bestirred himself to such an extent that one of our visitors tried to secure his services for himself, convinced we were throwing away a treasure.

In that fortnight we had several visitors, travellers passing through the station, and as each stayed a day or two, a few of the visits overlapped, and some merry hours were spent in the little homestead.

Some of the guests knew beforehand of the arrival of a Missus at the station, and came ready groomed from their last camp; but others only heard of her arrival when inside the homestead enclosure, and there was a great application of soap, and razors, and towels before they considered themselves fit for presentation.

With only one room at our disposal it would seem to the uninitiated that the accommodation of the homestead must have been strained to bursting point; but "out-bush" every man carries a "bluey" and a mosquito net in his swag, and as the hosts slept under the verandah, and the guests on the garden paths, or in their camps among the forest trees, spare rooms would only have been superfluous. With a billabong at the door, a bathroom was easily dispensed with; and as everyone preferred the roomy verandahs for lounging and smoking, the House had only to act as a dressing-room—for the hosts and a dining-room for all.

The meals, of course, were served on the dining-table; but no apology seemed necessary for the presence of a four-poster bed and a washing-stand in the reception-room. They were there, and our guests knew why they were there, and words, like the spare rooms, would have been superfluous.

Breakfast at sun-up or thereabouts, dinner at noon, and supper at sun-down is the long-established routine of meals on all cattle-runs of the Never-Never; and at all three meals Sam waited, bland and smiling.

The missus, of course, had one of the china cups, and the guests enamel ware; and the flies hovering everywhere in dense clouds, saucers rested on the top of the cups by common consent. Bread, scones, and such things were covered over with serviettes throughout all meals, while hands were kept busy "shooing" flies out of prospective mouthfuls.

Everything lacked conventionality, and was accepted as a matter of course; and although at times Sam sorely taxed my gravity by using the bed for a temporary dumb-waiter, the bushmen showed no embarrassment, simply because they felt none, and retained their self-possession with unconscious dignity. They sat among the buzzing swarms of flies, light-hearted and self-reliant, chatting of their daily lives—of lonely vigils, of cattle-camps and stampedes, of dangers and priva-tions, and I listened with a dawning consciousness that life "out-bush" is something more than mere existence.

Being within four miles of the Overland Telegraph—that backbone of the overland route—rarely a week was to pass without someone coming in, and at times our travellers came in twos and threes; and as each brought news of that world out-side our tiny circle, carrying in perhaps an extra mail to us, they formed a strong link in the chain that bound us to Outside.

In them every rank in bush life was represented, from cattle-drovers and stockmen to the owners of stations, from swag-men and men "down in their luck" to telegraph operators and heads of government departments, men of various nationalities with, foremost among them, the Scots, sons of that fighting race that has everywhere fought with and conquered the Australian bush. Yet, whatever their rank or race, our travellers were men, not riff-raff; the long, formidable stages that wall in the Never-Never have seen to that, turning back the weaklings and worth-less to the flesh-pots of Egypt, and proving the worth and mettle of the brave-hearted: all men, every one of them, and all in need of a little hospitality, whether of the prosperous and well-doing or "down in their luck", and each was welcomed accord-ing to that need; for out-bush rank counts for little: we are only men and women there. And all who came in, and went on, or remained, gave us of their best while with us; for there was that in the Maluka that drew the best out of all men. In life we generally find in our fellow-men just what we seek; and the Maluka, seeking only the good, found only the good, and drew much of it into his own sympathetic, sunny nature. He demand-ed the best and was given the best, and while with him, men found they were better men than at other times.

Some of our guests sat with us at table, some with the men, and some "grubbed in their camps". All of them rode in strangers and many of them rode out life-long friends, for such is the way of the bush-folk: a little hospitality, a day or two of mutual understanding, and we have become part of the other's life. For bush hospitality is something better than the bare housing and feeding of guests, being just the simple sharing of our daily lives with a fellow-man—a literal sharing of all that we have; of our plenty or scarcity, our joys or sorrows, our comforts or discomforts, our security or danger; a democratic hospitality, where all men are equally welcome, yet so refined in its simplicity and wholesomeness, that fulsome thanks or vulgar apologies have no part in it, although it was whispered among the bush-folk that those "down in their luck" learned that when the Maluka was filling tucker-bags, a timely word in praise of the missus filled tucker-bags to overflowing.

Two hundred and fifty guests was the tally for that year, and earliest among them came a telegraph operator, who—as is the way with telegraphic operators out-bush—invited us to "ride across to the wire for a shake hands with Outside"; and within an hour we came in sight of the telegraph wire as our horses mounted the stony ridge that overlooks the Warloch Ponds, when the wire was forgotten for a moment in the kaleidoscope of moving, everchanging colour that met our eyes.

Two wide-spreading, limpid ponds, the Warloch lay before us, veiled in a glory of golden-flecked heliotrope and purple water-lilies, and floating deep green leaves, with here and there gleaming little seas of water, opening out among the lilies, and standing knee-deep in the margins a rustling fringe of light reeds and giant bulrushes. All round the ponds stood dark groves of pandanus palms, and among and beyond the palms tall grasses and forest trees, with here and there a spreading coolibah festooned from summit to trunk with brilliant crimson strands of mistletoe, and here and there a gaunt dead old giant of the forest, and everywhere above and beyond the timber deep sunny blue and flooding sunshine. Sunny blue reflected, with the gaunt old trees, in the tiny gleaming seas among the lilies, while everywhere upon the floating leaves myriads and myriads of grey and pink "galah" parrots and sulphur-crested cockatoos preened feathers, or rested, sipping at the water—grey and pink verging to heliotrope and snowy white, touched here and there with gold, blending, flower-like, with the golden-flecked glory of the lilies.

For a moment we waited, spell-bound in the brilliant sunshine; then, the dogs running down to the water's edge, the galahs and cockatoos rose with gorgeous sunrise effect: a floating grey-and-pink cloud, backed by sunlit flashing white. Direct to the forest trees they floated and, settling there in their myriads, as by a miracle the gaunt, gnarled old giants of the bush all over blossomed with garlands of grey, and pink, and white, and gold.

But the operator, being unpoetical, had ridden on to the "wire", and presently was "shinning up" one of its slender galvanized iron posts as a preliminary to the "handshake"; for, tapping the line being part of the routine of a telegraph operator in the Territory, "shinning up posts" is one of his necessary accomplishments.

In town, dust, and haste, and littered papers, and nerve-racking bustle seem indispensable to the sending of a telegram; but when the bush-folk "shake hands" with Outside all is sunshine and restfulness, soft beauty and leisurely peace. With the murmuring bush about us, in the clear space kept always cleared beneath those quivering wires, we stood all dressed in white, first looking up at the operator as, clinging to his pole, he tapped the line, and then looking down at him as he knelt at our feet with his tiny transmitter beside him clicking out our message to the South folk. And as we stood with our horses' bridles over our arms and the horses nibbling at the sweet grasses, in touch with the world in spite of our isolation, a gorgeous butterfly rested for a brief space on the tiny instrument, with gently swaying purple wings, and away in the great world men were sending telegrams amid clatter and dust, unconscious of that tiny group of bush-folk, or that Nature, who does all things well, can beautify even the sending of a telegram.

In the heart of the bush we stood, yet listening to the clatter of the townsfolk, for, business over, the little clicking instrument was gossiping cheerfully with us—the telegraph wire in the Territory being such a friendly wire. Daily it gathers gossip, and daily it whispers it up and down the line, and daily news and gossip fly hither and thither: who's Inside, who has gone out, whom to expect, where the mail-man is, the newest arrival in Darwin and the latest rainfall at Powell's Creek.

Daily the telegraph people hear all the news of the Territory, and in due course give the news to the public, when the travellers, gathering it, carry it out to the bushfolk, scattering it broadcast, until everybody knows everyone else, and all his business, and where it has taken him; and because of that knowledge, and in spite of those hundreds of thousands of square miles of bushland, the people of the Territory are held together in one great brotherhood.

Among various items of news the little instrument told us that Dan was "packing up for the return trip"; and in a day or two he came in, bringing a packet of garden seeds and a china teapot from Mine Host, Southern letters from the telegraph, and, from Little Johnny, news that he was getting "tools together and would be along in no time".

Being in one of his whimsical moods, Dan withheld congratulations.

"I've been thinking things over, boss," he said, assuming his most philosophical manner, "and I reckon any more rooms'll only interfere with getting the missus educated."

Later on he used the servant question to hang his argument on. "Just proves what I was saying," he said. "If the cleaning of one room causes all this trouble and worry, where'll she be when she's got four to look after? What with white ants, and blue mould, and mildew, and wrastling with lubras, there won't be one minute to spare for education."

He also professed disapproval of the Maluka's devices for making the homestead more habitable. "If this goes on we'll never learn her nothing but loafin'," he declared, when he found that a couple of yards of canvas and a few sticks had become a comfortable lounge chair. "Too much luxury!" and he sat down on his own heels to show how he scorned luxuries. A tree sawn into short lengths to provide verandah seats for all comers, he passed over as doubtful. He was slightly reassured, however, when he heard that my revolver practice had not been neglected, and condescended to own that some of the devices were "handy enough". A neat little tray made from the end of a packing-case and a few laths interested him, in particular. "You'll get him dodged for ideas one of these days," he said, alluding to the Maluka's ingenuity; and when, a day or two later, I broke the spring of my watch and asked helplessly, "However was I going to tell the time till the waggons came with the clock?" Dan felt sure I had set and solved the problem.

"That 'ud get anybody dodged," he declared; but it took more than that to "dodge" the Maluka's resourcefulness. He spent a little while in the sun with a compass and a few wooden pegs, and a sundial lay on the ground just outside the verandah.

Dan declared it just "licked creation", and wondered if "that 'ud settle 'em" when I asked for some strong iron rings for a curtain. But the Dandy took a hobble chain to the forge, and breaking the links asunder, welded them into smooth round rings.

The need for curtain rings was very pressing, for, scanty as it was, the publicity of our wardrobe hanging in one corner of the reception-room distressed me; but with the Dandy's rings and a checkered rug for curtain, a corner wardrobe was soon fixed up.

Dan looked at it askance, and harked back to the sundial and education. "It's cute enough," he said. "But it won't do, boss. She should have been taught how to tell the time by the sun. Don't you let 'em spoil your chances of education, missus. You were in luck when you struck this place; never saw luck to equal it. And if it holds good, something'll happen to stop you from ever having a house, so as to get you properly educated."

My luck "held good" for the time being; for when Johnny came along in a few days he announced, in answer to a very warm welcome, that "something had gone wrong at No. 3 Well", and that he'd "promised to see to it at once".

"Oh, Johnny!" I cried reproachfully, but the next moment was "toeing the line" even to the Head Stockman's satisfaction; for with a look of surprise Johnny had added: "I—I thought you'd reckon that travellers' water for the Dry came before your rooms." Out-bush we deal in hard facts.

"Thought I'd reckon!" I said, appalled to think my comfort

should even be spoken of when men's lives were in question. "Of course I do; I didn't understand, that was all."

"We haven't finished her education yet," Dan explained, and the Maluka added, "But she's learning."

Johnny looked perplexed. "Oh, well! That's all right, then," he said, rather ambiguously. "I'll be back as soon as possible, and then we shan't be long."

Two days later he left the homestead bound for the well, and as he disappeared into the Ti-Tree that bordered the south track, most of us agreed that "luck was out". Only Dan professed to think differently. "It's more wonderful than ever," he declared; "more wonderful than ever, and if it holds good we'll never see Johnny again."

8

Considering ourselves homeless, the Maluka decided that we should "go bush" for a while during Johnny's absence beginning with a short tour of inspection through some of the southern country of the run; intending, if all were well there, to prepare for a general horse-muster along the north of the Roper. Nothing could be done with the cattle until after the Wet.

Only Dan and the inevitable black "boy" were to be with us on this preliminary walk-about; but all hands were to turn out for the muster, to the Quiet Stockman's dismay.

"Thought they mostly sat about and sewed," he said in the quarters. Little did the Sanguine Scot guess what he was doing when he "culled" needlework from the "mob" at Pine Creek.

The walk-about was looked upon as a reprieve; and when a traveller, expressing sympathy, suggested that "it might sicken her a bit of camp life", Jack clung to that hope desperately.

Most of the nigger world turned up to see the "missus mount", that still being something worth seeing. Apart from the mystery of the side-saddle, and the joke of seeing her in an enormous mushroom hat, there was the interest of the mounting itself; Jackeroo having spread a report that the Maluka held out his hands, while the missus ran up them, and sat herself upon the horse's back.

"They reckon you have escaped from a Wild West show," Dan said, tickled at the look of wonder on some of the faces as I settled myself in the saddle. We learned later that Jackeroo had tried to run up Jimmy's hands to illustrate the performance in camp, and, failing, had naturally blamed Jimmy, causing report to add that the Maluka was a very Samson in strength.

"A dress rehearsal for the cattle-musters later on," Dan called the walk-about, looking with approval on my cartridge belt and revolver; and after a few small mobs of cattle had been rounded up and looked over, he suggested "rehearsing that part of the performance where the missus gets lost, and catches cows and milks 'em".

"Now's your chance, missus," he shouted, as a scared, frightened beast broke from the mob in hand, and went crashing through the undergrowth. "There's one all by herself to practise on." Dan's system of education, being founded on object-lessons, was mightily convincing; and for that trip, anyway, he had a very humble pupil to instruct in the "ways of telling the signs of water at hand".

All day as we zigzagged through scrub and timber, visiting the water-holes and following up cattle-pads, the solitude of the bush seemed only a pleasant seclusion; and the deep forest glades, shady pathways leading to the outside world; but at night, when the camp had been fixed up in the silent depths of a dark Leichhardt-pine forest, the seclusion had become an isolation that made itself felt, and the shady pathways, miles of dark treacherous forest between us and our fellow-men.

There is no isolation so weird in its feeling of cut-offness as that of a night camp in the heart of the bush. The flickering camp-fires draw all that is human and tangible into its charmed circle, and without, all is indefinable darkness and uncertainty. Yet it was in this night camp among the dark pines, with even the stars shut out, that we learnt that outbush "Houselessness" need not mean "Homelessness"—a discovery that destroyed all hope that "this would sicken her a bit".

As we were only to be out one night, and there was little chance of rain, we had nothing with us but a little tucker, a bluey each, and a couple of mosquito nets. The simplicity of our camp added intensely to the isolation; and as I stood among the dry rustling leaves, looking up at the dark broad-leaved canopy above us, with my "swag" at my feet, the Maluka called me a "poor homeless little coon".

A woman with a swag sounds homeless enough to Australian ears, but Dan, with his habit of looking deep into the heart of things, "didn't exactly see where the homelessness came in".

We had finished supper, and the Maluka, stretching himself luxuriously in the firelight, made a nest in the warm leaves for me to settle down in. "You're right, Dan," he said, after a short silence, "when I come to think of it: I don't exactly see myself where the homelessness comes in. A bite and a sup and a faithful dog, and a guidwife by a glowing hearth, and what more is needed to make a home? Eh, Tiddle'ums?"

Tiddle'ums, having for some time given the whole of her heart to the Maluka, nestled closer to him, and Dan gave an appreciative chuckle, and pulled Sool'ems ears. The conversation promised to suit him exactly.

"Never got farther than the dog myself," he said. "Did I, Sool'em, old girl?" But Sool'em becoming effusive, there was a pause until she could be persuaded that "nobody wanted none of her licking tricks". As she subsided, Dan went on with his thoughts uninterrupted: "I've seen others at the guidwife business, though, and it didn't seem too bad, but I never struck it in a camp before. There was Mrs Bob now. You've heard me tell of her? I didn't know how it was, but while she was out at the 'Downs' things seemed different. She never interfered, and we went on just the same, but everything seemed different somehow."

The Maluka suggested that perhaps he had "got father than the dog" without knowing it, and the idea appealing to Dan, he "reckoned it must have been that". But his whimsical mood had slipped away, as it usually did when his thoughts strayed to Mrs Bob; and he went on earnestly: "She was the right sort if ever there was one. I know 'em, and she was one of 'em. When you were all right you told her yarns, and she'd enjoy 'em more'n you would yourself, which is saying something; but when you were off the track a bit you told her other things, and she'd heave you on again. See her with the sick travellers!" And then he stopped unexpectedly as his voice became thick and husky.

Camp-fire conversations have a trick of coming to an abrupt end without embarrassing anyone. As Dan sat looking into the

fire, with his thoughts far away in the past, the Maluka began
to croon contentedly at "Home, Sweet Home", and, curled up
in the warm, sweet nest of leaves, I listened to the crooning, and,
watching the varying expression of Dan's face, wondered if
Mrs Bob had any idea of the bright memories she had left
behind her in the bush. Then as the Maluka crooned on, everything but the crooning became vague and indistinct, and,
beginning also to see into the heart of things, I learned that
when a woman finds love and comradeship out-bush, little else
is needed to make even the glowing circle of a camp-fire her
home-circle.

Without any warning the Maluka's mood changed. "There
is nae luck aboot her house, there is nae luck at a'," he shouted
lustily, and Dan, waking from his reverie with a start, rose to the
tempting bait.

"No *luck* about *her* house!" he said. "It was Mrs Bob that had
no luck. She struck a good, comfortable, well-furnished house
first go off, and never got an ounce of educating. She was chained to that house as surely as ever a dog was chained to its kennel.
But it'll never come to that with the missus. Something's bound
to happen to Johnny, just to keep her from ever having a house.
Poor Johnny, though," he added, warming up to the subject.
"It's hard for him. He's a decent little chap. We'll miss him";
and he shook his head sorrowfully, and looked round for
applause.

The Maluka said it seemed a pity that Johnny had been
allowed to go to his fate; but Dan was in his best form.

"It wouldn't have made any difference," he said tragically.
"He'd have got fever if he'd stayed on, or a tree would have
fallen on him. He's doomed if the missus keeps him to his
contract."

"Oh, well! He'll die in a good cause," I said cheerfully, and
Dan's gravity deserted him.

"You're the dead finish!" he chuckled; and without further
ceremony, beyond the taking off of his boots, rolled into his
mosquito net for the night.

We heard nothing further from him until that strange
rustling hour of the night—that hour half-way between mid-

night and dawn, when all Nature stirs in its sleep, and murmurs drowsily in answer to some mysterious call.

Nearly all bushmen who sleep with the warm earth for a bed will tell of this strange wakening moment, of that faint touch of half-consciousness, that whispering stir, strangely enough, only perceptible to the *sleeping* children of the bush—one of the mysteries of Nature that no man can fathom, one of the delicate threads with which the Wizard of Never-Never weaves his spells. "Is all well, my children?" comes the cry from the watch-man of the night; and with a gentle stirring the answer floats back, "All is well."

Softly the pine forest rustled with the call and the answer; and as the camp roused to its dim half-consciousness, Dan murmured sleepily, "Sool'em, old girl"; then, after a vigorous rustling among the leaves (Sool'em's tail returning thanks for the attention), everything slipped back into unconsciousness until the dawn. As the first grey streak of dawn filtered through the pines, a long-drawn-out cry of "Day-li-ght"—Dan's camp reveille—rolled out of his net, and Dan rolled out after it, with even less ceremony than he had rolled in.

On our way back to the homestead, Dan suggested that the "missus might like to have a look at the dining-room"; we turned into the towering timber that borders the Reach, and for the next two hours rode on through soft, luxurious shade; and all the while the fathomless, spring-fed Reach lay sleeping on our left.

The Reach always slept; for nearly twelve miles it lay, a swaying garland of heliotrope and purple water-lilies, gleaming through a graceful fringe of palms and rushes and scented shrubs, touched here and there with shafts of sunlight and murmuring and rustling with an attendant host of gorgeous butterflies and flitting birds and insects.

Dan looked on the scene with approving eyes. "Not a bad place to ride through, is it?" he said. But gradually, as we rode on, a vague depression settled down upon us, and when Dan finally decided he "could do with a bit more sunshine", we followed him into the blistering noontide glare with almost a sigh of relief.

It is always so. These wondrous waterways have little part in that mystical holding power of the Never-Never. They are only pleasant places to ride through and—leave behind; for their purring slumbrous beauty is vaguely suggestive of the beauty of a sleeping tiger—a sleeping tiger with deadly fangs and talons hidden under a wonder of soft allurement; and when exiles in the towns sit and dream, their dreams are all of stretches of scorched grass and quivering, sun-flecked shade.

In the honest sunlight Dan's spirits rose, and as I investigated various byways he asked "where the sense came in of tying-up a dog that was doing no harm running loose". "It waren't as though she'd taken to chivvying cattle," he added, as, a mob of inquisitive steers trotting after us, I hurried Roper in among the riders; and then he wondered "how she'll shape at her first muster".

The rest of the morning he filled in with tales of cattle-musters —tales of stampedes and of cattle rushing over camps and "mincing chaps into saw-dust"—until I was secretly pleased that the coming muster was for horses.

But Jack's reprieve was to last a little longer. When all was ready for the muster, word came in that outside blacks were in all along the river, and the Maluka deciding that the risks were too great for the missus in long-grass country, the plans were altered, and I was left at the homestead in the Dandy's care.

"It's an ill wind that blows nobody any good," the Maluka said, drawing attention to Jack's sudden interest in the proceedings.

Apart from sterling worth of character, the Dandy was all contrast to the Quiet Stockman: quick, alert, and sociable, and brimming over with quiet tact and thoughtfulness, and the Maluka knew I was in good hands. But the Dandy had his work to attend to; and after watching till the bush had swallowed up the last of the pack-team, I went to the wood-heap for company and consolation. Had the Darwin ladies seen me then, they would have been justified in saying, "I told you so."

There was plenty of company at the wood-heap, but the consolation was doubtful in character. Goggle-Eye and three other old black fellows were gossiping there, and after a peculiar grin of welcome, they expressed fear lest the homestead should be attacked by "outside" blacks during the Maluka's absence. "Might it," they said, and offered to sleep in the garden near me, as no doubt "missus would be frightened fellow" to sleep alone.

"Me big mob frightened fello longa wild black fellow," Goggle-Eye said, rather overdoing the part; and the other old rascals giggled nervously, and said, "My word!" But sly, watchful glances made me sure they were only probing to find if fear had kept the missus at the homestead. Of course, if it had, a little harmless bullying for tobacco could be safely indulged in when the Dandy was busy at the yards.

Fortunately, Dan's system of education provided for all emergencies; and remembering his counsel to "die rather than own to a black fellow that you were frightened of anything", I refused their offer of protection and declared so emphatically that there was nothing in heaven or earth that I was afraid to tackle single-handed, that I almost believed it myself.

There was no doubt *they* believed it, for they murmured in admiration: "My word! Missus big mob cheeky fellow all right." But in their admiration they forgot that they were supposed to be quaking with fear themselves, and took no precautions against the pretended attack. "Putting themselves away properly," the Dandy said when I told him about it.

"It was a try-on all right," he added. "Evidence was against you, but they struck an unexpected snag. You'll have to keep it up, though"; and deciding "there was nothing in the yarn", the Dandy slept in the Quarters, and I in the House, leaving the doors and windows open as usual.

When this was reported at dawn by Billy Muck, who had taken no part in the intimidation scheme, a wholesome awe crept into the old men's admiration; for a black fellow is fairly logical in these matters.

To him, the man who crouches behind barred doors is a coward, and may be attacked without much risk, while he who relies only on his own strength appears as a Goliath defying the armies of a nation, and is best left alone, lest he develop into a Samson annihilating Philistines. Fortunately for my reputation, only the Dandy knew that we considered open doors easier to get out of than closed ones, and that my revolver was to be fired to call him from the Quarters if anything alarming occurred.

"You'll have to live up to your reputation now," the Dandy said, and, brave in the knowledge that he was within cooee, I ordered the old men about most unmercifully, leaving little doubt in their minds that "missus was big mob cheeky fellow".

They were most deferential all day, and at sun-down I completed my revenge by offering these rulers of a nation the insult of a woman's protection. "If you are still afraid of the wild blacks, you may sleep near me tonight," I said, and apologized for not having made the offer for the night before.

"You've got 'em on toast," the Dandy chuckled as the offer was refused with a certain amount of dignity.

The lubras secretly enjoyed the discomfiture of their lords and masters, and taking me into their confidence, made it very plain that a lubra's life at times is anything but a happy one; particularly if "me boy all day krowl (growl)". As for the lords and masters themselves, the insult rankled so that they spent the next few days telling great and valiant tales of marvellous personal daring, hoping to wipe the stain of cowardice from their characters. Fortunately for themselves, Billy Muck and Jimmy had been absent from the wood-heap, and, therefore, not having committed themselves on the subject of wild blacks, bragged excessively. Had they been present, knowing the old fellows well, I venture to think there would have been no intimidation scheme floated.

As the Dandy put it, "altogether the time passed pleasantly", and when the Maluka returned we were all on the best of terms, having reached the phase of friendship when pet names are permissible. The missus had become "Gadgerrie" to the old men and certain privileged lubras. What it means I do not know, excepting that it seemed to imply fellowship. Perhaps it meant "old pal" or "mate", or, judging from the tone of voice that accompanied it, "old girl", but more probably, like "Maluka", untranslatable. The Maluka was always "Maluka" to the old men, and to some of us who imitated them.

Dan came in the day after the Maluka, and, hearing of our "affairs", took all the credit of it to himself.

"Just shows what a bit of educating'll do," he said. "The Dandy would have had a gay old time of it if I hadn't put you up to their capers"; and I had humbly to acknowledge the truth of all he said.

"I don't say you're not promising well," he added, satisfied with my humility. "If Johnny'll only stay away long enough, we'll have you educated up to doing without a house."

Within a week it seemed as though Johnny was aiding and abetting Dan in his scheme of education; for he sent in word that his "cross-cut saw", or something equally important, had "doubled up on him", and he was going back to Katherine to "see about it straight off".

9

Before the mustered horses were drafted out, everyone at the homestead, blacks, whites, and Chinese, went up to the stockyard to "have a look at them".

Dan was in one of his superior moods. "Let's see if she knows anything about horses," he said condescendingly, as the Quiet Stockman opened the mob up a little to show the animals to better advantage. "Show us your fancy in this lot, missus." "Certainly," I said, affecting particular knowledge of the subject, and Jack wheeled with a quick, questioning look, suddenly aware that, after all, a woman *might* be only a fellow-man; and as I glanced from one beautiful animal to another he watched keenly, half-expectant and half-incredulous.

It did not take long to choose. In the foreground stood a magnificent brown colt, that caught and held the attention, as it watched every movement with ears shot forward, and nostrils quivering; and as I pointed it out Jack's boyish face lit up with surprise and pleasure.

"Talk of luck!" Dan cried, as usual withholding the benefit of the doubt. "You've picked Jack's fancy."

But it was Jack himself who surprised everyone, for, forgetting his monosyllables, he said with an indescribable ring of fellowship in his voice, "She's picked out the best in the whole mob," and turned back to his work among the horses with his usual self-possession.

Dan's eyes opened wide. "Whatever's come to Jack?" he said; but seemed puzzled at the Maluka's answer that he was

Jeannie Gunn (Angela Punch McGregor), feels
frustrated and dissatisfied with her life at the
Station.

Jeannie Gunn (Angela Punch McGregor) enjoying a
horse ride.

"only getting educated". The truth is, that every man has his vulnerable point, and Jack's was horses.

When the mob had been put through the yards, all the unbroken horses were given into the Quiet Stockman's care, and for the next week or two the stockyard became the only place of real interest; for the homestead, waiting for the Wet to lift, had settled down to store lists, fencing, and stud books.

It was not the horses alone that were of interest at the yards; the calm, fearless, self-reliant man who was handling them was infinitely more so. Nothing daunted or disheartened him; and in those hours spent on the stockyard fence, in the shade of a spreading tree, I learnt to know the Quiet Stockman for the man he was.

If anyone would know the inner character of a fellowman, let him put him to horse-breaking, and he will soon know the best or the worst of him. Let him watch him handling a wild, unbroken colt, and if he is steadfast of purpose, just, brave, and true-hearted, it will all be revealed; but if he lacks self-restraint, or is cowardly, shifty, or mean-spirited, he will do well to avoid the test, for the horse will betray him.

Jack's horse-breaking was a battle for supremacy of mind over mind, nor mind over matter—a long course of careful training and schooling, in which nothing was broken, but all bent to the control of a master. To him no two horses were alike; carefully he studied their temperaments, treating each horse according to its nature—using the whip freely with some, and with others not at all; coercing, coaxing, or humouring, as his judgment directed. Working always for intelligent obedience, not cowed stupidity, he appeared at times to be almost reasoning with the brute mind, as he helped it to solve the problems of its schooling; penetrating dull stupidity with patient reiteration, or wearing down stubborn opposition with steady, unwavering persistence, and always rewarding ultimate obedience with gentle kindness and freedom.

Step by step, the training proceeded. Submission first, then an establishment of perfect trust and confidence between horse and man, without which nothing worth having could be attained.

After that, in orderly succession the rest followed; toleration of handling, reining, mouthing, leading on foot, and on horseback, and in due time saddling and mounting. One thing at a time and nothing new until the old was so perfected that when all was ready for the mounting—from a spectacular point of view—the mounting was generally disappointing. Just a little rearing and curvetting, then a quiet, trusting acceptance of this new order of things.

Half a dozen horses were in hand at once, and, as with children at school, some quickly got ahead of the others, and every day the interest grew keener and keener in the individual character of the horses. At the end of a week Jack announced that he was "going to catch the brown colt" next day. "It'll be worth seeing," he said; and from the Quiet Stockman that was looked upon as a very pressing invitation.

From the day of the draughting he had ceased altogether to avoid me, and in the days that followed had gradually realized that a horse could be more to a woman than a means of locomotion; and now no longer drew the line at conversations.

When we went up to the yards in the morning, the brown colt was in a small yard by itself, and Jack was waiting at the gate, ready for its "catching".

With a laugh at the wild rush with which the colt avoided him, he shut himself into the yard with it, and moved quietly about, sometimes towards it and sometimes from it; at times standing still and looking it over, and at other times throwing a rope or sack carelessly down, waiting until his presence had become familiar, and the colt had learned that there was nothing to fear from it.

There was a certain calmness in the man's movements, a fearless repose that utterly ignored the wild rushes, and as a natural result they soon ceased; and within just a minute or two the beautiful creature was standing still, watching in quivering wonder.

Gradually a double rope began to play in the air with ever-increasing circles, awakening anew the colt's fears and as these in turn subsided, without any apparent effort, a long running noose flickered out from the circling rope, and falling over the strong young head, lay still on the arching neck.

The leap forward was terrific; but the rope brought the colt up with a jerk; and in the instant's pause that followed the Quiet Stockman braced himself for the mad rearing plunges that were coming. There was literally only an instant's pause, and then with a clatter of hoofs the plungings began, and were met with muscles of iron, and jaw set like a vice, as the man, with heels dug into the ground, dragged back on the rope, yielding as much as his judgment allowed—enough to ease the shocks, but not an inch by compulsion.

Twice the rearing, terrified creature circled round him, and then the rope began to shorten to a more workable length. There was no haste, no flurry. Surely and steadily the rope shortened (but the horse went to the man, not the man to the horse; that was to come later). With the shortening of the rope the compelling power of the man's will forced itself into the brute mind; and, bending to that will, the wild leaps and plungings took on a vague suggestion of obedience—a going *with* the rope, not against it; that was all. An erratic going, perhaps, but enough to tell that the horse had acknowledged a master. That was all Jack asked for at first, and, satisfied, he relaxed his muscles, and as the rope slackened the horse turned and faced him; and the marvel was how quickly it was all over.

But something was to follow, that once seen could never be forgotten—the advance of the man to the horse.

With barely perceptible movement, the man's hands stole along the rope at a snail's pace. Never hurrying, never stopping, they slid on, the colt watching them as though mesmerized. When within reach of the dilated nostrils, they paused and waited, and slowly the sensitive head came forward snuffing, more in bewilderment than fear at this new wonder, and as the dark twitching muzzle brushed the hands, the head drew sharply back, only to return again in a moment with greater confidence.

Three or four times the quivering nostrils came back to the hands before they stirred, then one lifted slowly and lay on the muzzle, warm and strong and comforting, while the other, creeping up the rope, slipped on to the glossy neck, and the catching was over.

For a little while there was some gentle patting and fondling, to a murmuring accompaniment of words; the horse standing still with twitching ears the while. Then came the test of the victory—the test of the man's power and the creature's intelligence. The horse was to go to the man, at the man's bidding alone, without force or coercion. "The better they are the sooner you learn 'em that," was one of Jack's pet theories, while his proudest boast—his only boast, perhaps—was that "he'd never been beaten on that yet".

"They have to come sooner or later if you stick at 'em," he had said, when I marvelled at first to see the great creatures come obediently to the click of his tongue or fingers. So far in all his wide experience the latest had been the third day. That, however, was rare; more frequently it was a matter of hours, sometimes barely an hour, while now and then—incredulous as it may seem to the layman—only minutes.

Ten minutes before Jack put the brown colt to the test it had been a wild, terrified, plunging creature, and yet, as he stepped back to try its intelligence and submission, his face was confident and expectant.

Moving slowly backwards, he held out one hand—the hand that had proved all kindness and comfort—and, snapping a finger and thumb, clicked his tongue in a murmur of invitation.

The brown ears shot forward to attention at the sound, and as the head reached out to investigate, the snapping fingers repeated the invitation, and without hesitation the magnificent creature went forward obediently until the hand was once more resting on the dark muzzle.

The trusting beauty of the surrender seemed to break some spell that had held us silent since the beginning of the catching. "Oh, Jack! Isn't he a beauty?" I cried, unconsciously putting my admiration into a question.

But Jack no longer objected to questions. He turned towards us with soft, shining eyes. "There's not many like him," he said, pulling at one of the flexible ears. "You could learn him anything." It seemed so, for after trying to solve the problem of the roller and bit with his tongue when it was put into his mouth, he accepted the mystery with quiet, intelligent trust; and as soon as he was freed from it, almost courted further fondling. He would let no one but Jack near him, though. When we entered the yard the ears went back and the whites of the eyes showed. "No one but me for a while," Jack said, with a strange ring of ownership in his voice, telling that it is a good thing to have a horse that is yours, and yours only.

Within a week "Brownie" was mounted, and ridden down to the House for final inspection, before "going bush" to learn the art of rounding up cattle. "He'll let you touch him now," Jack said; and after a snuffing inquiry at my hands the beautiful creature submitted to their caresses.

Dan looked at him with approving eyes. "To think she had the luck to choose him too, out of all that crowd," he said.

"*We* always call it instinct, I think," the Maluka said teasingly, twitting me on one of my pet theories; and the Dandy politely suggested, "It might be knowledge."

Then the Quiet Stockman gave his opinion, making it very clear that he no longer felt that women had nothing in common with men. "It never *is* anything *but* instinct," he said, with quiet decision in his voice. "No one ever *learns* horses."

While the Quiet Stockman had been busy rearranging his ideas of womanhood, a good many things had been going wrong at the homestead. Sam began by breaking both china cups, and letting the backbone slip out of everything in his charge.

Fowls laid out and eggs became luxuries. Cream refused to rise on the milk. It seemed impossible to keep meat sweet. Jimmy lost interest in the gathering of firewood and the carrying of water; and as a result, the water-butts first shrank, then leaked, and finally lay down, a medley of planks and iron hoops. A swarm of grasshoppers passed through the homestead, and to use Sam's explicit English, "Vegetable bin finissem all about"; and by the time fresh seeds were springing the Wet returned with renewed vigour, and flooded out the garden. Then stores began to fail, including soap and kerosene, and writing-paper and ink threatened to "peter out". After that the lubras, in a private quarrel during the washing of clothes, tore one of the "couple of changes" of blouses sadly; and the mistress of a cattle station was obliged to entertain guests at times in a pink cambric blouse patched with a washed calico flour-bag; no provision having been made for patching. Then just as we were wondering what else could happen, one night, without the slightest warning, the very birds migrated from the lagoon, carrying away with them the promise of future pillows, to say nothing of mattress, and the Maluka was obliged to go far afield in search of non-migrating birds.

Dan wagged his head and talked wise philosophy, with these disasters for the thread of his discourse; but even he was obliged to own that there was a limit to education when Sam announced that "Tea bin finissem all about."

He had found that the last eighty-pound tea-chest contained tinware when he opened it to replenish his tea-caddy. Tea had been ordered, and the chest was labelled tea clearly enough, to show that the fault lay in Darwin; but that was poor consolation to us, the sufferers.

The necessities of the bush are few; but they are necessities; and Billy Muck was sent in to the Katherine post-haste, to beg, borrow, or buy tea from Mine Host. At the least, a horseman would take six days for the trip, irrespective of time lost in packing up; but knowing Billy's untiring, swinging stride, we hoped to see him within four days.

Billy left at midday, and we drank our last cup of tea at supper; the next day learned what slaves we can be to our bodies. Because we lacked tea, the interest went out of everything. Listless and unsatisfied, we sat about and developed headaches, not thirsty—for there was water in plenty—but craving for the uplifting influence of tea. Never drunkards craved more intensely for strong drink! Sam made coffee; but coffee only increased the headaches and cravings, and so we sat peering into the forest, hoping for travellers; and all we learnt by the experience was that tea is a necessity of life out-bush.

On the second evening a traveller came in from the south track. "He wouldn't refuse a woman, surely," everyone said, and we welcomed him warmly.

He had about three ounces of tea. "Meant to fill up here meself," he said in apology, as, with the generosity of a bush-man, he offered it all unconditionally. Let us hope the man has been rewarded, and has never since known what it is to be tealess out-bush! We never heard his name, and I doubt if any one of us would know the man again if we saw him. All we saw was a dingy tucker-bag, with its one corner bulging heart-shaped with tea!

We accepted one half, for the man had a three-days' journey before him, and Sam doled it out so frugally that we spent two comparatively happy days before fixing our attention on the north track, along which Billy would return.

In four and a half days he appeared, carrying a five-pound tea-tin on his head, and was hailed with a yell of delight. We were all in the stockyard, and Billy, in answer to the hail, came there.

Dan wanted a "sniff of it right off", so it was then and there opened; but as the lid flew back the yell of delight changed to a howl of disappointment. By some hideous mistake, Billy had brought *raisins*.

Like so many philosophers, Dan could not apply his philosophy to himself. "It's the dead finish," he said dejectedly; "never struck anything like it before. Twice over too," he added. "First tinware and now this foolery"; and he kicked savagely at the offending tin, sending a shower of raisins dancing out into the dust.

Everyone but Dan was speechless, while Billy, not being a slave to tea-drinking, gathered the raisins up, failing to see any cause for disappointment, particularly as most of the raisins fell to his share for his prompt return.

He also failed to see any advantage in setting out again for the Katherine. "Might it catch raisins nuzzer time," he said, logically enough.

Dan became despondent at the thought. "They're fools enough for anything," he said. I tried to cheer him up on the law of averages, as Goggle-Eye was sent off with instructions to travel "quick-fellow, quick-fellow, big mob quick-fellow", and many promises of reward if he was back in "four fellow sleeps".

For two more days we peered into the forest for travellers, but none appeared, and Dan became retrospective. "We might have guessed this 'ud happen," he said, declaring it was a "judgment on the missus" for chucking good tea away just because a fly got into it. "Luck's cleared right out because of it, missus," he said; "and if things go on like this Johnny'll be coming along one of these days." (Dan was the only one of us who could joke on the matter.) "Luck's smashed all to pieces," he insisted later, when he found that the first pillow was finished; but at sun-down was inclined to think it might be "on the turn again", for Goggle-Eye appeared on the north track, stalking majestically in front of a horseman.

"Me bin catch traveller," he said triumphantly, claiming his rewards. "Me bin come back two fellow sleep"; and before we could explain *that* was hardly what we had meant, the man had ridden up.

"Heard you were doing a famish here, sitting with your tongues hanging out," he laughed, "so I've brought you a few more raisins." And, dismounting, he drew out from a pack-bag a long calico bag containing quite ten pounds of tea.

"You struck the Wag's tin," he said, explaining the mistake, as everyone shouted for Sam to boil a kettle instantly, and with the tea came a message from the Wag himself:

"I'll trouble you for my raisins"; and we could almost hear the Wag's slow dry chuckle underlying the words.

Mine Host also sent a message, saying he would "send further supplies every opportunity, to keep things going until the waggons came through", and underlying *his* message we felt his kindly consideration. As a further proof of his thoughtfulness we found two china cups embedded in the tea. He had heard of Sam's accident. Tea in china cups! and as much and as strong as we desired! But in spite of Mine Host's efforts to keep us going, twice again, before the waggons came, we found ourselves begging tea from travellers.

Our energies revived with the very first cup of tea and we went for our usual evening stroll through the paddocks, with all our old appreciation; and on our return found the men stretched out on the grass beyond the Quarters, optimistic and happy, sipping at further cups of tea. (Sam's kettle was kept busy that night.)

The men's optimism was infectious, and presently the Maluka "supposed the waggons would be starting before long".

It was only March, and the waggons had to wait till the Wet lifted; but just then everyone felt sure that "the Wet would lift early this year".

"Generally does with the change of moon before Easter," the traveller said, and flying off at a tangent, I asked when Easter was, unwittingly setting the homestead a tough problem.

Nobody "could say for certain". But Dan "knew a chap once who could reckon it by the moon"; and the Maluka felt inspired to work it out. "It's simple enough," he said. "The first Friday —or is it Sunday?—*after* the first full moon, *after* the twenty-first of March."

"Twenty-fifth, isn't it?" the Dandy asked, complicating matters from the beginning.

The traveller reckoned it'd be new moon about Monday or Tuesday, which seemed near enough at the time; and full moon was fixed for the Tuesday or Wednesday fortnight from that.

"That ought to settle it," Dan said; and so it might have if anyone had been sure of Monday's date; but we all had different convictions about that, varying from the ninth to the thirteenth.

After much ticking off of days upon fingers, with an old newspaper as "something to work from", the date of the full moon was fixed for the twenty-fourth or twenty-fifth of March, unless the moon came in so late on Tuesday that it brought the full to the morning of the twenty-sixth.

"Seems getting a bit mixed," Dan said, and matters were certainly complicated.

If we were to reckon from the twenty-first, Easter was in March, but if from the twenty-fifth, in April—if the moon came in on Monday, but March in either case if the full was on the twenty-sixth.

Dan suggested "giving it best". "It'd get anybody dodged," he said, hopelessly at sea; but the Maluka wanted to "see it through". "The new moon should clear most of it up," he said; "but you've given us a teaser this time, little 'un."

The new moon should have cleared everything up if we could have seen it, but the Wet coming on in force again, we saw nothing till Thursday evening, when it was too late to calculate with precision.

Dan was for having two Easters, and "getting even with it that way"; but Sam unexpectedly solved the problem for us.

"What was the difficulty?" he asked, and listened to the explanation attentively. "Bunday!" he exclaimed at the finish, showing he had fully grasped the situation. Of course, he knew all about Bunday! Wasn't it so many weeks after the China-man's New Year festival? And in a jargon of pidgin-English he swept aside all moon discussions, and fixed the date of "Bunday" for the twenty-eighth of March, which, as Dan wisely remark-ed, "proved that somebody was right", but whether the Maluka or the Dandy, or the moon, he forgot to specify. "The old heathen to beat us all too," he added, "just when it had got us all dodged." Dan took all the credit of the suggestion to him-self. Then he looked philosophically on the toughness of the problem. "Anyway," he said, "the missus must have learnt a bit about beginning at the beginning of things. Just think what she'd have missed if anyone had known when Easter was right off!"

"What she'd have missed indeed. Exactly what the towns-man misses, as long as he remains in a land where everything can be known right off."

But a new idea had come to Dan. "Of course," he said, "as far as that goes, if Johnny does turn up she ought to learn a thing or two, while he's moving the dining-room up the house"; and he decided to welcome Johnny on his return.

He had not long to wait, for in a day or two Johnny rode into the homestead, followed by a black boy carrying a cross-cut saw. This time he hailed us with a cheery:

"*Now* we shan't be long."

10

It had taken over six weeks to "get hold of Little Johnny"; but as the Dandy had prophesied, once he started, he "made things hum in no time".

"Now we shan't be long," he said, flourishing a tape-measure; and the Dandy was kept busy for half a day, "wrestling with the calculating".

That finished, the store was turned inside out and a couple of "boys" sent in for "things needed", and after them more "boys" for more things; and then other "boys" for other things, until travellers must have thought the camp blacks had entered into a walking competition. When everything necessary was ordered, "all hands" were put on to sharpen saws and tools, and the homestead shrieked and groaned all day with harsh discordant raspings. Then a camp was pitched in the forest, a mile or so from the homestead; a saw-pit dug, a platform erected, and before a week had passed an invitation was issued for the missus to "come and see a tree felled". "Laying the foundation-stone," the Maluka called it.

Johnny of course welcomed us with a jovial "Now we shan't be long," and shouldering a tomahawk, led the way out of the camp into the timber.

House-hunting in town does not compare favourably with timber-hunting for a house, in a luxuriant tropical forest. Sheltered from the sun and heat, we wandered about in the feathery undergrowth, while the Maluka tested the height of the giant timber above us with shots from his bull-dog revolver, bringing down twigs and showers of leaves from the topmost branches, and sending flocks of white cockatoos up into the air with squawks of amazement.

Tree after tree was chosen and marked with the tomahawk, each one appearing taller and straighter and more beautiful than any of its fellows—until, finding ourselves back at the camp, Johnny went for his axe and left us to look at the beauty around us.

"Seems a pity to spoil all this, just to make four walls to shut the missus in from anything worth looking at," Dan murmured as Johnny reappeared. "They won't make anything as good as this up at the house." Johnny the unpoetical, hesitated, perplexed. Philosophy was not in his line. " 'Tisn't too bad," he said, suddenly aware of the beauty of the scene; and then the tradesman came to the surface. "I reckon *my* job'll be a bit more on the plumb, though," he chuckled, and, delighted with his little joke, shouldered his axe and walked towards one of the marked trees, while Dan speculated aloud on the chances a man had of "getting off alive" if a tree fell on him.

"Trees don't fall on a man that knows how to handle timber," the unsuspecting Johnny said briskly; and as Dan feared that "fever was her only chance then", he spat on his hands, and, sending the axe home into the bole of the tree with a clean, swinging stroke, laid the foundation-stone—the foundation-stone of a tiny home in the wilderness, that was destined to be the dwelling-place of great joy, and happiness, and sorrow.

The Sanguine Scot had prophesied rightly. There being "time enough for everything in the Never-Never", there was time for "many pleasant rides along the Reach, choosing trees for timber".

But the rides were the least part of the pleasure. For the time being, the silent Reach forest had become the hub of our little universe. All was life and bustle and movement there. Every day fresh trees were felled and chopping contests entered into by Johnny and the Dandy; and as the trees fell in quick succession, black boys and lubras, armed with tomahawks, swarmed over them, to lop away the branches, before the trunks were dragged by the horses to the mouth of the saw-pit. Everyone was happy and light-hearted, and the work went merrily forward, until a great pile of tree-trunks lay ready for the saw-pit.

Then a new need arose; Johnny wanted several yards of strong string, and a "sup" of ink, to make guiding lines on the timber for his saw; but as only sewing cotton was forthcoming, and the Maluka refused to part with one drop of his precious ink, we were obliged to do down to the beginning of things once more: two or three lubras were set to work to convert the sewing-cotton into tough, strong string, while others prepared a substitute for the ink from burnt water-lily roots.

The sawing of the tree-trunks lasted for nearly three weeks, and the Dandy, being the under-man in the pit, had anything but a merry time. Down in the pit, away from the air, he worked; pulling and pushing, pushing and pulling, hour after hour, in a blinding stream of sawdust.

When we offered him sympathy and a gossamer veil, he accepted the veil gratefully, but waved the sympathy aside, saying it was "all in the good cause". Nothing was ever a hardship to the Dandy, excepting dirt.

Johnny, being a past-master in his trade, stood on the platform in the upper air, guiding the saw along the marked lines; and as he directed us all in the fine art of pit-sawing, Dan decided that the building of a house, under some circumstances, could be an education in itself.

"Thought she might manage to learn a thing or two out of it," he said. "The building of it is right enough. It all depends what she uses it for when Johnny's done with it."

As the pliant saw coaxed beams, and slabs, and flooring boards out of the forest trees, I grew to like beginning at the beginning of things, and realized there was an underlying truth in Dan's whimsical reiteration, that "the missus was in luck when she struck this place"; for beams and slabs and flooring-boards wrested from Nature amid merry-making and philosophical discourses are not as other beams and slabs and flooring-boards. They are old friends and fellow-adventurers, with many a good tale to tell, recalling comical situations in their reminiscences with a vividness that baffles description.

Perhaps those who live in homes with the beginning of things left behind in forests they have never seen, may think chattering planks a poor compensation for unpapered, rough-boarded walls and unglazed window-frames. Let them try it before they judge; remembering always, that before a house can be built of old friends and memories, the friends must be made and the memories lived through.

But other things besides the sawing of timber were in progress. Things were also "humming" in the dog world. A sturdy fox-terrier, Brown by name, had been given by a passing traveller to the Maluka; given almost of necessity, for Brown—as is the way with fox-terriers at times—quietly changed masters, and lying down at the Maluka's feet, had refused to leave him. The station dogs resented his presence there, and persecuted him as an intruder; and, being a peace-loving dog, Brown bore it patiently for two days, hoping, no doubt, the persecution would wear itself out. On the third day, however, he quietly changed his tactics—for sometimes the only road to peace is through fighting—and, accepting a challenge, took on the station dogs one by one in single combat.

Only a full-sized, particularly sturdy-looking fox-terrier against expert cattle dogs; and yet no dog could stand against him. One by one he closed with them, and one by one they went before him; and at the end of the week he was "cock of the walk", and lay down to enjoy his well-earned peace. His death-stroke was a flashing lunge, from a grip of a fore-leg to a sharp, grinding grip of the enemy's tongue. How he managed it was a puzzle, but sooner or later he got his grip in, to let go at the piercing yell of defeat that invariably followed. But Brown was a gentleman, not a bully, and after each fight buried the hatchet, appearing to shake hands with his late adversary. No doubt if he had had a tail he would have wagged it, but Brown had been born with a large, perfectly round, black spot at the root of his tail, and his then owner, having an eye for the picturesque, had removed his white tail entirely, even to its last joint, to allow no break in the spot; and when the spirit moved Brown to wag a tail, a violent stirring of hairs in the centre of this spot betrayed his desire to the world. It goes without saying that

Brown did not fight the canine women-folk; for, as someone has said, man is the only animal that strikes his women-folk.

Most of the battles were fought in the station thoroughfare, all of them taking on the form of a general *mêlée*. As soon as Brown closed with an enemy, the rest of the dogs each sought an especial adversary, hoping to wipe out some past defeat; while the pups, having no past to wipe out, diverted themselves by skirmishing about on the outskirts of the scrimmage, nipping joyously at any hind-quarters that came handy, bumping into other groups of pups, thoroughly enjoying life, and accumulating material for future fights among themselves.

Altogether we had a lively week. To interfere in the fights only prolonged them, and, to add to the general hubbub, the servant question had opened up again. Jimmy's Nellie, who had been simmering for some time, suddenly rebelled, and refused to consider herself among the rejected.

We said there was no vacancy on the Staff for her, and she immediately set herself to create one, by pounding and punching at the Staff in private. Finding this of no avail, she threatened to "sing" Maudie dead, also in private, unless she resigned. Maudie proving unexpectedly tough and defiant, Nellie gave up all hope of creating a vacancy, and changing front, adopted a stone-walling policy. Every morning, quietly and doggedly, she put herself on the Staff, and every morning was as quietly and doggedly dismissed from office.

Doggedness being an unusual trait in a black fellow, the homestead became interested. "Never say die, little 'un," the Maluka laughed each morning; but Dan was inclined to bet on Nellie.

"She's got nothing else to do, and can concentrate all her thoughts on it," he said, "and besides, it means more to her."

It meant a good deal to me, too, for I particularly objected to Jimmy's Nellie: partly because she was an inveterate smoker and a profuse spitter upon floors; partly because—well, to be quite honest—because a good application of carbolic soap would have done no harm; and partly because she appeared to have a passion for exceedingly scanty garments, her favourite costume being a skirt made from the upper half of a fifty-pound calico flour-bag. Her blouses had, apparently, been all mislaid.

Nellie, unconscious of my real objections, daily and doggedly put herself on the Staff, and was daily and doggedly dismissed. But as she generally managed to do the very thing that most needed doing, before I could find her to dismiss, Dan was offering ten to one on Nellie by Easter-time.

"Another moon'll see her on the Staff," he prophesied, as we prepared to go out-bush for Easter.

The Easter moon had come in dry and cool, and at its full the Wet lifted, as our traveller had foretold. Only a bushman's personal observation, remember, this lifting of the Wet with the full of the Easter moon, not a scientific statement; but by an insight peculiarly their own, bushmen come at more facts than most men.

Sam did his best with Bunday, serving hot rolls with mysterious markings on them for breakfast, and by midday he had the homestead to himself, the Maluka and I being camped at Bitter Springs and everyone else being elsewhere. Our business was yard-inspection, with Goggle-Eye as general factotum. We, of course, had ridden out, but Goggle-Eye had preferred to walk. "Me all day knock up longa horse," he explained, striding comfortably along beside us.

Several exciting hours were spent with boxes of wax matches burning the rank grass back from the yard at the Springs (at Goggle-Eye's suggestion the missus had been pressed into the service); and then we rode through the rank grass along the river, scattering matches as we went like sparks from an engine. As soon as the rank grass seeds it must be burnt off before the soil loses its moisture, to ensure a second shorter spring, and everywhere we went now clouds of dense smoke rose behind us.

That walk-about with the Maluka and "Gadgerrie" lived like a red-letter day in old Goggle-Eye's memory; for did he not himself strike a dozen full boxes of matches?

Dan was away beyond the northern boundary, going through the cattle, judging the probable duration of "outside waters" for that year, burning off too as he rode. The Quiet Stockman was away beyond the southern boundary, rounding up wanderers and stragglers among the horses, and the station was face to face with the year's mustering and branding—for with the lifting of the Wet everything in the Never-Never begins to move.

"After the Wet" rivers go down, the north-west monsoon giving place to the south-east Trades; bogs dry up everywhere, opening all roads; travellers pass through the stations from all points of the compass—cattle buyers, drovers, station-owners, telegraph people—all bent on business, and all glad to get moving after the long compulsory inaction of the Wet; and lastly that great yearly cumbrous event takes place: the starting of the "waggons", with their year's stores for Inside.

The first batch of travellers had little news for us. They had heard that the teams were loading up, and couldn't say for certain, and, finding them unsatisfactory, we looked forward to the coming of the Fizzer, our mailman, who was almost due.

Eight mails a year was our allowance, with an extra one now and then through the courtesy of travellers. Eight mails a year against eight hundred for the townsfolk. Was it any wonder that we all found we had business at the homestead when the Fizzer was due there?

When he came this trip he was, as usual, brimming over with news: personal items, public gossip, and the news that the horse teams had got most of their loading on, and that the Macs were getting their bullocks under way. Two horse-waggons and a dray for far Inside, and three bullock waggons for the nearer distances, comprised the "waggons" that year. The teamsters were English; but the bullock-punchers were three "Macs"— an Irishman, a Highlander, and the Sanguine Scot.

Six waggons, and about six months' hard travelling, in and out, to provide a year's stores for three cattle stations and two telegraph stations. It is not surprising that the freight per ton was what it was—twenty-two pounds per ton for the Elsey, and upwards of forty pounds for Inside. It is this freight that makes the grocery bill such a big item on stations out-bush, where several tons of stores are considered by no means a large order.

Close on the heels of the Fizzer came other travellers, with the news that the horse teams had "got going" and the Macs had "pulled out" to the Four Mile. "Your trunks'll be along in no time now, missus," one of them said. "They've got 'em all aboard."

The Dandy did some rapid calculations: "Ten miles a day on good roads," he said: "one hundred and seventy miles. Tens into that seventeen days. Give 'em a week over for unforeseen emergencies, and call if four weeks." It sounded quite cheerful and near at hand, but a belated thunderstorm or two, and consequent bogs, nearly doubled the four weeks.

Almost every day we heard news of the teams from the now constant stream of travellers; and by the time the timber was all sawn and carted to the House to fulfil the many promises there, they were at the Katherine.

But if the teams were at the Katherine, so were the teamsters, and so was the Pub; and when teamsters and a pub get together it generally takes time to separate them, when that pub is the last for over a thousand miles. One pub at the Katherine and another at Oodnadatta, and between them over a thousand miles of bush, and desert, and dust, and heat, and thirst. That, from a teamster's point of view, is the Overland Route from Oodnadatta to the Katherine.

A pub had little attraction for the Sanguine Scot, and provided he could steer the other Macs safely past the one at the Katherine, there would be no delay there with the trunks; but the year's stores were on the horse teams, and the station, having learnt bitter experience from the past, now sent in its own waggon for the bulk of the stores, as soon as they were known to be at the Katherine; and so the Dandy set off at once.

"You'll see me within a fortnight, bar accidents," he called back, as the waggon lurched forward towards the slip-rails; and the Pub also having little attraction for the Dandy, we decided to expect him, "bar accidents". For that matter, a pub had little attraction for any of the Elsey men, the Quiet Stockman being a total abstainer, and Dan knowing "how to behave himself", although he owned to having "got a bit merry once or twice".

The Dandy out of sight, Johnny went back to his work, which happened to be hammering the curves out of sheets of corrugated iron.

"Now we shan't be long," he shouted, hammering vigorously; and when I objected to the awful din, he reminded me, with
a grin, that it was "all in the good cause". When "smoothed
out", as Johnny phrased it, the iron was to be used for capping
the piles that the house was built upon, "to make them little
white ants stay at home".

"We'll smooth all your troubles out, if you give us time," he
shouted, returning to the hammering after his explanation with
even greater energy. But by dinner-time someone had waddled
into our lives who was to smooth most of the difficulties out of it,
to his own and our complete satisfaction.

Just as Sam announced dinner a cloud of dust creeping along
the horizon attracted our attention.

"Foot travellers!" Dan decided; but something emerged out
of the dust, as it passed through the slip-rails, that looked very
like a huge mound of white jelly on horse-back.

Directly it sighted us it rolled off the horse, whether inten-
tionally or unintentionally we could not say, and leaving the
beast to the care of chance, unfolded two short legs from somewhere and waddled towards us—a fat, jovial Chinese John
Falstaff.

"Good day, boss! Good day, missus! Good day, all about,"
he said in cheerful salute, as he trundled towards us like a ship's
barrel in full sail. "Me new cook, me——" and then Sam
appeared and towed him into port.

"Well, I'm blest!" Dan exclaimed, staring after him. "What
have we struck?"

But Johnny knew, as did most Territorians. "You've struck
Cheon, that's all," he said. "Talk of luck! He's the jolliest old
josser going."

The "jolliest old josser" seemed difficult to express; for
already he had eluded Sam, and, reappearing in the kitchen
doorway, waddled across the thoroughfare towards us.

"Me new cook!" he repeated, going on from where he had
left off. "Me Cheon!" and then, in queer pidgin-English, he
solemnly rolled out a few of his many qualifications.

"Me savey all about," he chanted. "Me savey cook 'im, and
gard'in', and milk 'im, and chuckie, and fishin', and shootin'

wild duck." On and on he chanted through a varied list of accomplishments, ending up with an application for the position of cook. "Me sit down? Eh, boss," he asked, moon-faced and serious.

"Please yourself!" the Maluka laughed, and with a flash of white teeth and an infectious chuckle Cheon laughed and nodded back; then, still chuckling, he waddled away to the kitchen and took possession there, while we went to our respective dinners, little guessing that the truest-hearted, most faithful, most loyal old "josser" had waddled into our lives.

I I

Cheon rose at cock-crow ("fowl-sing-out", he preferred to call it), and began his duties by scornfully refusing Sam's bland offer of instruction in the "ways" of the homestead.

"Me savey all about," he said, with a majestic wave of his hands, after expressing supreme contempt for Sam's caste and ways; so Sam applied for his cheque, shook hands all round, and withdrew smilingly.

Sam's account being satisfactorily "squared", Cheon's name was then formally entered in the station books as cook and gardener, at twenty-five shillings a week. That was the only vacancy he ever filled in the books; but in our life at the homestead he filled almost every vacancy that required filling, and there were many.

There was nothing he could not and did not do for our good; and it was well that he refused to be instructed in anybody's ways, for his own were delightfully disobedient and unexpected and entertaining. Not only had we "struck the jolliest old josser going", but a born ruler and organizer into the bargain. He knew best what was good for us, and told us so, and, meekly bending to his will, our orders became mere suggestions to be entertained and carried out if approved of by Cheon, or dismissed as "silly-fellow" with a Podsnappian wave of his arm if they in no way appealed to him.

Full of wrath for Sam's ways, and bubbling over with trundling energy, he calmly appropriated the whole Staff, as well as Jimmy, Billy Muck, and the Rejected, and within a week had

93

put backbone into everything that lacked it, from the water-butts to old Jimmy.

The first two days were spent in a whirlwind of dust and rubbish, turned out from unguessed-at recesses, and Cheon's jovial humour suiting his helpers to a nicety, the rubbish was dealt with amid shouts of delight and enjoyment; until Jimmy, losing his head in his lightness of heart, dug Cheon in the ribs, and, waving a stick over his head, yelled in mock fierceness: "Me wild-fellow, black fellow. Me myall-fellow."

Then Cheon came out in a new role. Without a moment's hesitation, his arms and legs appeared to fly out all together in Jimmy's direction, completely doubling him up.

"Me myall-fellow, too," Cheon said calmly, master of himself and the situation. Then, chuckling at Jimmy's discomfiture, he went on with his work, while his helpers stared open-eyed with amazement; an infuriated Chinese catherine-wheel being something new in the experience of a black fellow. It was a wholesome lesson, though, and no one took liberties with Cheon again.

The rubbish disposed of, leaking water-butts, and the ruins of collapsed water-butts, were carried to the billabong, swelled in the water, hammered and hooped back into steadfast, reliable water-butts, and trundled along to their places in a merry, joyous procession.

With Cheon's hands on the helm, cream rose on the milk from somewhere. The meat no longer turned sour. An expert fisherman was discovered among the helpers—one Bob by name. Cheon's shot-gun appeared to have a magnetic attraction for wild duck. A garden sprang up as by magic, grasshoppers being literally chased off the vegetables. The only thing we lacked was butter; and after a week of order and cleanliness and dazzlingly varied menus, we wondered how we had ever existed without them.

It was no use trying to wriggle from under Cheon's foot once he put it down. At the slightest neglect of duty, lubras or boys were marshalled and kept relentlessly to their work until he was satisfied; and woe betide the lubras who had neglected to wash hands, and pail, and cows, before sitting down to their milking.

The very fowls that laid out-bush gained nothing by their subtlety. At the faintest sound of a cackle, a dosing lubra was roused by the point of Cheon's toe, as he shouted excitedly above her: "Fowl sing out! That way! Catch 'im egg! Go on!" pointing out the direction with much pantomime; and as the egg-basket filled to overflowing, he either chuckled with glee or expressed further contempt for Sam's ways.

But his especial wrath was reserved for the fowl-roosts over his sleeping quarters. "What's 'er matter! Fowl sit down close up kitchen!" he growled in furious gutturals, whenever his eyes rested on them; and as soon as time permitted he mounted to the roof and, boiling over with righteous indignation, hurled the offending roosts into space.

New roosts were then nailed to the branches of a spreading coolibah tree, a hundred yards or so to the north of the buildings, the trunk encircled with zinc to prevent snakes or wild cats from climbing into the roosts; a movable ladder staircase made, to be used by the fowls at bedtime, and removed as soon as they were settled for the night, lest the cats or snakes should make unlawful use of it (Cheon always foresaw every contingency); and finally, "boys" and lubras were marshalled to wean the fowls from their old love.

But the weaning took time, and proved most entertaining; and while the fowls were being taught by bitter experience to bend to Cheon's will, the homestead pealed with shoutings and laughter.

Every evening the fun commenced about sun-down, and the entire community assembled to watch it; for it was worth watching—fowls dodged, and scurried, and squawked, as the Staff and the Rejected, under Cheon's directions, chivvied and danced and screamed between them and their desire, the lubras cheering to the echo every time one of the birds gave in, and stalked, cackling and indignant, up the ladder into the branches of the coolibah; or pursuing runaways that had outwitted them, in shrieking, pell-mell disorder, while Cheon, fat and perspiring, either shouted orders and cheered lustily, bounded wrathfully after both runaways and lubras, or collapsed, doubled up with uncontrollable laughter, at the squawk of amazement from fowls which, having gained their old haunt, had found Jimmy there waiting to receive them. As for ourselves, I doubt if we ever enjoyed anything better. A simple thing, perhaps, to amuse grown-up white folk—a fat, perspiring Chinaman, and eight or ten lubras chivvying fowls; but it is this enjoyment of simple things that makes life in the Never-Never all it is.

Busy as he was, Cheon found time to take the missus also under his ample wing, and protect her from everything—even herself. "Him too muchee little fellow," he said to the Maluka, to explain his attitude towards his mistress; and the Maluka, chuckling, shamefully encouraged him in his ways.

Every suggestion the missus made was received with an amused: "No good that way, missus! Me savey all about." Her methods with lubras were openly disapproved, and her gardening ridiculed to all comers: "White woman no good, savey gard'n," he reiterated; but was fated to apologize handsomely in that direction later on.

Still, in other things the white woman was honoured as became her position as never Sam honoured her. Without any discrimination, Sam had summoned all at meal-times with a booming teamster's bell, thus placing the gentry on a level with the Quarters; but as Cheon pointed out, what could be expected of one of Sam's ways and caste? It was all very well to ring a peremptory bell for the Quarters—its caste expected to receive and obey orders; but gentry should be graciously notified that all was ready, when it suited their pleasure to eat; and from the day of Sam's departure, the House was honoured with a sing-song, "Din-ner! Boss! Mis-sus!" at midday, with changes rung at "Bress-fass" or "Suppar"; and no written menu being at its service, Cheon supplied a chanted one, so that before we sat down to the first course we should know all others that were to come.

The only disadvantage we could associate with his coming was that by some means Jimmy's Nellie had got on to the Staff. No one seemed to know when or how it had happened, but she was there, grimly established, working better than anyone else, and Dan was demanding payment of his bets.

Cheon would not hear of her dismissal. She was his "right hand", he declared; and so I interviewed Nellie, and stated my objections in cold, brutal English, only to hate myself the next moment; for poor Nellie, with a world of longing in her eyes, professed herself more than willing to wear "good-fellow clothes" *if she could get any.*

"Missus got big mob," she suggested as a hint; and, although that was a matter of opinion and comparison, in remorse I recklessly gave her my only bath wrapper, and for weeks went to the bath in a mackintosh.

Nellie was also willing to use as much carbolic soap as the station could afford; but as the smoking and spitting proved more difficult to cope with, and I had discovered that I could do all the "housework" in less time than it took to superintend it, I made Cheon a present of the entire Staff, only keeping a lien on it for the washing and scrubbing. The lubras, however, refused to be taken off my visitor's list, and Cheon insisting on them waiting on the missus while she was attending to the housework, no one gained or lost by the transfer.

Cheon had a scheme all his own for dealing with the servant question: the Maluka should buy a little Chinese maiden to wait on the missus. Cheon knew of one in Darwin, going cheap, for ten pounds, his—*cousin's* child. "A real bargain!" he assured the Maluka, finding him lacking in enthusiasm; "docile, sweet, and attentive, and"—yes, Cheon was sure of that—"devoted to the missus", and also a splendid pecuniary investment (Cheon always had an eye on the dollars). Being only ten years of age, for six years she could serve the missus, and would then bring at least eighty pounds in the Chinese matrimonial market in Darwin—Chinese wives being scarce there. If she grew up moon-faced, and thus "good-looking", there seemed no end to the wealth she would bring us.

It took time to convince Cheon of the abolition of slavery throughout the Empire, and even when convinced, he was for buying the treasure, and saying nothing about it to the Governor. It was not likely he would come in person to the Elsey, he argued, and, unless told, would know nothing about it.

But another fat, roundabout roly-poly of humanity was to

settle the servant question finally, within a day or two. "Larrikin" had been visiting foreign parts at Wandin, towards the west, and returning with a new wife, stolen from one "Jacky Big-Foot", presented her to the missus.

"Him Rosy!" he said, thus introducing his booty, and without further ceremony Rosy requested permission to "sit down" on the staff. Like Cheon, she carried her qualifications on the tip of her tongue: "Me savey scrub 'im, and sweep 'im, and wash 'im, and blue 'im, and starch 'im," she said glibly, with a flash of white teeth against a babyish pink tongue. She was wearing a freshly washed bright blue dress, hanging loosely from her shoulders, and looked so prettily jolly, clean, capable, and curly-headed, that I immediately made her housemaid and Head of the Staff.

"Great Scott!" the Maluka groaned, "that makes four of them at it!" But Rosy had appealed to me, and I pointed out that it was a chance not to be missed, and that she was worth the other three all put together. "Life will be a perennial picnic," I said, "with Rosy and Cheon at the head of affairs; and for once I prophesied correctly.

Rosy, having been brought up among white folk, proved an adept little housemaid; and Cheon looked with extreme favour upon her, and held her up as a bright and shining example to Jimmy's Nellie. But the person Cheon most approved of at the homestead was Johnny; for not only had Johnny helped him in many of his wild efforts at carpentry, but was he not working in the good cause?

"What's 'er matter, missus only got one room?" Cheon had said, angry with circumstances, and daily and hourly he urged Johnny to work quicker.

"What's the matter indeed!" Johnny echoed, mimicking his furious gutturals, and sawing, planing, and hammering, with untiring energy, pointed out that he was doing his best to give her more.

Finding the progress slow with only one man at work, Cheon suggested the Maluka might lend a hand in his spare time (station books being considered recreation); and when Dan came in with a mob of cattle from the Reach country, he hinted that cattle could wait, and that Dan could employ his time better.

But Dan also was out of patience with circumstances, and growled out that "they'd waited quite long enough as it was", for the work of the station was at a deadlock for want of stores. They had been sadly taxed by the needs of travellers, and we were down to our last half-bag of flour and sugar, and a terrifyingly small quantity of tea; soap, jams, fruits, kerosene, and all such had long been things of the past. The only food we had in quantities was meat, vegetables, and milk. Where we would have been without Cheon no one can tell.

To crown all, we had just heard that the Dandy was delayed in a bog with a broken shaft, but he eventually arrived in time to save the situation, but not before we were quite out of tea. He had little to complain of in the way of welcome when his great piled-up waggon lumbered into the homestead avenue and drew up in front of the store.

The horse teams were close behind, the Dandy said, but Mac was "having a gay time" in the sandy country, and sent in a message to remind the missus that she was still in the Land of Wait-awhile. The reminder was quite unnecessary.

There was also a message from Mine Host. "I'm sending a few cuttings for the missus," it read. Cuttings he called them; but the back of the waggon looked like a nurseryman's van; for all a-growing and a-blowing and waiting to be planted out stood a row of flowering, well-grown plants in tins: crimson hibiscus, creepers, oleanders, and all sorts. A man is best known by his actions, and Mine Host best understood by his kindly thoughtfulness.

The store was soon full to overflowing, and so was our one room, for everything ordered for the House had arrived—rolls of calico heavy and unbleached, mosquito netting, blue matting for the floors, washstand ware, cups and saucers, and dozens of smaller necessities piled in every corner of the room.

"There won't be many idle hands round these parts for a while," a traveller said, looking round the congested room, and he was right, for having no sewing-machine, a gigantic hand-sewing contract was to be faced. The ceilings of both rooms were to be calico, and a dozen or so of seams were to be oversewn for that; the strips of matting were to be joined together and bound into squares, and after that a herculean task undertaken: the making of a huge mosquito-netted dining-room, large enough to enclose the table and chairs, so as to ensure our meals in comfort—for the flies, like the poor, were to be with us always.

This net was to be nearly ten feet square and twelve high, with a calico roof of its own drawn taut to the ceiling of the room, and walls of mosquito netting, weighted at the foot with a deep fold of calico, and falling from ceiling to floor, with a wide double overlapping curtain for a doorway. Imagine an immense four-poster bed-net, ten by ten by twelve, swung taut within a large room, and a fair idea of the dining-net will have been formed. A room within a room, and within the inner-room we hoped to find a paradise at meal-time in comparison with the purgatory of the last few months.

But the sewing did not end at that. The lubras' methods of washing had proved most disastrous to my meagre wardrobe; and the resources of the homestead were taxed to the utmost to provide sufficient patching material to keep the missus even decently clothed.

"Wait for the waggons," the Maluka sang cheerily every time he found me hunting in the store (unbleached calico or mosquito netting being unsuitable for patching).

Cheon openly disapproved of this state of affairs, and was inclined to blame the Maluka. A good husband usually provides his wife with sufficient clothing, he insinuated; but when he heard that further supplies were on the bullock waggons, he apologized, and as he waddled about kept one ear cocked to catch the first sound of the bullock bells. "Bullocky jump four miles," he informed us; from which we inferred that the sound of the bells would travel four miles. Cheon's English generally required paraphrasing.

Almost every day some fresh garment collapsed, and I bitterly regretted my recklessness in giving Jimmy's Nellie the bath wrapper. Fortunately a holland dress was behaving beautifully. "A staunch little beast," the Maluka called it. That, however, had to be washed, every alternate day; and

fearing possible contingencies, I was beginning a dress of unbleached calico, when the Maluka, busy among the stores,
came on a roll of bright pink galatea ordered for lubras' dresses,
and brought it to the house in triumph.

Harsh, crudely pink, galatea! Yet it was received as joyfully
as ever a woman received a Paris gown; for although necessity
may be the mother of invention, she more often brings thankful hearts into this world.

A hank of coarse, bristling white braid was also unearthed
from among the stores, and within three days the galatea had
become a sturdy white-braided blouse and skirt, that promised
to rival the "staunch little beast" in staunch-heartedness.

By the time it was finished, Johnny and the Dandy had all the
flooring-boards down in the dining-room, and before the last
nail was in, Cheon and the Maluka had carried in every
available stick of furniture, and spread it about the room to the
greatest possible advantage. The walls were still unfinished, and
doors and window-frames gaped; but what did that matter?
The missus had a dining-room, and as she presided at her
supper-table in vivid pink and the pride of possession, Cheon
looked as though he would have liked to shake hands with
everyone at once, but particularly with Johnny.

"Looks A1," the Maluka said, alluding to the stiff, aggressive
frock, and took me "bush" with him, wearing the blouse and a
holland riding-skirt that had also proved itself a true, staunch
friend.

Dan, the Quiet Stockman, and the Dandy had already gone
"bush" in different directions; for with the coming of the year's
stores, horse-breaking, house-building, trunks, and waggons
had all stepped into their proper places—a very secondary one
—and cattle had come to the front, and would stay there, as
far as the men were concerned, until next Wet.

Cattle, and cattle only, would be the work of the Dry. Dan
and the Quiet Stockman, with a dozen or so of cattle "boys" to
help them, had the year's musterings and brandings to get
through; the Dandy would be wherever he was most needed;
yard-building, yard-repairing, carting stores or lending a
hand with mustering when necessity arose, while the Maluka

would be everywhere at once, in organization if not in body.

Where runs are huge, and fenceless, and freely watered, the year's mustering and branding is no simple task. Our cattle were scattered through a couple of thousand square miles of scrub and open timbered country, and therefore each section of the run had to be gone over again and again; each mob, when mustered, travelled to the nearest yard and branded

Every available day of the Dry was needed for the work; but there is one thing in the Never-Never that refuses to take a secondary place—the mailman; and at the end of a week we all found, once again, that we had business at the homestead; for six weeks had slipped away since our last mail-day, and the Fizzer was due once more.

12

The Fizzer was due at sun-down, and for the Fizzer to be due meant that the Fizzer would arrive; and by six o'clock we had all got cricks in our necks, with trying to go about as usual, and yet keep an expectant eye on the north track.

The Fizzer is unlike every type of man excepting a bush mail-man. Hard, sinewy, dauntless, and enduring, he travels day after day and month after month, practically alone—"on me Pat Malone", he calls it—with or without a black boy, according to circumstances, and five trips out of his yearly eight throwing dice with death along his dry stages, and yet at all times as merry as a grig, and as chirrupy as a young grass-hopper.

With a light-hearted "So long, chaps," he sets out from the Katherine on his thousand-mile ride, and with a cheery "What ho, chaps! Here we are again!" rides in again within five weeks with that journey behind him.

A thousand miles on horseback "on me Pat Malone", into the Australian interior and out again, travelling twice over three long dry stages and several shorter ones, and keeping strictly within the Government time-limit, would be a life-experience to the men who set that limit—if it wasn't a death-experience. "Like to see one of 'em doing it 'emselves," says the Fizzer. Yet never a day late, and rarely an hour, he does it eight times a year, with a "So long, chaps", and a "Here we are again."

The Fizzer was due at sun-down, and at sun-down a puff of dust rose on the track, and as a cry of "Mail oh!" went up all round the homestead, the Fizzer rode out of the dust.

"Hullo! What ho, boys!" he shouted in welcome, and the next moment we were in the midst of his clattering team of pack-horses.

For five minutes everything was in confusion; horse bells and hobbles jingling and clanging, harness rattling, as horses shook themselves free, and pack-bags, swags, and saddles came to the ground with loud, creaking flops. Everyone was lending a hand, and the Fizzer, moving in and out among the horses, shouted a medley of news and instructions and welcome.

"New? Stacks of it!" he shouted. The Fizzer always shouted. "The gay time we had at the Katherine! Here, steady with that pack-bag. It's breakables! How's the raisin market? Eh, lads!" with many chuckles. "Sore back here, fetch along the balsam. What ho, Cheon!" as Cheon appeared and greeted him as an old friend. "Heard you were here. You're the boy for my money. You *bally* ass! Keep 'em back from the water there." This last was for the black boy. It took discrimination to fit the Fizzer's remarks on to the right person. Then as a pack-bag dropped at the Maluka's feet, he added: "That's the station lot, boss. Full bags, missus! Two on 'em. You'll be doing the disappearing trick in half a mo'."

In "half a mo'" the seals were broken, and the mail-matter shaken out on the ground. A cascade of papers, magazines, and books, with a fat, firm little packet of letters among them: forty letters in all—thirty of them falling to my lot—thirty fat, bursting envelopes, and in another "half mo'" we had all slipped away in different directions—each with our precious mail matter—doing the "disappearing trick" even to the Fizzer's satisfaction.

The Fizzer smiled amiably after the retreating figures, and then went to be entertained by Cheon. He expected nothing else. He provided feasts all along his route, and was prepared to stand aside while the bush-folk feasted. Perhaps in the silence that fell over the bush homes, after his mail-bags were opened, his own heart slipped away to dear ones, who were waiting somewhere for news of our Fizzer.

Eight mails *only* in a year is not all disadvantage. Townsfolk

who have eight hundred tiny doses of mail-matter doled out to
them, like men on sick diet, can form little idea of the pleasure
of that feast of "full bags and two on 'em", for like thirsty camels
we drank it all in—every drop of it—in long, deep, satisfying
draughts. It may have been a disadvantage, perhaps, to have
been so thirsty; but then only the thirsty soul knows the sweetness of slaking that thirst.

After a full hour's silence the last written sheet was laid down,
and I found the Maluka watching and smiling.

"Enjoyed your trip South, little 'un?" he said, and I came
back to the bush with a start, to find the supper dead cold. But
then supper came every night and the Fizzer once in forty-two.

At the first sound of voices, Cheon bustled in. "New-fellow
tea, I think," he said, and bustled out again with the teapot
(Cheon had had many years' experience of bush mail-days),
and in a few minutes the unpalatable supper was taken
away, and cold roast beef and tomatoes stood in its place.

After supper, as we went for our evening stroll, we stayed for
a little while where the men were lounging, and after a general
interchange of news the Fizzer's turn came.

News! He had said he had stacks of it, and he now bubbled
over with it. The horse teams were "just behind", and the
"Macs" almost at the front gate. The Sanguine Scot? Of course
he was all right; always was, but reckoned bullock-punching
wasn't all it was cracked up to be; thought his troubles were
over when he got out of the sandy country, but hadn't reckoned
on the black soil flats. "Wouldn't be surprised if he took to
punching something else besides bullocks before he's through
with it," the Fizzer shouted, roaring with delight at the recollection of the Sanguine Scot in a tight place. On and on he
went with his news, and for two hours afterwards, as we sat
chewing the cud of our mail-matter, we could hear him laughing and shouting and "chiacking".

At daybreak he was at it again, shouting among his horses, as
he culled his team of "done-ups", and soon after breakfast was
at the head of the south track with all aboard.

"So long, chaps," he called. "See you again half past eleven
four weeks"; and by "half past eleven four weeks" he would

have carried his precious freight of letters to the yearning, waiting men and women hidden away in the heart of Australia, and be out again, laden with Inside letters for the Outside world.

At all seasons of the year he calls the first two hun .red miles of his trip a "kid's game". "Water somewhere nearly every day, and a decent camp most nights." And although he speaks of the next hundred and fifty as being a "bit off during the Dry", he faces its seventy-five-mile dry stage, sitting loosely in the saddle, with the same cheery "So long, chaps."

Five miles to "get a pace up"—a drink and then that seventy-five miles of Dry, with any "temperature they can spare from other parts", and not one drop of water in all its length for the horses. Straight on top of that, with the same horses and the same temperature, a run of twenty miles, mails dropped at Newcastle Waters, and another run of fifty into Powell's Creek, dry or otherwise according to circumstances.

"Takes a bit of fizzing to get into the Powell before the fourth sun-down," the Fizzer says—for, forgetting that there can be no change of horses, and leaving no time for a "spell" after the "seventy-five-mile dry", the time limit for that one hundred and fifty miles, in a country where four miles an hour is good travelling on good roads, has been fixed at three and a half days. "Four, they call it," said the Fizzer, "forgetting I can't leave the water till midday. Takes a bit of fizzing all right"; and yet at Powell's Creek no one has yet discovered whether the Fizzer comes at sun-down, or the sun goes down when the Fizzer comes.

"A bit off," he calls that stage, with a school-boy shrug of his shoulders; but at Renner's Springs, twenty miles farther on, the shoulders set square, and the man comes to the surface. The dice-throwing begins there, and the stakes are high—a man's life against a man's judgment.

Some people speak of the Fizzer's luck, and say he'll pull through, if anyone can. It is luck, perhaps—but not in the sense they mean—to have the keen judgment to know to an ounce what a horse has left in him, judgment to know when to stop and when to go on—for that is left to the Fizzer's discretion; and with that judgment the dauntless courage to go on with, and win through, every task attempted.

The Fizzer changes horses at Renner's Springs for the "Downs trip"; and as his keen eyes run over the mob, his voice raps out their verdict like an auctioneer's hammer. "He's fit. So is he. Cut that one out. That colt's A1. The chestnut's done. So is the brown. I'll risk that mare. That black's too fat." No hesitation: horse after horse rejected or approved, until the team is complete; and then driving them before him he faces the Open Downs—the Open Downs, where the last mail-man perished; and only the men who know the Downs in the Dry know what he faces.

For five trips out of the eight, one hundred and thirty miles of sun-baked, crab-holed, practically trackless plains, no sign of human habitation anywhere, cracks that would swallow a man —"hardly enough wood to boil a quart pot", the Fizzer says, and a sun-temperature hovering about 160 degrees (there is no shade-temperature on the Downs); shadeless, trackless, sun-baked; crab-holed plains, and the Fizzer's team a moving speck in the centre of an immensity that, never diminishing and never changing, moves onward with the team; an immensity of quivering heat and glare, with that one tiny living speck in its centre, and in all that hundred and thirty miles one drink for the horses at the end of the first eighty. That is the Open Downs.

"Fizz!" shouts the Fizzer. "That's where the real fizzing gets done, and nobody that hasn't tried it knows what it's like."

He travels its first twenty miles late in the afternoon, then, unpacking his team, "lets 'em go for a roll and a pick, while he boils a quart pot" (the Fizzer carries a canteen for himself); "spells" a bare two hours, packs up again and travels all night, keeping to the vague track with a bushman's instinct, "doing another twenty miles before daylight"; unpacks for another spell, pities the poor brutes "nosing round too parched to feed", may "doze a bit with one ear cocked", and then packing up again, "punches 'em along all day", with or without a spell. Time is precious now. There is a limit to the number of hours a horse can go without water, and the thirst of the team fixes the time limit on the Downs. "Punches 'em along all day, and into water close up sun-down", at the deserted Eva Downs station.

"Give 'em a drink at the well there," the Fizzer says as unconcernedly as though he turned on a tap. But the well is old and out of repair, ninety feet deep, with a rickety old wooden windlass; fencing wire for a rope; a bucket that the Fizzer has "seen fit to plug with rag on account of it leaking a bit", and a trough, stuffed with mud at one end by the resourceful Fizzer. Truly the Government is careful for the safety of its servants. Added to all this, there are eight or ten horses so eager for a drink that the poor brutes have to be tied up, and watered one at a time; and so parched with thirst that it takes three hours' drawing before they are satisfied—three hours' steady drawing, on top of twenty-three hours out of twenty-seven spent in the saddle, and half that time "punching" jaded beasts along; and yet they speak of the "Fizzer's luck".

"Real fine old water too," the Fizzer shouts in delight, as he tells his tale. "Kept in the cellar for our special use. Don't indulge in it much myself. Might spoil my palate for newer stuff, so I carry enough for the whole trip from Renner's."

If the Downs have left deep lines on the Fizzer's face, they have left none in his heart. Yet at that well the dicethrowing goes on just the same.

Maybe the Fizzer feels "a bit knocked out with the sun", and the water for his perishing horses ninety feet below the surface; or "things go wrong" with the old windlass, and everything depends on the Fizzer's ingenuity. The odds are very uneven when this happens—a man's ingenuity against a man's life, and death playing with loaded dice. And every letter the Fizzer carries past that well costs the public just twopence.

A drink at the well, an all-night's spell, another drink, and then away at midday, to face the toughest pinch of all—the pinch where death won with the other mail-man. Fifty miles of rough, hard, blistering, scorching, "going", with worn and jaded horses.

The old programme all over again. Twenty miles more, another spell for the horses (the Fizzer never seems to need a spell for himself), and then the last lap of thirty, the run into

Anthony's Lagoon, "punching the poor beggars along some-how". "Keep 'em going all night," the Fizzer says: "and if you should happen to be at Anthony's on the day I'm due there you can set your watch for eleven in the morning when you see me coming along." I have heard somewhere of the Pride of Harness.

Sixteen days is the time-limit for those five-hundred miles, and yet the Fizzer is expected because the Fizzer is due, and to a man who loves his harness no praise could be sweeter than that. Perhaps one of the brightest thoughts for the Fizzer as he "punches" along those desolate Downs is the knowledge that a little before eleven o'clock in the morning Anthony's will come out, and, standing with shaded eyes, will look through the quivering heat, away into the Downs, for that tiny moving speck. When the Fizzer is late there, death will have won at the dice-throwing.

I suppose he got a salary. No one ever troubled to ask. He was expected, and he came, and in our selfishness we did not concern ourselves beyond that.

It is men like the Fizzer who, "keeping the roads open", lay the foundation-stones of great cities; and yet when cities creep into the Never-Never along the Fizzer's mail route, in all probability they will be called after Members of Parliament and the Prime Ministers of that day, grandsons, perhaps, of the men who forgot to keep the old well in repair, while our Fizzer and the mail-man who perished will be forgotten; for townsfolk are apt to forget the beginnings of things.

Three days' spell at Anthony's, to wait for the Queensland mail-man from the "other-side" (another Fizzer no doubt, for the bush mail-service soon culls out the unfitted), an exchange of mail-bags, and then the Downs must be faced again with the same team of horses. Even the Fizzer owns that "tackling the Downs for the return trip's a bit sickening; haven't had time to forget what it feels like, you know", he explains.

Inside to Anthony's, three days' spell, over the Downs again, stopping for another drink at that well, along the stage "that's a bit off", and back to the "kid's game", dropping mail-bags in twos and threes as he goes in, and collecting others as he comes out, to say nothing of the weary packing and unpacking of his team. That is what the Fizzer had to do by half past eleven four weeks.

"And will go hopelessly on the spree at the end of the trip," say uncharitable folk; but they do not know our Fizzer. "Once upon a time I was a bad little boy," our Fizzer says now, "but since I learnt sense a billy of tea's good enough for me."

And our Fizzer is not the only man out-bush who has "learnt sense". Man after man I have met who found tea "good enough", and many more who "know how to behave themselves". Sadly enough, there are others in plenty who find their temptations too strong for them—temptations that the world hardly guesses at.

But I love the bush-folk for the good that is in them, hidden, so often, carefully away deep down in their brave, strong hearts —hearts and men that ring true, whether they have "learnt sense", or "know how to behave", or are only of the others. But every man's life runs parallel with other lives, and while the Fizzer was "punching along" his dry stages events were moving rapidly with us; while perhaps, away in the hearts of towns, men and women were "winning through dry stages" of their lives there.

13

Soon after the Fizzer left us the horse-teams came in, and went on, top-heavy with stores for Inside; but the Macs were now thinking of the dry stages ahead, and were travelling at the exasperating rate of about four miles a day, as they "nursed the bullocks" through the good grass country.

Dan had lost interest in waggons, and was anxious to get among the cattle again; but with the trunks so near, the House growing rapidly, the days of sewing waiting, I refused point-blank to leave the homestead just then.

Dan tried to taunt me into action, and reviewed the "kennel" with critical eyes. "Never saw a dog making its own chain before," he said to the Maluka as I sat among billows of calico and mosquito netting. But the home-making instinct is strong in a woman, and the musterers went out west without the missus. The Dandy being back at the Bitter Springs superintending the carting of new posts for the stockyard there, the missus was left in the care of Johnny and Cheon.

"Now we shan't be long," said Johnny, and Cheon, believing him, expressed great admiration for Johnny, and superintended the scrubbing of the walls, while I sat and sewed, yard after yard of over sewing, as never woman sewed before.

The walls were erected on what is known as the drop-slab-panel system—upright panels formed of three-foot slabs cut from the outside slice of tree-trunks, and dropped horizontally, one above the other, between grooved posts—a simple arrangement, quickly run up and artistic in appearance—outside, a horizontally fluted surface, formed by the natural curves of the timber, and inside, flat, smooth walls. As in every third panel there was a door or a window, and as the horizontal slabs stopped within two feet of the ceiling, the building was exceedingly airy, and open on all sides.

Cheon, convinced that the system was all Johnny's, was delighted with his ingenuity. But as he insisted on the walls being scrubbed as soon as they were up, and before the doors and windows were in, Johnny had one or two good duckings, and narrowly escaped many more; for lubras' methods of scrubbing are as full of surprises as all their methods.

First soap is rubbed on the dry boards, then vigorously scrubbed into a lather with wet brushes, and after that the lather is sluiced off with artificial waterspouts whizzed up the walls from full buckets. It was while the sluicing was in progress that Johnny had to be careful; for many buckets missed their mark, and the waterspouts shot out through the doorways and window-frames.

Wearing a mackintosh, I did what I could to prevent surprises, but without much success. Johnny fortunately took it all as a matter of course. "It's all in the good cause," he chuckled, shaking himself like a water-spaniel after a particularly bad misadventure; and described the "performance" with great zest to the Maluka when he returned. The sight of the clean walls filled the Maluka also with zeal for the cause; and in the week that followed walls sprouted with corner shelves and brackets—three wooden kerosene cases became a handy series of pigeon-holes for magazines and papers. One panel in the dining-room was completely filled with bookshelves, one above the other for our coming books. Great sheets of bark, stripped by the blacks from the Ti Tree forest, were packed a foot deep above the rafters to break the heat reflected from the iron roof, while beneath it the calico ceiling was tacked up. And all the time Johnny hammered and whistled and planed, finishing the bathroom and "getting on" with the office.

The Quiet Stockman coming in was pressed into the service, and grew quite enthusiastic, suggesting substitutes for necessities, until *I* suggested cutting off the tail of every horse on the run, to get enough horsehair for a mattress.

"Believe the boss'ud do it himself if she asked him," he said in the Quarters; and in his consternation suggested bang-tailing the cattle during the musters.

"Just the thing," Dan decided; and we soon saw, with his assistance, a vision of our future mattress walking about the run on the ends of cows' tails.

"Looks like it's going to be a dead-heat," Johnny said, still hammering, when the Dandy brought in word that the Macs were within twelve miles of the homestead. And when I announced next day that the dining-net was finished and ready for hanging, he also became wildly enthusiastic.

"Told you from the beginning we shouldn't be long," he said, flourishing a hammer and brimming over with suggestions for the hanging of the net. "Rope'll never hold it," he declared; "fencing wire's the thing," so fencing wire was used, and after a hard morning's work pulling and straining the wire and securing it to uprights, the net was in its place, the calico roof smooth and flat against the ceiling, and its curtains hanging to the floor, with strong, straight saplings run through the folded hem to weight it down. Cheon was brimming over with admiration for it.

"My word, boss! Missus plenty savey," he said. (Cheon invariably discussed the missus in her presence.) "Chinaman woman no more savey likee that," and bustling away, dinner was soon served inside the net.

Myriads of flies, balked in their desire, settled down on the outside, and while we enjoyed our dinner in peace and comfort, Cheon hovered about, like a huge bloated buzzfly himself, chuckling around the outside among the swarms of balked flies, or coming inside to see if "any fly sit down inside".

"My word, boss! Hear him sing-out sing-out. Missus plenty savey," he reiterated, and then calling a Chinese friend from the kitchen, stood over him, until he also declared that "missus *blenty* savey", with good emphasis on the *blenty*.

The net was up by midday, and at ten o'clock at night the slow, dull clang of a bullock-bell crept out of the forest. Cheon was the first to hear it. "Bullocky come on," he called, waddling to the house and waking us from our first sleep; and as the deep-throated bell boomed out again the Maluka said drowsily: "The homestead's only won by a head. Mac's at the Warlochs."

At "fowl-sing-out" we were up, and found Bertie's Nellie behind the black boys' humpy shyly peeping round a corner. With childlike impetuosity she had scampered along the four miles from the Warlochs, only to be overcome with unaccountable shyness.

" 'Allo, missus!" was all she could find to say, and the remainder of the interview she filled in with wriggling and giggles.

Immediately after breakfast Mac splashed through the creek at a hand-gallop and, dashing up to the house, flung himself from his horse, the same impetuous, warmhearted "Brither Scot".

"Patience rewarded at last," he called in welcome; and when invited to "come ben the hoose to the dining-room", was, as usual, full of congratulations. "My! We are some!" he said, examining every detail. But as he also said that "the Dandy could get the trunks right off if we liked to send him across with the dray", he naturally "liked", and Johnny and the Dandy, harnessing up, went with him, and before long the verandah and rooms were piled with trunks.

Fortunately Dan was "bush" again among the cattle, or his heart would have broken at this new array of links for the chain.

Once the trunks were all in, Mac, the Dandy, and Johnny retired to the Quarters after a few more congratulations, Johnny continuing his flourishes all the way across. Cheon, however, with his charming disregard for conventionality, being interested, settled himself on one of the trunks to watch the opening up of the others.

To have ordered him away would have clouded his beaming happiness; so he remained, and told us exactly what he thought of our possessions, adding much to the pleasure of the opening of the trunks. If any woman would experience real pleasure, let her pack all her belongings into trunks—all but a couple of changes of everything—and go away out-bush, leaving them to follow "after the Wet" per bullock waggon, and when the reunion takes place the pleasure will be forthcoming. If she can find a Cheon to be present at the reunion, so much the better.

Some of our belongings Cheon thoroughly approved of; others were passed over as unworthy of notice, and others were held up to chuckling ridicule. A silver teapot was pounced upon with a cry of delight (tinware being considered far beneath the dignity of a missus, and seeing Sam had broken the china pot soon after its arrival, tinware had graced our board for some time), pictures were looked at askance, particularly an engraving of Psyche at the Pool; while the case for a set of carvers received boundless admiration, although the carvers in no way interested him.

The photographs of friends and relatives were looked carefully over, the womenfolk being judged by what they might bring in a Chinese matrimonial market.

"My word! That one good-looking. Him close up sixty pound longa China," was rather disconcerting praise of a very particular lady friend.

A brass lamp was looked upon as a monument of solid wealth. "Him gold," he decided, insisting it was in the face of all denials. "Him gold. Me savey gold all right. Me live longa California long time," he said, bringing forward a most convincing argument; and, dismissing the subject with one of his Podsnappian waves, he decided that a silver-coloured composition flower-bowl in the form of a swan was solid silver; "Him sing out all a same silver," he said, making it ring with a flick of his finger and thumb when I differed from him; and knowing Cheon by now, we left it at that for the time being.

After wandering through several trunks and gloating over blouses, and skirts, and house-linen, and old friends, the books were opened up, and before the Maluka became lost to the world Cheon favoured them with a passing glance. "Big mob book," he said indifferently, and turned his attention to the last trunk of all.

Near the top was a silver filigree candlestick moulded into the form of a convolvulus flowers and leaf—a dainty little thing, but it appeared ridiculous to Cheon's commonsense mind.

"Him silly fellow," he scoffed, and appealed to the Maluka

for his opinion. "Him silly fellow? Eh, boss?" he asked.

The Maluka was half-buried in books. "Um," he murmured absently, and that clinched the matter for all time. "Boss bin talk silly fellow!" Cheon said, with an approving nod towards the Maluka, and advised packing the candle-stick away again. "Plenty room sit down longa box," he said, truthfully enough, putting it into an enormous empty trunk and closing the lid, leaving the candlestick a piece of lonely splendour hidden under a bushel.

But the full glory of our possessions was now to burst upon Cheon. The trunk we were at was half-filled with all sorts of cunning devices for kitchen use, intended for the mistress's pantry of that commodious station home of past ignorant imagination. A mistress's pantry forsooth, in a land where houses are superfluous and luxuries barred, and at a homestead where the mistress had long ceased to be anything but the little missus—something to rule or educate or take care of, according to the nature of her subordinates.

In a flash I knew all I had once been, and quailing before the awful proof before me, presented Cheon with the whole collection of tin and enamel ware, and packed him off to the kitchen before the Maluka had time to lose interest in the books.

Everything was exactly what Cheon most needed, and he accepted everything with gleeful chuckles—everything excepting a kerosene Primus burner for boiling a kettle. That he refused to touch. "Him go bang," he explained, as usual explicit and picturesque in his English.

After gathering his treasure together he waddled away to the kitchen, and at afternoon tea we had sponge cakes, light and airy beyond all dreams of airy lightness, no one having yet combined the efforts of Cheon, a flour dredge, and an egg-beater, in his dreams. And Cheon's heart being as light as his cookery, in his glee he made a little joke at the expense of the Quarters, summoning all there to afternoon tea with a chuckling call of "Cognac!"—chuckles that increased tenfold at the mock haste of the Quarters. A little joke, by the way, that never lost in freshness as the months went by.

At intervals during the days that followed Cheon surveyed

his treasures, and during these intervals the whirr of the flour dredge or egg-beater was heard from the kitchens, and invariably the whirr was followed by a low, distinct chuckle of appreciation.

All afternoon we worked, and by the evening the dining-room was transformed; blue cloths and lace runners on the deal side-table and improvised pigeon-holes; nick-nacks here and there on tables and shelves and brackets; pictures on the walls; "kent" faces in photograph frames among the nick-nacks; a folding carpet-seated arm-chair in a position of honour; cretonne curtains in the doorway between the rooms, and inside the shimmering white net a study in colour effect—blue-and-white matting on the floor, a crimson cloth on the table, and on the cloth Cheon's "silver" swan sailing in a sea of purple, blue, and heliotrope water-lilies. But best of all were the books—row upon row of old familiar friends; nearly two hundred of them filling the shelved panel as they looked down upon us.

Mac was dazzled with the books. Hadn't seen so many together since he was a nipper, he said; and after we had introduced him to our favourite, we played with our new toys like a parcel of children, until supper-time.

When supper was over we lit the lamp, and shutting doors and windows, shut the Sanguine Scot in with us, and made believe we were living once more within sound of the rumble of a great city. Childish behaviour, no doubt, but to be expected from folk who can find entertainment in the going to bed of fowls; when the heart is happy it forgets to grow old.

"A lighted lamp and closed doors, and the outside world is what you will it to be," the Maluka theorized, and to disprove it Mac drew attention to the distant booming of the bells that swung from the neck of his grazing bullocks.

"The city clocks," we said. "We hear them distinctly at night."

But the night was full of sounds all around the homestead, and Mac, determined to mock, joined in with the "Songs of the Frogs".

"Quart pot! Qua-rt pot!" he croaked, as they sang outside in rumbling monotone.

"The roll of the tramcars," the Maluka interpreted gravely, as the long flowing gutturals blended into each other; and Mac's mood suddenly changing he entered into our sport, and soon put us to shame in make-believing spoke of "pining for a breath of fresh air"; "hoped" to get away from the grime and dust of the city as soon as the session was over; wondered how he would shape "at camping out", with an irrepressible chuckle. "Often thought I'd like to try it," he said, and invited us to help him make up a camping party. "Be a change for us city chaps," he suggested; and then exploding at what he called his "tom-foolery", set the dining-net all a-quivering and shaking.

"Gone clean dilly, I believe," he declared, after thinking that he had "better be making a move for the last train". Then, mounting his waiting horse, he splashed through the creek again, and disappeared into the moonlight grove of pandanus palms beyond it.

The waggons spelled for two days at the Warlochs, and we saw much of the Macs. Then they decided to "push on"; for not only were others farther In waiting for the waggons, but daily the dry stages were getting longer and drier; and the shorter his dry stages are, the better a bullock-puncher likes them.

With well-nursed bullocks, and a full complement of them— the "Macs" had twenty-two per waggon for their dry stages—a "thirty-five-mile dry" can be "rushed", the waggoners getting under way by three o'clock one afternoon, travelling all night with a spell or two for the bullocks by the way, and "punching" them into water within twenty-four hours.

'Getting over a fifty-mile dry" is, however, a more complicated business, and suggests a treadmill. The waggons are "pulled out" ten miles in the late afternoon, the bullocks unyoked and brought back to the water, spelled most of the next day, given a last drink and travelled back to the waiting waggons by sundown; yoked up and travelled on all that night and part of the next day; once more unyoked at the end of the forty miles of the stage; taken *forward* to the next water, and spelled and nursed upon again at this water for day or two; travelled back again to the waggons, and again yoked up, and finally brought forward in the night with the loads to the water.

Fifty miles dry with loaded waggons being the limit for mortal bullocks, the Government breaks the "seventy-five" with a "drink" sent out in tanks on one of the telegraph station waggons. The stage thus broken into "a thirty-five-mile dry", with another of forty on top of that, becomes complicated to giddiness in its backings, and fillings, and goings, and comings, and returnings.

As each waggon carries only five tons, all things considered, from thirty to forty pounds a ton is not a high price to pay for the cartage of stores to Inside.

But although the "getting in" with the stores means much to the bush-folk, "getting out" again is the ultimate goal of the waggoners.

There is time enough for the trip, but only good time, before the roads will be closed by the dry stages growing to impossible lengths for the bullocks to recross; and if the waggoners lose sight of their goal, and loiter by the way, they will find themselves "shut in" Inside, with no prospect of getting out until the next Wet opens the road for them.

The Irish Mac held records for getting over stages; but even he had been "shut in" once, and had sat kicking his heels all through a long Dry, wondering if the showers would come in time to let him out for the next year's loading, or if the Wet would break suddenly, and further shut him in with floods and bogs. The horse teams had been "shut in" the same year, but as the Macs explained, the teamsters had broached their cargo that year, and had a "glorious spree" with the cases of grog —a "glorious spree" that detained them so long on the road that by the time they were in there was no chance of getting out, and they had more than enough time to brace themselves for the interview that eventually came with their employers.

"Might a bullock puncher have the privilege of shaking hands with a lady?" the Irish Mac asked, extending an honest, horny hand; and the privilege, if it were one, was granted. Finally all was ready, and the waggons, one behind the other, each with its long swaying line of bullocks before it, slid away from the Warloch Ponds and crept into the forest, looking like three huge snails with shells on their backs, Bertie's Nellie watching, wreathed in smiles.

Nellie had brought to the homestead her bosom friend and crony, Biddy, and the Staff had increased to five. It would have numbered six, only Maudie, discovering that the house was infested with debbil-debbils, had resigned and "gone bush". The debbil-debbils were supposed to haunt the Maluka's telescope, for Maudie, on putting her eye to the sight opening, to find out what interested the Maluka so often, had found the trees on the distant plain leaping towards her.

"Debbil-debbil, sit down!" she screamed, as, flinging the telescope from her in a frenzy of fear, she found the distance still and composed.

"No more touch him, missus!" she shrieked, as I stooped to pick up the telescope. " 'Spose you touch him, all about there come on quick fellow. Me bin see him! My word him race!"

After many assurances, I was allowed to pick it up, Maudie crouching in a shuddering heap the while behind the office, to guard against surprises. Next morning she applied for leave of absence and "went bush". Jimmy's Nellie, however, was not so easily scared, and after careful investigation treated herself to a pleasant half-hour with the telescope.

"Tree all day walk about," she said, explaining the mystery to the Staff; and the looking-glass speedily lost in favour. The telescope proved full of delights. But although it was a great sight to see a piccaninny "come on big-fellow", nothing could compare with the joy of looking through the reversed end of the glass, into a world where great men became "little fellow", unless it were the marvel of watching dim, distant specks as they took on the forms of birds, beasts, or men.

The waggons gone, and with them Nellie's shyness, she quietly ousted Rosy from her position at the head of the staff. "Me sit down first time," she said; and happy, smiling Rosy, retiring, obeyed orders as willingly as she had given them. With Nellie and Rosy at the head of affairs, house-cleaning passed unnoticed, and although, after the arrival of unlimited changes of everything, washing-day threatened to become a serious business, they coped with that difficulty by continuing to live in

Jeannie Gunn (Angela Punch McGregor) with local Aboriginal woman.

Aeneas Gunn (Arthur Dignam), Manager of the
Elsey Station, at work.

a cycle of washing days—every alternate day only, though, so as to leave time for gardening.

The gardening staff, which consisted of a king, an heir-apparent, and a royal councillor, had been engaged to wheel barrow-loads of rich loamy soil from the billabong to the garden beds; but as its members preferred gossiping in the shade to work of any kind, the gardening took time and supervision.

"That'll do, Gadgerrie?" was the invariable question after each load, and the staff prepared to sit down for a gossip; and "Gadgerrie" had to start everyone afresh, after deciding whose turn it was to ride back to the billabong in the barrow.

Six loads in a morning was a fair record, for "Gadgerrie" was not often disinclined for a gossip on court matters, but although nothing was done while we were out-bush, the garden was gradually growing.

Two of the beds against the verandah were gaily flourishing, others "coming on", and outside the broad pathway a narrow bed had been made all round the garden for an hibiscus hedge; while outside this bed again; one at each corner of the garden, stood four posts—the Maluka's promise of a dog-proof, goat-proof, fowl-proof fence. So far Tiddle'ums had acted as fence, when we came in, at the homestead, scattering fowls, goats, and dairy cows in all directions if they dared come over a line she had drawn in her mind's eye. When Tiddle'ums was out-bush with us, Bett-Bett acted as fence.

Johnny, generally repairing the homestead now, admired the garden and declared everything would be "A1 in no time".

"Wouldn't know the old place," he said, a day or two later, surveying his own work with pride. Then he left us, and for the first time I was sorry the house was finished. Johnny was one of the men who had not "learnt sense", but the world would be a better place if there were more Johnnies in it.

Just as we were preparing to go out-bush for reports, Dan came in with a mob of cattle for branding and the news that a yard on the northern boundary was gone from the face of the earth.

"Clean gone since last Dry," he reported; "burnt or washed away, or both."

Rather than let his cattle go, he had travelled in nearly thirty miles with the mob in hand, but "reckoned" it wasn't "good enough". "The time I've had with them staggering bobs," he said, when we pitied the poor, weary, footsore little calves; "could 'ave brought in a mob of snails quicker. 'Tisn't good enough."

The Maluka also considered it not "good enough", and decided to run up a rough branding wing at once on to the holding yard at the Springs; and while Dan saw to the branding in the mob the Maluka looked out his plans.

"Did you get much hair for the mattress?" I asked, all in good faith, when Dan came down from the yards to the House to discuss the plans, and Dan stood still, honestly vexed with himself.

"Well, I'm blest!" he said, "if I didn't forget all about it," and then tried to console me by saying I wouldn't need a mattress till the mustering was over. "Can't carry it round with you, you know," he said, "and it won't be needed anywhere else." Then he surveyed the house with his philosophical eye.

"Wouldn't know the old place," Johnny had said, and Dan "reckoned" it was "all right as houses go." Adding with a chuckle, "Well, she's wrastled with luck for more'n four months to get it, but the question is, what's she going to use it for now she's got it?"

14

For over four months we had wrestled with luck for a house, only to find we had very little use for it for the time being, that is, until next Wet. It couldn't be carried out-bush from camp to camp, and finding us at a loss for an answer, Dan suggested one himself.

"Of course," he said, as he eyed the furnishings with interest, "it 'ud come in handy to pack the chain away in, while the dog was out enjoying itself"; and we left it at that. It *came* in handy to pack the chain away in while the dog was enjoying itself, for within twenty-four hours we were camped at the Bitter Springs, and two weeks passed before the homestead saw us again.

After our experience of "getting hold of Johnny", Dan called it foolishness to wait for an expert, and the Dandy being away for the remainder of the stores, and the Quiet Stockman having his hands full to overflowing, the Maluka and Dan, with that adaptability peculiar to bushmen, set to work themselves at the yard, with fifteen or twenty boys as apprentices.

As most of the boys had their lubras with them, it was an immense camp, but exceedingly pretty. One small tent "fly" for a dressing-room for the missus, and the remainder of the accommodation—open-air and shady bough gundies, tiny, fresh, cool, green shade-houses here, there, and everywhere for the blacks; one set apart from the camp for a larder, and an immense one—all green waving boughs—for the missus to rest in during the heat of the day. "The Cottage", Dan-called it.

Of course, Sool'em and Brown were with us, Little Tiddle-

'ums being in at the homestead on the sick list with a broken leg; and in addition to Sool'em and Brown an innumerable band of nigger dogs, Billy Muck being the adoring possessor of fourteen, including pups, which fanned out behind him as he moved hither and thither like the tail of a comet.

Our camp, being a stationary one, was, by comparison with our ordinary camps, a *camp-de-luxe*; for, apart from the tent-fly, in it were books, pillows, and a canvas lounge, as well as some of the flesh-pots of Egypt, in the shape of eggs, cakes, and vegetables sent out every few days by Cheon, to say nothing of scrub turkey, fish, and such things.

Dan had no objection to the eggs, cakes, or vegetables, but the pillows and canvas lounge tried him sorely. "Thought the chain was to be left behind in the kennel," he said, and decided that the "next worst thing to being chained up" was "for a dog to have to drag a chain round when it was out for a run. Look at me!" he said, "never been chained up all me life, just because I never had enough permanent property to make a chain—never more than I could carry in one hand: a bluey, a change of duds, a mosquito net and a box of Cockle's pills."

We suggested that Cockle's pills were hardly permanent property, but Dan showed that they were, with him.

"More permanent than you'd think," he said. "When I've got 'em in me swag, I never need 'em, and when I've left 'em somewhere else I can't get 'em: so you see the same box does for always."

Yard-building lacking in interest, lubras and piccaninnies provided entertainment, until Dan, failing to see that "niggers could teach her anything", decided on a course of camp cookery.

Roast scrub turkey was the first lesson, cooked in the most correct style: a forked stick, with the fork upper-most, was driven into the ground near the glowing heap of wood ashes; then a long sapling was leant through the fork, with one end well over the coals; a doubled string, with the turkey turned round and round until the string was twisted to its utmost, and finally string and turkey were left to themselves, to wind and unwind slowly, an occasional winding-up being all that was necessary.

The turkey was served at supper, and with it an enormous boiled cabbage—one of Cheon's successes. Dan was in clover, boiled cabbage being considered nectar fit for the gods; and after supper he put the remnants of the feast away for his breakfast. "Cold cabbage goes all right," he said, as he stowed it carefully away—"particularly for breakfast."

Then the daily damper was to be made, and I took the dish without a misgiving. I felt at home there, for bushmen have long since discarded the old-fashioned damper, and use soda and cream-of-tartar in the mixture. But ours was an immense camp, and I had reckoned without any thought. An immense camp requires an immense damper; and, the dish containing pounds and pounds of flour, when the mixture was ready for kneading the kneading was beyond a woman's hands—a fact that provided much amusement to the bushmen.

"Hit him again, little 'un," the Maluka cried encouragingly, as I punched and pummelled at the unwieldy mass.

"Give it to him, missus," Dan chuckled. "That's the style! Now you've got him down."

Kneeling in front of the dish, I pounded obediently at the mixture; and as they alternately cheered and advised, and I wrestled with circumstances, digging my fists vigorously into the spongy, doughy depths of the damper, a traveller rode into the camp.

"Good evening, mates," he said, dismounting. "Saw your fires, and thought I'd camp near for company." Then discovering that one of the "mates" was a woman, backed a few steps, dazed and open-mouthed—a woman, dough to the elbows, pounding blithely at a huge damper, being an unusual sight in a night camp in the heart of one of the cattle runs in the Never-Never.

"We're conducting a cooking class," the Maluka explained, amused at the man's consternation.

The traveller grinned a sickly grin, and "begging pardon, ma'am, for intruding", said something about seeing to his camp, and backed to a more comfortable distance; and the damper-making proceeded.

"There's a billy just thinking of boiling here you can have, mate, seeing it's late," Dan called, when he heard the man rattling tinware, as he prepared to go for water; and once more "begging pardon, ma'am, for intruding", the traveller came into our camp circle, and busied himself with the making of tea.

The tea made to his satisfaction, he asked diffidently if there was a "bit of meat to spare", as his was a "bit off"; and Dan went to the larder with a hospitable "Stacks!"

"How would boiled cabbage and roast turkey go?" Dan called, finding himself confronted with the great slabs of cabbage; and the traveller, thinking it was supposed to be a joke, favoured us with another nervous grin and a terse "Thanks!" Then Dan reappeared, laden, and the man's eyes glistened as he forgot his first surprise in his second. "Real cabbage!" he cried. "Gosh, ain't tasted cabbage for five years"; and, the Maluka telling him to "sit right down, then, and begin, just where you are"—beside our camp-fire—with a less nervous "begging your pardon, ma'am", he dropped down on one knee and began.

"Don't be shy of the turkey," the Maluka said presently, noticing that he had only taken a tiny piece, and the man looked sheepishly up. "'Taint exactly that I'm shy of it," he said, "but I'm scared to fill up any space that might hold cabbage. That is," he added, again apologetic, "if it's not wanted, ma'am "

It wasn't wanted; and as the man found room for it, the Maluka and Dan offered further suggestions for the construction of the damper and its conveyance to the fire.

The conveyance required judgment and watchful diplomacy, as the damper preferred to dip in a rolling valley between my extended, arms, or hang over them like a table-cloth, rather than keep its desired form. But with patience, and the loan of one of Dan's huge palms, it finally fell with an unctuous, dusty "whouf" into the open-out bed of ashes.

By the time it was hidden away, buried in the heart of the fire, a woman's presence in a camp had proved less disturbing than might be imagined, and we learned that our traveller had "come from Beyanst", with a backward nod towards the Queensland border, and was going west; and by the time the cabbage and tea were finished he had become quite talkative.

"Ain't see cabbage, ma'am, for more'n five years," he said, leaning back on to a fallen tree-trunk, with a satisfied sigh (cabbage and tea being inflating), adding, when I sympathized, "nor a woman, neither, for that matter."

Neither a cabbage nor a woman for five years! Think of it, townsfolk! Neither a cabbage nor a woman—with the cabbage placed first. I wonder which will be longest remembered.

"Came on this, though, in me last camp, east there," he went on, producing a hairpin, with another nod eastwards. "Wondered how it got there. Your'n, I s'pose"; then, sheepish once more, he returned it to his pocket, saying he "s'posed he might as well keep it for luck".

It being a new experience to one of the plain sisterhood to feel a man was cherishing one of her hairpins, if only "for luck", I warmed towards the "man from Beyanst", and grew hopeful of rivalling even that cabbage in his memory. "You didn't expect to find hairpins, and a woman, in a camp in the back blocks," I said, feeling he was a character, and longing for him to open up. But he was even more of a character than I guessed.

"Back blocks!" he said in scorn. "There ain't no back blocks left. Can't travel a hundred miles nowadays without running into somebody! You don't know what back blocks is, begging your pardon, ma'am."

But Dan did; and the camp chat that night was worth travelling several hundred miles to hear: tales dug out of the beginning of things; tales of drought, and flood, and privation; cattle-duffing yarns, and long tales of the droving days; two years' reminiscences of getting through with a mob— reminiscences that finally brought ourselves and the mob to Oodnadatta.

"That's the place if you want to see drunks, ma'am," the traveller said, forgetting in his warmth his "begging your pardon, ma'am", just when it would have been most opportune, seeing I had little hankering to see "drunks".

"It's the desert does it, missus, after the overland trip," Dan explained. "It 'ud give anybody a 'drouth'. Got a bit merry meself there once and had to clear out to camp," he went on.

"Felt it getting a bit too warm for me to stand. You see, it was when the news came through that the old Queen was dead, and being something historical that had happened, the chaps felt it ought to be celebrated properly."

Poor old Queen! And yet, perhaps, her grand, noble heart would have understood these, her subjects, and known them for the men they were—as loyal-hearted and true to her as the highest in the land.

"They were lying two-deep about the place next morning," Dan added, continuing his tale; but the Maluka, fearing the turn the conversation had taken, suggested turning in.

Then Dan, having found a kindred spirit in the traveller, laid a favourite trap for one of his favourite jokes: shaking out a worn old bluey, he examined it carefully in the firelight.

"Blanket's a bit thin, mate," said the man from Beyanst, unconsciously playing his part. "Surely it can't keep you warm"; and Dan's eyes danced in anticipation of his joke.

"Oh, well!" he said, solemn-looking as an owl, as he tucked it under one arm, "if it can't keep a chap warm after ten years' experience, it'll never do it," and turned in at once, with his usual lack of ceremony.

We had boiled eggs for breakfast, and once more the traveller joined us. Cheon had sent the eggs out with the cabbage, and I had hidden them away, intending to spring a surprise on the men-folk at breakfast.

"How many eggs shall I boil for you, Dan?" I said airily, springing my surprise in this way on all the camp. But Dan, wheeling with an exclamation of pleasure, sprung a surprise of his own on the missus.

"Eggs!" he said. "Good enough! How many? Oh, a dozen'll do, seeing we've got steak"; and I limply showed all I had— fifteen.

Dan scratched his head trying to solve the problem. "Never reckon it's worth beginning under a dozen," he said; but finally suggested tossing for 'em after they were cooked.

"Not the first time I've tossed for eggs, either," he said, busy grilling steak on a gridiron made from bent-up fencing wire. "Out on the Victoria once they got scarce, and the cook used to boil all he had and serve the dice-box with 'em, the chap who threw the highest taking the lot."

"Ever try to boil an emu's egg in a quart pot?" the man from Beyanst asked, "lending a hand" with another piece of fencing wire, using it as a fork to turn the steak on the impromptu gridiron. "It goes in all right, but when it's cooked it won't come out, and you have to use the quart pot for an egg-cup and make tea later on."

"A course dinner," Dan called that; and then, nothing being forthcoming to toss with—dice or money not being among our permanent property—the eggs were distributed according to the "holding capacity" of the company: one for the missus, two for the Maluka, and half a dozen each for the other two.

The traveller had no objection to beginning under a dozen, but Dan used his allowance as a "relish" with his steak. "One egg!" he chuckled as he shelled his relish and I enjoyed my breakfast. "Often wonder however she keeps alive."

The damper proved "just a bit boggy" in the middle, so we ate the crisp outside slices and gave the boggy parts to the boys. They appeared to enjoy it, and seeing this, after breakfast the Maluka asked them what they thought of the missus as a cook. "Good damper, eh?" he said, and Billy Muck, rubbing his middle, full of damper and satisfaction, answered: "My word! That one damper good fellow. Him sit down long time"; and all the camp, rubbing middles, echoed his sentiments. The stodgy damper had made them feel full and uncomfortable; and to be full and uncomfortable after a meal spells happiness to a black fellow.

"Hope it won't sit too heavy on *my* chest," chuckled the man from Beyanst, then, remembering that barely twelve hours before he had ridden into the camp a stranger, began "begging pardon, ma'am" most profusely again, and hoped we'd excuse him "making so free with a lady".

"It's your being so friendly like, ma'am," he explained. "Most of the others I've struck seemed too good for rough chaps like us. Of course," he added hastily, "that's not saying that you're not as good as 'em. *You* ain't a Freezer on a pedestal, that's all."

"Thank Heaven," the Maluka murmured, and the man from Beyanst sympathized with him. "Must be a bit off for their husbands," he said; and his apologies were forgotten in the absorbing topic of "Freezers".

"A Freezer on a pedestal," *he* had said. "Goddess", the world prefers to call it; and tradition depicts the bushman worshipping afar off.

But a "Freezer" is what *he* calls it to himself; and contrary to all tradition, goes on his way unmoved, and why shouldn't he? He may be, and generally is, sadly in need of a woman friend, "someone to share his joys and sorrows with"; but because he knows few women is no reason why he should stand afar off and adore the unknowable. "Friendly like" is what appeals to us all; and the bushfolk are only men, not monstrosities—rough, untutored men for the most part. The difficult part to understand is how any woman can choose to stand aloof and freeze, with warm-hearted men all around her willing to take her into their lives.

As the men exchanged opinions, "Freezers" appeared solitary creatures—isolated monuments of awe-inspiring goodness and purity, and I felt thankful that circumstances had made me only the Little Missus—a woman, down with the bushmen at the foot of all pedestals, needing all the love and fellowship she could get, and with no more goodness than she could do with—just enough to make her worthy of the friendship of "rough chaps like us."

"Oh, well," said the traveller, when he was ready to start, after finding room in his swag for a couple of books, "I'm not sorry I struck this camp"; but whether because of the cabbage, or the woman, or the books, he did not say. Let us hope it was because of the woman, and the books, and the cabbage, with the cabbage placed last.

Then, with a pull of his hat, and a "good-bye, ma'am, good luck", the man from Beyanst rode out of the gundy camp, and out of our lives, to become one of its pleasant memories.

The man from Beyanst was our only visitor for the first week in that camp, and then after that we had someone every day.

Dan went into the homestead for stores, and set the ball

rolling by returning at sundown in triumph with a great find: a lady traveller, the wife of one of the Inland Telegraph masters. Her husband and little son were with her, but—well, they were only men. It was five months since I had seen a white woman, and all I saw at the time was a woman riding towards our camp. I wonder what she saw as *I* came to meet *her* through the leafy bough gundies. It was nearly two years since she had seen a woman.

It was a merry camp that night—merry and beautiful and picturesque. The night was very cold and brilliantly starry, as nights usually are in the Never-Never during the Dry; the camp-fires were all around us: dozens of them, grouped in and out among the gundies, and among the fires—chatting, gossiping groups of happy-hearted human beings.

Around one central fire sat the lubras, with an outer circle of smaller fires behind them: one central fire and one fire behind each lubra, for such is the wisdom of the black folk; they warm themselves both back and front. Within another circle of fires chirruped and gossiped the "boys", while around an immense glowing heap of logs sat the white folk—the "big-fellow fools" of the party, with scorching faces and freezing backs, too conservative to learn wisdom from their humbler neighbours.

At our fireside we women did most of the talking, and as we sat chatting on every subject under the sun, our husbands looked on in indulgent amusement. Dan soon wearied of the fleeting conversation and turned in, and the little lad slipped away to the black folk; but late into the night *we* talked: late into the night, and all the next day and evening and following morning—shaded from the brilliant sunshine all day in the leafy "Cottage", and scorching around the camp-fire during the evenings. And then these travellers, too, passed out of our camp to become, with the man from Beyanst, just pleasant memories.

"She'll find mere men unsatisfying after this," the Maluka said in farewell; and a mere man, coming in from the north-west before sun-down, greeted the Maluka with: "Thought you married a towny," as he pointed with eloquent forefinger at our supper circle.

"So I did," the Maluka laughed back. "But before I had time to dazzle the bushies with her the Wizard of the Never-Never charmed her into a bush-whacker."

"Into a *charming* bush-whacker, he *means*!" the traveller said, bowing before his introduction; and I wondered how the Maluka could have thought for one moment that "mere men" would prove unsatisfying. But as I acknowledged the gallantry, Dan looked on dubiously, not sure whether pretty speeches were a help or a hindrance to education.

But not one could call the Fizzer a "mere man"; and half past eleven four weeks being already past, the Fizzer was even then at the homestead, and before another midday, came shouting into our camp, and, settling down to dinner, kept the conversation ball rolling.

"Going to be a record Dry," he assured us—"all surface water gone along the line already"; and then he hurled various items of news at us: "The horse teams were managing to do a good trip; and Mac? Oh, Mac's getting along," he shouted; "struck him on a dry stage; seemed a bit light-headed; said dry stages weren't all beer and skittles—queer ideas. Beer and skittles! He won't find much beer on dry stages, and I reckon the man's dilly that 'ud play a game of skittles on any one of 'em."

Everyone was all right down the line! But the Fizzer was always a bird of passage, and by the time dinner was over, and a few postscripts added to the mail, he was ready to start, and rode off, promising the best mail the "Territory could produce in a fortnight".

Other travellers followed the Fizzer, and the cooking lessons proceeded until the fine art of making "puff de looneys", sinkers, and doughboys had been mastered, and then, before the camp had time to grow monotonous, the Staff appeared with a few of the station pups. "Might it missus like puppy dogs," it said to explain its presence, hinting also that the missus might require a little clothes-washing done.

Lately, washing-days at the homestead had lost all their vim, for the creek having stopped running, washing had to be conducted in tubs, so as to keep the billabong clear for drinking purposes. But at the Springs there was no necessity to think of anything but running water; and after a happy day, Bertie's Nellie, Rosy, and Biddy returned to the homestead—the goats had to be seen to, Nellie said, thinking nothing of a twenty-seven-mile walk in a day, with a few hours' washing for recreation in between whiles.

Part of the Staff, a shadow or two, and the puppy dogs filled in all time until the yard was pronounced finished; then a mob of cattle was brought in and put through, to test its strength; and just as we were preparing to return to the homestead the Dandy's waggon lumbered into camp with its loading of stores.

A box of new books kept us busy all afternoon, and then, before sun-down, the Maluka suggested a farewell stroll among the pools.

The Bitter Springs—a chain of clear, crystal pools, a long winding chain, doubling back on itself in loops and curves—form the source of the permanent flow of the Roper; pools only a few feet deep, irregular and wide-spreading, with mossy-green, deeply undermined, overhanging banks, and limestone bottoms washed into terraces that gleam azure-blue through the transparent water.

There is little rank grass along their borders, no sign of water-lilies, and few weeds within them; clumps of palms dotted here and there among the light timber, and everywhere sun-flecked, warm, dry shade. Nowhere is there a hint of that sinister suggestion of the Reach. Clear, beautiful, limpid, wide-spreading, irregular pools, set in an undulating field of emerald-green mossy turf, shaded with graceful foliage and gleaming in the sunlight with exquisite opal tints—a giant necklace of opals, set in links of emerald green, and thrown down at hazard, to fall in loops and curves within a forest grove.

It is in appearance only the pools are isolated; for although many feet apart in some instances, they are linked together throughout by a shallow underground river that runs over a rocky bed; while the turf, that looks so solid in many places, is barely a two-foot crust arched over five or six feet of space and water—a death-trap for heavy cattle; but a place of interest to white folk.

The Maluka and I wandered aimlessly in and out among the

pools for a while, and then, coming out unexpectedly from a
piece of bush, found ourselves face to face with a sight that
froze all movement out of us for a moment—the living, moving
head of a horse, standing upright from the turf on a few inches
of neck: a grey, uncanny, bodiless head, nickering piteously at
us as it stood on the ̤urf at our feet. I have never seen a ghost,
but I know exactly how I will feel if ever I do.

For a moment we stood spellbound with horror, and the
next, realizing what had happened, were kneeling down beside
the piteous head. The thin crust of earth had given way beneath
the animal's hindquarters as it grazed over the turf, and before
it could recover itself it had slipped bodily through the hole
thus formed, and was standing on the rocky bed of the underground river, with its head only in the upper air.

The poor brute was perishing for want of food and water. All
around the hole, as far as the head could reach, the turf was
eaten, bare, and although it was standing in a couple of feet of
water it could not get at it. While the Maluka went for help I
brought handfuls of grass, and his hat full of water, again and
again, and was haunted for days with the remembrance of those
pleading eyes and piteous, nickering lips.

The whole camp, black and white, came to the rescue; but it
was awful work getting the exhausted creature out of its death-
trap. The hole had to be cut back to a solid ridge of rocky soil,
saplings cut to form a solid slope from the bed of the river to the
ground above, and the poor brute roped and literally hauled up
the slope by sheer force and strength of numbers. After an hour's
digging, dragging, and rope-pulling, the horse was standing on
solid turf, a new pool had been added to the Springs, and none
of us had much hankering for riding over springy country.

The hour's work among the pools awakened the latent
geologist in all of us, excepting Dan, and set us rooting at the
bottom of one of the pools for a piece of the terraced limestone.

It was difficult to dislodge, and our efforts reminded Dan of a
night spent in the camp of a geologist—a man with many
letters after his name. "Had the chaps heaving rocks round for
him half his time," he said. "Couldn't see much sense in it
meself." Dan spoke of the geologist as "one of them old

Alphabets". "Never met a chap with so many letters in his brand," he exclaimed. "He was one of them taxydermy blokes, you know, that's always messing round with stones and things."

Out of the water, the opal tints died out of the limestone, and the geologist in us went to sleep again when we found that all we had for our trouble was a piece of dirty-looking rock. Like Dan, we saw little sense in "heaving rocks round", and went back to the camp and the business of packing up for the homestead.

About next midday we rode into the homestead thoroughfare, where Cheon and Tiddle'ums welcomed us with enthusiasm, but Cheon's enthusiasm turned to indignation when he found we were only in for a day or two.

"What's er matter?" he ejaculated. "Missus no more stockrider"; but a letter waiting for us at the homestead made "bush" more than ever imperative: a letter, from the foreman of the telegraphic repairing line party, asking for a mob of killers and fixing a date for its delivery to one "Happy Dick".

"Spoke just in the nick of time," Dan said; but as we discussed plans Cheon hinted darkly that the Maluka was not a fit and proper person to be entrusted with the care of a woman, and suggested that he should undertake to treat the missus as she should be treated, while the Maluka attended to the cattle.

Fate, however, interfered to keep the missus at the homestead, to persuade Cheon that, after all, the Maluka was a fit and proper person to have the care of a woman, and to find a very present use for the House; and influenza sore-throat breaking out in the camp, the missus developed it, and Dan went out alone to find the Quiet Stockman and the "killers" for Happy Dick.

15

Before a week was out the Maluka and Cheon had won each other's undying regard because of their treatment of the missus.

With the nearest doctor three hundred miles away in Darwin, and held there by hospital routine, the Maluka decided on bed and feeding-up as the safest course, and Cheon came out in a new character.

As medical adviser and reader-aloud to the patient, the Maluka was supposed to have his hands full, and Cheon, usurping the position of sick-nurse, sent everything, excepting the nursing, to the wall. Rice-water, chicken-jelly, barley-water, egg-flips, beef-tea, junket, and every invalid food he had ever heard of, were prepared, and, with the Maluka to back him up, forced on the missus; and when food was not being administered, the pillow was being shaken or the bed-clothes straightened. (The mattress being still on the ends of cows' tails, a folded rug served in its place.) There was very little wrong with the patient, but the wonder was she did not become really ill through over-eating and want of rest.

I pleaded with the Maluka, but the Maluka pleading for just a little more rest and feeding-up, while Cheon gulped and choked in the background, I gave in, and eating everything as it was offered, snatched what rest I could, getting as much entertainment as possible out of Cheon and the Staff in between times.

For three days I lay obediently patient, and each day Cheon grew more affectionate, patting my hands at times, as he confided to the Maluka that although he admired big, moon-faced women as a feast for the eyes, he liked them small and docile when he had to deal personally with them. Until I met Cheon I thought the Chinese incapable of affection; but many lessons are learned out-bush.

Travellers—house-visitors—coming in on the fourth day, I hoped for a speedy release, but visitors were considered fatiguing, and release was promised as soon as they were gone.

Fortunately the walls had many cracks in them—not being as much on the plumb as Johnny had predicted, and for a couple of days, watching the visitors through these cracks and listening to their conversation provided additional amusement. I could see them quite distinctly as, no doubt, they could see me; but we kept a decorous silence until the Fizzer came in, then at the Fizzer's shout the walls of Jericho toppled down.

"The missus sick!" I heard him shout. "Thought she looked in prime condition at the Springs." (Bush language frequently has a strong twang of cattle in it.)

"So I am now," I called; and then the Fizzer and I held an animated conversation through the walls. "I'm imprisoned for life," I moaned, after hearing the news of the outside world; and laughing and chuckling outside, the Fizzer vowed he would "do a rescue next trip if they've still got you down". Then, after appreciating fervent thanks, he shouted in farewell, "The boss is bringing something along that'll help to pass some of the time —the finest mail you ever clapped eyes on," and presently patient and bed were under a litter of mail-matter.

The Fizzer having brought down the walls of conventionality, the traveller-guests proffered greetings and sympathy through the material walls, after which we exchanged mail-news and general gossip for a day or two; then, just as these travellers were preparing to exchange farewells, others came in and postponed the promised release. As there seemed little hope of a lull in visitors, I was wondering if ever I should be considered well enough to entertain guests, when Fate once more interfered.

"Whatever's this coming in from the East?" I heard the Maluka call in consternation, and in equal consternation his traveller-guest called back, "Looks like a whole village settle-

ment." Then Cheon burst into the room in a frenzy of excitement. "Big mob traveller, missus. Two-fellow-missus, sit down,"
he began; but the Maluka was at his heels.

"Here's two women and a mob of youngsters," he gasped.
"I'm afraid you'll have to get up, little 'un, and lend a hand
with them."

Afraid! By the time the village settlement had "turned out"
and found its way to the house, I was out in the open air
welcoming its members with a heartiness that must have surprised them. Little did they guess that they were angels unaware.
Homely enough angels, though, they proved, as angels unaware
should prove: one man and two women from "Queensland
way", who had been Inside for fifteen years, and with them two
fine young lads and a wee, toddling baby—all three children
born in the bush and leaving it for the first time.·

Never before had Cheon had such a company to provide
for; but as we moved towards the house in a body—ourselves,
the village settlement, and the Maluka's traveller-guests, with a
stockman traveller and the Dandy looking on from the Quarters,
his hospitable soul rejoiced at the sight; and by the time seats
had been found for all comers, he appeared laden with tea and
biscuits, and within half an hour had conjured up a plentiful
dinner for all comers.

Fortunately the chairs were all "up" to the weight of the
ladies, and the remainder of the company easily accommodated
itself to circumstances, in the shape of sawn stumps, rough
stools, and sundry boxes; and although the company was large
and the dining-table small, and although, at times, we feared
the table was about to fulfil its oft-repeated threat and fall over,
yet the dinner was there to be enjoyed, and, being bush-folk,
and hungry, our guests enjoyed it, passing over all incon-
gruities with simple merriment—a light-hearted, bubbling
merriment, in no way comparable to that "laughter of fools",
that crackling of thorns under a pot, provoked by the incon-
gruities of the world's freak dinners. The one is the heritage of
the simple-hearted, and the other—all the world has to give in
exchange for this birthright.

The elder lads, one fourteen and one ten years of age, found

Cheon by far the most entertaining incongruity at the dinner, and when dinner was over—after we had settled down on the various chairs and stumps that had been carried out to the verandah again—they shadowed him wherever he went.

They were strangely self-possessed children; but knowing little more of the world than the black children their playmates, Cheon, in his turn, found them vastly amusing, and instructing them in the ways of the world—from his point of view—found them also eager pupils. But their education came to a standstill after they had mastered the mysteries of the Dandy's gramophone, and Cheon was no longer entertaining.

All afternoon brass-band selections, comic songs, and variety items blared out with ceaseless reiteration; and as the men-folk smoked and talked cattle, and the wee baby—a bonnie fair child—toddled about, smiling and contented, the women-folk spoke of their life "out-back"; and listening, I knew that neither I nor the telegraph lady had even guessed what roughness means.

For fifteen years things had been improving, and now everyone was to have a well-earned holiday. The children were to be christened and then shewn the delights of a large town! Darwin of necessity (Palmerston, by the way, on the map, but Darwin to Territorians). Darwin with its one train, its telegraph offices, two or three stores, banks and public buildings, its Residency, its Chinatown, its lovers' walk, its two or three empty, wide, grass-grown streets bordered with deep-verandahed, iron-built bungalow-houses, with their gardens planted in painted tins—a development of the white-ant pest—and lastly, its great sea, where ships wander without tracks or made ways! Hardly a typical town, but the best in the Territory.

The women, naturally, were looking forward to doing a bit of shopping, and as we slipped into fashions the traveller-guests became interested. "Haven't seen so many women together for years," one of them said. "Reminds me of when I was a nipper," and the other traveller "reckoned" he had struck it lucky for once. "Three on 'em at once," he chuckled with indescribable relish. "They reckon it never rains but it pours." And so it would seem with three women guests within three weeks at a homestead where women had been almost unknown for years.

But these women guests only stayed one night, the children being all impatience to get on to the telegraph line, to those wires that talked, and to the railway, where the iron monster ran.

Early in the morning they left us, and as they rode away the fair toddling baby was sitting on its mother's pommel-knee, smiling out on the world from the deep recesses of a sun-bonnet. Already it had ridden a couple of hundred miles, with its baby hands playing with the reins, and before it reached home again another five hundred would be added to the two hundred. Seven hundred miles on horseback in a few weeks, at one year old, compares favourably with one of the Fizzer's trips. But it is thus the bush develops her Fizzers.

After so much excitement Cheon feared a relapse, and was for prompt, preventive measures; but even the Maluka felt there was a limit to the Rest Cure, and the musterers coming in with Happy Dick's bullocks and a great mob of mixed cattle for the yards, Dan proved a strong ally; and besides, as the musterers were in and Happy Dick due to arrive by midday, Cheon's hands were full with other matters.

There was a roly-poly pudding to make for Dan, baked custard for the Dandy, jam-tarts for Happy Dick, cake and biscuits for all comers, in addition to a dinner and supper waiting to be cooked for fifteen black boys, several lubras, and half a dozen hungry white folk. Cheon had his own peculiar form of welcome for his many favourites, regaling each one of them with delicacies to their particular liking, each and every time they came in.

Happy Dick, also, had his own peculiar form of welcome. "Good day! Real glad to see you!" was *his* usual greeting. Sure of his own welcome wherever he went, he never waited to hear it, but hastened to welcome all men into his fellowship. "Real glad to see you," he would say, with a ready smile of comradeship: and it always seemed as though he had added, "I hope you'll make yourself at home while with me." In some mysterious way, Happy Dick was at all times the host giving liberally of the best he had to his fellow-men.

He was one of the pillars of the Line Party. "Born in it, I think," he would say. "Don't quite remember," adding with his ever-varying smile, "remember when it was born, anyway."

When the "Overland Telegraph" was built across the Australian continent from sea to sea, a clear broad avenue, two chains wide, was cut for it through bush and scrub and dense forests, along the backbone of Australia, and in this avenue the Line Party was "born" and bred—a party of axemen and mechanics under the orders of a foreman, whose duty it is to keep the "Territory section" of the line in repair, and this avenue free from the scrub and timber that spring up unceasingly in its length.

In unbroken continuity this great avenue runs for hundreds upon hundreds of miles, carpeted with feathery grasses and shooting shrubs, and walled in on either side with dense, towering forest or lighter and more scattered timber. On and on it stretches in utter loneliness, zigzagging from horizon to horizons beyond, and guarding those two sensitive wires at its centre, as they run along their single line of slender galvanized posts, from the great bush that never ceases in its efforts to close in on them and engulf them. A great broad highway, waiting in its loneliness for the generations to come, with somewhere in its length the Line Party camp, and here and there, within its thousand miles, a chance traveller or two; here and there a horseman with pack-horse ambling and grazing along behind him; here and there a trudging speck with a swag across its shoulders, and between them one, two, or three hundred miles of solitude; here and there a horseman riding, and here and there a footman trudging on, each unconscious of the others.

From day to day they travel on, often losing the count of the days, with those lines always above them, and those beckoning posts ever running on before them; and as they travel, now and then they touch a post for company—shaking hands with Outside: touching now and then a post for company, and daily realizing the company and comfort those posts and wires can be. Here at least is something in touch with the world, something vibrating with the lives and actions of men, and an ever-present friend in dire necessity. With those wires above him, any day a traveller can cry for help to the Territory, if he call while he yet has strength to climb one of those friendly posts and cut that quivering wire—for help that will come speedily, for the cutting of the telegraph wire is as the ringing of an alarm-bell throughout the Territory. In all haste the break is located, and food, water, and every human help that suggests itself sent out from the nearest telegraph station. There is no official delay—there rarely is in the Territory—for by some marvellous good fortune, there everything belongs to the Department in which it finds itself.

Just as Happy Dick is one of the pillars of the Line Party, so the Line Party is one of the pillars of the line itself. Up and down this great avenue, year in, year out, it creeps along, cutting scrub and repairing as it goes, and moving cumbrous main camps from time to time, with its waggon-loads of stores, tents, furnishings, flocks of milking goats, its fowls, its gramophone, and the Chinese cook. Month after month it creeps on, until, reaching the end of the section, it turns round to creep out again.

Year in, year out, it had crept in and out, and for twenty years Happy Dick had seen to its peace and comfort. Nothing ever ruffled him. "All in the game" was his nearest approach to a complaint, as he pegged away at his work, in between whiles going to the nearest station for killers, carting water in tanks out to "dry-stage camps", and doing any other work that found itself undone. Dick's position was as elastic as his smile.

He considered himself an authority on three things only: the Line Party, dog-fights, and cribbage. All else, including his dog Peter and his cheque-book, he left to the discretion of his fellow-men.

Peter—a speckled, drab-coloured, prick-eared creation, a few sizes larger than a fox-terrier—could be kept in order with a little discretion, and by keeping hands off Happy Dick; but all the discretion in the Territory, and a unanimous keeping off of hands, failed to keep order in the cheque-book.

The personal payment of salaries to men scattered through hundreds of miles of bush country being impracticable, the department pays all salaries due to its servants into their bank accounts at Darwin, and therefore when Happy Dick found himself the backbone of the Line Party, he also found himself the possessor of a cheque-book. At first he was inclined to look upon it as a poor substitute for hard cash; but after the foreman had explained its mysteries, and taught him to sign his name in magic tracery, he became more than reconciled to it, and drew cheques blithely, until one for five pounds was returned to a creditor: no funds—and in due course returned to Happy Dick.

"No good?" he said to the creditor, looking critically at the piece of paper in his hands. "Must have been writ wrong. Well, you've only yourself to blame, seeing you wrote it"; then added magnanimously, mistaking the creditor's scorn: "Never mind, write yourself out another. I don't mind signing 'em."

The foreman and the creditor spent several hours trying to explain banking principles, but Dick, "couldn't see it". "There's stacks of 'em left!" he persisted, showing his book of fluttering bank cheques. Finally, in despair, the foreman took the cheque-book into custody, and Dick found himself poor once more.

But it was only for a little while. In an evil hour he discovered that a cheque from another man's book answered all purposes if it bore that magic tracery, and Happy Dick was never solvent again. Gaily he signed cheques, and the foreman did all he could to keep pace with him on the cheque-book block; but as no one, excepting the accountant in the Darwin bank, knew the state of his account from day to day, it was like taking a ticket in a lottery to accept a cheque from Happy Dick.

"Real glad to see you," Happy Dick said in hearty greeting to us all as he dismounted, and we waited to be entertained. Happy Dick had his favourite places and people, and the Elsey community stood high in his favour. "Can't beat the Elsey for a good dog-fight and a good game of cribbage," he said, every time he came in or left us; and that from Happy Dick was high praise. At times he added, "Nor for a square meal, neither," thereby inciting Cheon to further triumphs for his approval.

As usual, Happy Dick "played" the Quarters cribbage and related a good dog-fight—"Peter's latest"—and, as usual before he left us, his pockets were bulging with tobacco—the highest stakes used in the Quarters—and Peter and Brown had furnished him with materials for a still newer dog-fight recital. As usual, he rode off with his killers, assuring all that he would "be along again soon", and, as usual, Peter and Brown were tattered and *hors-de-combat*, but both still aggressive. Peter's death lunge was the death lunge of Brown, and both dogs knew that lunge too well to let the other "get in".

As usual, Happy Dick had hunted through the store, and taken anything he "really needed", paying, of course, by cheque; but when he came to sign that cheque, after the Maluka had written it, he entered the dining-room for the first time since its completion.

With calm scrutiny he took in every detail, including the serviettes as they lay folded in their rings on the waiting dinner-table, and before he left the homestead he expressed his approval in the Quarters:

"Got everything up to the knocker, haven't they?" he said. "Often heard toffs decorated their tables with rags in hobble rings, but never believed it before."

Happy Dick gone, Cheon turned his attention to the health of the missus; but Dan persuading the Maluka that "all she needed was a breath of fresh air", we went bush on a tour of inspection.

16

Within a week we returned to the homestead, and for twenty-four hours Cheon gloated over us, preparing every delicacy that appealed to him as an antidote to an out-bush course of beef and damper. Then a man rode into our lives who was to teach us the depth and breath of the meaning of the word mate—a sturdy, thick-set man, with haggard, tired eyes and deep lines about his firm, strong mouth that told of recent and prolonged tension.

"Me mate's sick; got a touch of fever," he said simply, dismounting near the verandah. "I've left him camped back there at the Warlochs"; and as the Maluka prepared remedies —making up the famous Gulf mixture—the man, with grateful thanks, found room in his pockets and saddle-pouch for eggs, milk, and brandy, confident that "these'll soon put him right", adding, with the tense lines deepening about his mouth as he touched on what had brought them there: "He's been real bad, ma'am. I've had a bit of a job to get him as far as this." In the days to come we were to learn, little by little, that the "bit of a job" had meant keeping a sick man in his saddle for the greater part of the fifty-mile dry stage, with forty miles of "bad going" on top of that, and fighting for him every inch of the way that terrible symptom of malaria—that longing to "chuck it", and lie down and die.

Bad water after that fifty-mile Dry made men with a touch of fever only too common at the homestead; and knowing how much the comforts of the homestead could do, when the Maluka came out with the medicines he advised bringing the sick man on as soon as he had rested sufficiently. "You've only to ask for it and we'll send the old station buck-board across," he said; and the man began fumbling uneasily at his saddle-girths, and said something evasive about "giving trouble"; but when the Maluka—afraid that a man's life might be the forfeit of another man's shrinking fear of causing trouble—added that on second thoughts we would ride across as soon as horses could be brought in, he flushed hotly and stammered: "If you please, ma'am. If the boss'll excuse me, me mate's dead set against a woman doing things for him. If you wouldn't mind not coming. He'd rather have me. Me and him's been mates this seven years. The boss'll understand."

The boss did understand, and rode across to the Warlochs alone, to find a man as shy and reticent as a bushman can be, and full of dread lest the woman at the homestead would insist in visiting him. "You see, that's why he wouldn't come on," the mate said. "He couldn't bear the thought of a woman doing things for him"; and the Maluka explained that the missus understood all that. That lesson had been easily learned; for again and again men had come in "down with a touch of fever", whose temperatures went up at the very thought of a woman doing things for them, and always the actual nursing was left to the Maluka or the Dandy, the woman seeing to egg-flips and such things, exchanging at first perhaps only an occasional greeting, and listening at times to strange life-histories later on.

But in vain the Maluka explained and entreated: the sick man was "all right where he was". His mate was worth "ten women fussing round", he insisted, ignoring the Maluka's explanations. Had he not "lugged him through the worst pinch already?" And then he played his trump card. "He'll stick to me till I peg out," he said—"nothing's too tough for him"; and as he lay back, the mate, deciding "arguing'll only do for him", dismissed the Maluka with many thanks, refusing all offers of nursing help with a quiet "He'd rather have me," but accepting gratefully broths and milk and anything of that sort the homestead could furnish. "Nothing ever knocks me out," he reiterated, and dragged on through sleepless days and nights, as the days dragged by finding ample reward in the knowledge that "he'd rather have me"; and when there came that deep word of praise from his stricken comrade, "A good mate's harder to find than a good wife," his gentle, protecting devotion increased tenfold.

Bushmen are instinctively protective. There is no other word that so exactly defines their tender helpfulness to all weakness and helplessness. Knowing how hard the fight is out-bush for even the strong and enduring, all their magnificent strength and courage stand ready for those who would go to the wall without it. A lame dog, a man down in his luck, an old soaker, little women, any woman in need or sickness—each and all call forth this protectiveness; but nothing calls it forth in its self-sacrificing tenderness like the helplessness of a strong man stricken down in his strength.

Understanding this also, we stood aside; and rejoicing, as the sick man, benefiting by the comparative comfort, and satisfied to have his own way, seemed to improve. For three days he improved steadily, and then, after standing still for another day, slipped back inch by inch to weakness and prostration, until the homestead, without coercion, was the only chance for his life.

But there was a woman there; and as the mate went back to his pleading, the woman did what the world may consider a strange thing—but a man's life depended on it—she sent a message out to the sick man, to say that if he would come to the homestead, she would not go to him until he asked her.

He pondered over the message for a day, sceptical of a woman's word—surely some woman had left that legacy in his heart—but eventually decided he wouldn't risk it. Then the chief of the telegraph coming in— a man widely experienced in fever—and urging one more attempt, the Dandy volunteered to help us in our extremity, and, driving across to the Warlochs in the chief's buggy, worked one of his miracles; he spent only a few minutes alone with the man (and the Dandy alone knows now what passed), but within an hour the sick traveller was resting quietly between clean sheets in the Dandy's bed. There were times when the links in the chain seemed all blessing.

Waking warm and refreshed, the sick man faced the battle

of life once more, and the chief taking command, and the man quietly and hopefully obeying orders, the woman found her promise easy to keep; but the mate's hardest task had come, the task of waiting with folded hands. With the same quiet steadfastness he braced himself for this task, and when, after weary hours, the chief pronounced "all well" and turned to him with an encouraging, "I think he'll pull through now, my man," the sturdy shoulders that had borne so much drooped and quivered beneath the kindly words, and with dimming eyes he gave in at last to the Maluka's persuasions, and lay down and slept, sure of the Dandy's promise to wake him at dawn.

At midnight the Maluka left the Quarters, and going back just before the dawn to relieve the Dandy, found the sick man lying quietly restful, with one arm thrown lightly across his brow. He had spoken in his sleep a short while before, the Dandy said, as the Maluka bent over him with a cup of warm milk; but the cup was returned to the table untasted. Many travellers had come into our lives and passed on with a bright nod of farewell; but at the first stirring of the dawn, without one word of farewell, this traveller had passed on and left us; left us, and the faithful mate of those seven strong young years and those last few days of weariness. "Unexpected heart failure," our chief said, as the Dandy went to fulfil his promise to the sleeping mate. He promised to wake him at the dawn; and leaving that awakening in the Dandy's hands, as we thought of that lonely Warloch camp, our one great thankfulness was that when the awakening came the man was not to be alone there with his dead comrade. The bush can be cruel at times, and yet, although she may leave us alone with our beloved dead, her very cruelty brings with it a fierce, consoling pain; for out-bush our dead are all our own.

Beyond those seven faithful years the mate could tell us but little of his comrade's life. He was William Neaves, born at Wollongong, with a mother living somewhere there. That was all he knew. "He was always a reticent chap," he reiterated. "He never wanted anyone but me about him," and the unspoken request was understood. He was *his* mate, and no one but himself must render the last services.

Dry-eyed and worn, the man moved about, doing all that should be done, the bushmen only helping where they dared; then, shouldering a pick and shovel, he went to the little rise beyond the slip rails, and set doggedly to work at a little distance from two lonely graves already there. Doggedly he worked on; but, as he worked, gradually his burden lost its overwhelming weight, for the greater part of it had somehow slipped on to the Dandy's shoulders—those brave, unflinching shoulders, that carried other men's burdens so naturally and so willingly that their burdens always seemed the Dandy's own. The Dandy may have had that power of finding "something decent" in everyone he met, but in the Dandy all men found the help they needed most.

Quietly and unassumingly the Dandy put all in order, and then, soon after midday, with brilliant sunshine all about us, we stood by an open grave in the shade of the drooping glory of a crimson flowering bauhenia. Some scenes live undimmed in our memories for a lifetime—scenes where we have seemed onlookers rather than actors, seeing every detail with minute exactness—and that scene, with its mingling of glorious beauty, human pathos, and soft, subdued sound, will live, I think, in the memory of most of us for many years to come.

"In the midst of life we are in death," the Maluka read, standing among that drooping crimson splendour, and at his feet lay the open grave, preaching silently its great lesson of Life and Death, with, beside it, the still, quiet form of the traveller whose last weary journey had ended; around it, bareheaded and all in white, a little band of bush-folk, silent and reverent and awed; above it, that crimson glory, and all around and about it, soft sun-flecked bush, murmuring sounds, flooding sunshine, and deep azure-blue distances. Beyond the bush, deep azure-blue; within it and throughout it, flooding sunshine and golden ladders of light; and at its sun-flecked heart, under that drooping crimson-starred canopy of soft grey-green, that little company of bush-folk, standing beside that open grave, as Mother Nature, strewing with flowers the last resting-place of one of her children, scattered gently falling scarlet blossoms into it and about it. Here and there a dog lay, stretched out in the shade, sniffing in idle curiosity at the blossoms as they fell, well satisfied with what life had to give them; while at their master's feet lay the traveller who was to leave such haunting memories behind him: William Neaves, born at Wollongong, with somewhere there a mother going quietly about her work, wondering vaguely perhaps where her laddie was that day.

Poor mother! Yet, when even that knowledge came to her, it comforted her in her sorrow to know that a woman had stood beside that grave mourning for her boy in her name.

Quietly the Maluka read on to the end; and then in the hush that followed the mate stooped, and, with deep lines hardening rigidly, picked up a spade. There was no mistaking his purpose; but as he straightened himself the Dandy's hand was on the spade and the Maluka was speaking. "Perhaps you'll be good enough to drive the missus back to the house right away," he was saying. "I think she has had almost more than she can stand."

The man looked hesitatingly at him. "If you'll be good enough," the Maluka added, "I should not leave here myself till all is completed."

Unerringly the Maluka had read his man: no hint of *his* strength failing, but a favour asked, and with it a service for a woman.

The stern lines about the man's mouth quivered for a moment, then set again as he sacrificed his wishes to a woman's need, and relinquishing the spade, turned away; and as we drove down to the house in the chief's buggy—the buggy that a few minutes before had borne our sick traveller along that last stage of his earthly journey—he said gently, almost apologetically, "I should have reckoned on this knocking you out a bit, missus." Always others, never self, with the bush-folk.

Then, this service rendered for the man who had done what he could for his comrade, his strong, unflinching heart turned back to its labour of love, and, all else being done, found relief for itself in softening and smoothing the rough outline of the new-piled mound; and as the man toiled, Mother Nature went on with her work, silently and sweetly healing the scar on her bosom, hiding her pain from the world, as she shrouded in starry crimson the burial-place of her brave, enduring son—a service to be renewed from day to day until the mosses and grasses grew again.

But there were still other services for the mate to render; and as the bush-folk stood aside, none daring to trespass here, a rough wooden railing rose about the grave. Then the man packed his comrade's swag for the last time, and, that done, came to the Maluka, as we stood under the house verandah, and held out two sovereigns in his open palm. The man was yet a stranger to the ways of the Never-Never.

"I'll have to ask for tick for meself for a while," he said. "But if that won't pay for all me mate's had, there's another where they came from. He was always independent, and would never take charity."

The hard lines about his mouth were very marked just then, and the outstretched hand seemed fiercely defiant; but the Maluka, reading in it only a man's proud care for a comrade's honour, put it gently aside, saying: "We give no charity here; only hospitality to our guests. Surely no man would refuse that."

They speak of a woman's delicate tact. But daily the bushman put the woman to shame, while she stood dumb or stammering. The Mulaka had touched the one chord in the man's heart that was not strained to breaking-point, and instantly the fingers closed over the sovereigns, and the defiant hand fell to his side, as with a husky, "Not from your sort, boss," he turned sharply on his heel; and as he walked away a hand was brushed hastily across the weary eyes.

With that brushing of the hand the inevitable reaction began, and for a little while we feared we would have another sick traveller on our hands. But only for a little while. After a day or two of rest and care his strength came back, but his thoughts were ever of those seven years of steadfast comradeship. Simply and earnestly he spoke of them and of that mother, all unconscious of the heartbreak that was speeding only too surely to her. Poor mother! And yet those other two nameless graves on that little rise deep in the heart of the bush bear witness that other mothers have even deeper sorrows to bear. Their sons are gone from them, and they, knowing nothing of it, wait patiently through the long silent years for the word that can never come to them.

For a few days the man rested, and then, just when work—hard work—was the one thing needful, Dan came in for a consultation, and with him a traveller, the bearer of a message from our kind, great-hearted chief to say that work was waiting for the mate at the Line Party. Our chief was the personification of all that is best in the bush-folk, as all bushmen will testify to his memory—men's lives crossed his by chance just here and there, but at those crossing-places life had been happier and better. For one long weary day the mate's life had run parallel with our chief's, and because of that, when he left us his heart was lighter than ever we had dared to hope for. But this man was not to fade quite out of our lives, for deep in that loyal heart the Maluka had been enshrined as "one in ten thousand".

Jeannie Gunn (Angela Punch McGregor), joining in
the fun with the Aboriginal women, whilst they try
to catch a goanna for dinner.

Angela Punch McGregor and Arthur Dignam on
the set with Aboriginal actor, Donald Blitner
(Goggle-Eye).

17

The bearer of the chief's message had also carried out an extra mail for us, and, opening it, we found the usual questions of the South folk.

"Whatever do you do with your time?" they all asked. "The monotony would kill me," some declared. "Every day must seem the same," said others: everyone agreeing that life out-bush was stagnation, and all marvelling that we did not die of ennui.

"Whatever do you do with your time?" The day Neaves's mate left was devoted to housekeeping duties—"spring-cleaning", the Maluka called it—while Dan drew vivid word-pictures of dogs cleaning their own chains. The day after that was filled in with preparations for a walk-about, and the next again found us camped at Bitter Springs. Monotony, when of the thirty days that followed these three every day was alike only in being different from any other, excepting in their almost unvarying menu; beef and damper and tea for a first course, and tea and damper and jam for a second. They also resembled each other, and all other days out-bush, in the necessity of dressing in a camp mosquito-net. "Stagnation!" they called it, when no day was long enough for its work, and almost every night found us camped a day's journey from our breakfast camp.

It was August, well on in the Dry, and on a cattle station in the Never-Never "things hum" in August. All the surface waters are drying up by then, and the outside cattle—those scattered away beyond the borders—are obliged to come in to the permanent waters, and must be gathered in and branded before the showers scatter them again.

We were altogether at the Springs: Dan, the Dandy, the Quiet Stockman, ourselves, every horse-"boy" that could be mustered, a numerous staff of camp "boys" for the Dandy's work, and an almost complete complement of dogs, little Tiddle'ums only being absent, detained at the homestead this time with the cares of a nursery. A goodly company all told as we sat among the camp-fires, with our horses clanking through the timber in their hobbles: forty horses and more, pack teams and relays for the whole company and riding hacks, in addition to both stock and camp horses for active mustering; for it requires over two hundred horses to get through successfully a year's work on a "little place like the Elsey".

Every one of the company had his special work to attend to; but everyone's work was concerned with cattle, and cattle only. The musterers were to work every area of country again and again, and the Dandy's work began in the building of the much-needed yard to the north-west.

We breakfasted at the Springs all together, had dinner miles apart, and all met again at the Stirling for supper. Dan and ourselves dined also at the Stirling on damper and "push" and vile-smelling blue-black tea. The damper had been carried in company with some beef and tea, in Dan's saddle-pouch; the tea was made with the thick, muddy, almost putrid water of the fast-drying water-hole, and the "push" was provided by force of circumstances, the pack teams being miles away with the plates, knives, and forks.

Out-bush we take the good with the bad as we find it; so we sat among towering white-ant hills, drinking as little of the tea as possible and enjoying the damper and "push" with hungry relish.

Around the Stirling are acres of red-coloured, queer-shaped, uncanny white-ant hills, and camped among these we sat, each served with a slice of damper that carried a smaller slice of beef upon it, providing the "push" by cutting off small pieces of the beef with a pen-knife, and "pushing" them along the damper to the edge of the slice, to be bitten off from there in hearty mouthfuls.

No butter, of course. In Darwin, eight months before, we had tasted our last butter on ship-board, for tinned butter, out-bush in the tropics, is as palatable as castor oil. The tea had been made in the Maluka's quart pot, our cups having been carried dangling from our saddles, in the approved manner of the bush-folk.

We breakfasted at the Springs, surrounded by the soft forest beauty; ate our dinner in the midst of grotesque ant-hill scenery, and spent the afternoon looking for a lost water-hole.

The Dandy was to build his yard at this hole when it was found, but the difficulty was to find it. The Sanguine Scot had "dropped on it once", by chance, but lost his bearing later on. All we knew was that it was there, to be found somewhere in that corner of the run—a deep, permanent hole "back in the scrub somewhere", according to the directions of the Sanguine Scot.

Of course, the black boys could have found it; but it is the habit of black boys to be quite ignorant of the whereabouts of all lost or unknown waters, for when a black fellow is "wanted" he is looked for at water, and in his wisdom keeps any "water" he can a secret from the white folk, an unknown "water" making a safe hiding-place when it suits a black fellow to obliterate himself for a while.

Eventually we found our hole, after long wanderings and futile excursions up gullies and by-ways, riding always in single file, with the men in front to break down a track through scrub and grass, and the missus behind on old Roper.

"Like a cow's tail," Dan said, mentally reviewing the order of the procession, as, after dismounting, we walked round our find—a wide-spreading sheet of deep, clay-coloured water, snugly hidden behind scrubby banks.

As we clambered on, two bushmen all in white, a dog or two, and a woman in a holland riding-dress, the Maluka pointed out the inaptness of the simile.

"A cow's tail," he said, "is wanting in expression, and takes no interest in its owner's hopes and fears," and suggested a dog's tail as a more happy comparison. "Has she not wagged along behind her owner all afternoon?" he asked, "drooping in sympathy whenever his hopes came to nothing; stiffening expectantly at other times, and is even now vibrating with pleasure in this his hour of triumph."

Bush-folk being old-fashioned, no one raised any objection to the term "owner", as Dan chuckled over the amendment.

After thinking the matter well out, Dan decided he was "what you might call a tail-less tyke", "We've had to manage without any wagging, haven't we, Brown, old chap?" he said, unconscious of the note in his voice that told of lonely years and vague longings.

As Brown acknowledged this reference to himself, by stirring the circle of hairs that expressed his sentiments to the world, Dan further proved the expansiveness of the Maluka's simile.

"You might have noticed," he went on, "that when a dog does own a tail he generally manages to keep it out of the fight somehow." In marriage as Dan had known it, strong men had stood between their women and the sharp cuffs and blows of life; "keeping her out of the fight somehow". Then the procession preparing to re-form, as the Maluka, catching Roper, mounted me again. Dan completely rounded off the simile. "Dogs seem able to wrestle through somehow without a tail," he said, "but I reckon a tail 'ud have a bit of a job getting along without a dog." As usual, Dan's whimsical fancy had burrowed deep into the heart of a great truth; for, in spite of what "tails" may say, how few there are of us who have any desire to "get along without the dog".

We left the water-hole about five o'clock, and riding into the Stirling Camp at sun-down, found the Dandy there, busy at the fire, with a dozen or so of large silver fish spread out on green leaves beside him.

"Good enough!" Dan cried at the first sight of them, and the Dandy explained that the boys had caught "shoals of 'em" at his dinner-camp at the Fish Hole, assuring us that the water there was "stiff with 'em". But the Dandy had been busy elsewhere. "Good enough!" Dan had said at the sight of the fish, and pointing to a billy full of clear, sweet water that was just thinking of boiling, the Maluka echoed the sentiment if not the words.

"Dug a soakage along the creek a bit and got it," the Dandy explained; and as we blessed him for his thoughtfulness, he lifted up a clean cloth and displayed a pile of crisp Johnny cakes. "Real slap-up ones," he assured us, breaking open one of the crisp, spongy rolls. It was always a treat to be in camp with the Dandy: everything about the man was so crisp and clean and wholesome.

As we settled down to supper, the Fizzer came shouting through the ant-hills, and, soon after, the Quiet Stockman rode into camp. Our Fizzer was always the Fizzer. "Managed to escape without help!" he shouted in welcome as he came to the camp-fire, alluding to his promise "to do a rescue"; and then he surveyed our supper. "Struck it lucky, as usual," he declared, helping himself to a couple of fish from the fire, and breaking open one of the crisp Johnny cakes. "Can't beat grilled fish and hot rolls by much, to say nothin' of tea." The Fizzer was one of those happy, natural people who always find the supply exactly suited to the demand.

But if our Fizzer was just our Fizzer, the Quiet Stockman was changing every day. He was still the Quiet Stockman, and always would be, speaking only when he had something to say, but he was learning that he had much to say that was worth saying, or, rather, much that others found worth listening to; and that knowledge was squaring his shoulders and bringing a new ring into his voice.

Around the camp-fires we touch on any subject that suggests itself, but at the Stirling that night, four of us being Scots, we found Scotland and Scotsmen an inexhaustible topic, and before we turned in were all of Jack's opinion, that "you can't beat the Scots". Even the Dandy and the Fizzer were converted; and Jack having realized that there are such things as Scotswomen—Scotch-hearted women—a new bond was established between us.

No one had much sleep that night, and before dawn there was no doubt left in our minds about the outside cattle coming in. It seemed as though every beast on the run must have come in to the Stirling that night for a drink. Every water-hole out-bush is as the axis of a great circle, cattle pads narrowing into it like the spokes of a wheel, from every point of the compass, and along these pads around the Stirling mob after mob of cattle came in in single file, treading carelessly, until each old bull leader, scenting the camp, gave its low, deep, drawn-out warning call that told of danger at hand. After that rang out, only an occasional snapping twig betrayed the presence of the cattle as they crept cautiously in for the drink that must be procured at all hazards. But after the drink the only point to be considered was safety, and in a crashing stampede they rushed out into the timber. Till long after midnight they were at it, and as Brown and I were convinced that every mob was coming straight over our net, we spent an uneasy night. To make matters worse, just as the camp was settling down to a deep sleep after the cattle had finally subsided, Dan's camp reveille rang out.

It was barely three o'clock, and the Fizzer raised an indignant protest of, "Moonrise, you bally ass."

"Not it," Dan persisted, unfortunately bent on argument; "not at this quarter of the moon, and besides it was moonlight all evening," and, that being a strong peg to hang his argument on, investigation heads appeared from various nets. "Seem to think I don't know dawn when I see it," Dan added, full of scorn for the camp's want of observation; but before we had time to wither before his scorn, Jack turned the tables for us with his usual quiet finality. "That's the west you're looking at," he said. "The moon's just set"; and the curtain of Dan's net dropped instantly.

"Told you he was a bally ass," the Fizzer shouted in his delight, and promising Dan something later on, he lay down to rest.

Dan, however, was hopelessly roused. "Never did that before," gurgled out of his net, just as we were dropping off once more; but a withering request from the Dandy to "gather experience somewhere else" silenced him till dawn, when he had the wisdom to rise without further reveille.

After breakfast we all separated again: the Dandy to his yard-building at the Yellow Hole, and the rest of us, with the cattle boys, in various directions, to see where the cattle were, each party with its team of horses, and carrying in its packs a bluey, an oilskin, a mosquito net, a plate, knife, and fork apiece, as well as a "change of duds" and a bite of tucker for all: the bite of tucker to be replenished with a killer when necessary, the change of duds to be washed by the boys also when necessary, and the plate to serve for all courses, the fastidious turning it over for the damper and jam course.

The Maluka spent one day with Dan beyond the "front gate"—his tail wagging along behind as a matter of course— another day passed boundary-riding, inspecting waterholes, and doubling back to the Dandy's camp to see his plans; then, picking up the Quiet Stockman, we struck out across country, riding four abreast through the open forest lands, and were camped at sun-down, in the thick of the cattle, miles from the Dandy's camp, and thirty miles due north from the homestead. "Whatever do you do with your time?" asked the South folk.

Dan was in high spirits: cattle were coming in everywhere, and another beautiful permanent "water" had been discovered in unsuspected ambush. To know all the waters of a run is important; for they take the part of fences, keeping the cattle in certain localities; and as cattle must stay within a day's journey or so of water, an unknown water is apt to upset a man's calculations.

As the honour of finding the hole was all Dan's it was named DS in his honour, and we had waited beside it while he cut his initials deep into the trunk of a tree, deploring the rustiness of his education as he carved. The upright stroke of the D was simplicity itself, but after that complications arose.

"It's always got me dodged which way to turn the darned thing," Dan said, scratching faint lines both ways, and standing off to decide the question. We advised turning to the right, and the D was satisfactorily completed, but S proved the "dead finish", and had to be wrestled with separately.

"Can't see why they don't name a chap with something that's easily wrote," Dan said, as we rode forward, with our united team of horses and boys swinging along behind us, and M and T and O were quoted as examples. "Reading's always had me dodged," he explained. "Left school before I had time to get it down and wrestle with it."

"There's nothing like reading and writing," the Quiet Stockman broke in, with an earnestness that was almost startling; and as he sat that evening in the firelight poring over the *Cardinal's Snuff-box*, I watched him with a new interest.

Jack's reading was very puzzling. He always had the same book—that *Cardinal's Snuff-box*—and pored over it with a strange persistence, that could not have been inspired by the book. There was no expression on his face of lively interest or pleasure, just an intent, dogged persistence; the strong, firm chin set as though he were colt-breaking. Gradually, as I watched him that night, the truth dawned on me: the man was trying to teach himself to read. The *Cardinal's Snuff-box*, and the only clue to the mystery, a fair knowledge of the alphabet learned away in a childish past. In truth, it takes a deal to "beat the Scots", or, what is even better, to make them feel that they are beaten.

As I watched, full of admiration for the proud, strong character of the man, he looked up suddenly, and, in a flash knew that I knew. Flushing hotly, he rose, and "thought he would turn in"; and Dan, who had been discussing education most of the evening, decided to "bottle off a bit of sleep too for the next day's use", and opened up his swag.

"There's one thing about not being too good at the reading trick," he said, surveying his permanent property: "a chap doesn't need to carry books round with him to put in the spare time."

"Exactly," the Maluka laughed. He was lying on his back, with an open book face downwards on his chest, looking up at the stars. He always had a book with him, but, book-lover as he was, it rarely got farther than his chest when we were in camp. Life out-bush is more absorbing than books.

"Of course reading's handy enough for them as don't lay much stock on education," Dan owned, stringing his net between his mosquito-pegs; then, struck with a new idea, he wondered why "the missus never carries books around. Anyone 'ud think she wasn't much at the reading trick herself," he said. "Never see you at it, missus, when I'm around."

"Lay too much stock on education," I answered, and, chuckling, Dan retired into his net, little guessing that when he was "round" his own self, his quaint outlook on life, and the underlying truth of his inexhaustible, whimsical philosophy, were infinitely more interesting than the best book ever written.

But the Quiet Stockman seemed perplexed at the answer. "I thought reading 'ud learn you most things," he said, hesitating beside his own net; and before we could speak, the corner of Dan's net was lifted and his head reappeared. "I've learned a deal of things in my time," he chuckled, "but *reading* never taught me none of 'em. Then his head once more disappeared, and we tried to explain matters to the Quiet Stockman. The time was not yet ready for the offer of a helping hand.

At four in the morning we were roused by a new camp reveille of Star-light. "Nothing like getting off early when mustering's the game," Dan announced. By sun-up the musterers were away, and by sun-down we were coming into Bitter Springs, driving a splendid mob of cattle before us.

The Maluka and I had had nothing to do with the actual gathering in of the mob, for the missus had not "shaped" too well at her first muster and preferred travelling with the pack teams when active mustering was in hand. Ignominious perhaps, but safe, and safety counts for something in this world; anyway, for the poor craven souls. Riding is one thing; but crashing through timber and undergrowth, dodging over-hanging branches, leaping fallen logs, and stumbling and plunging over crab-holed and rat-burrowed areas, to say nothing of charging bulls turning up at unexpected corners, is quite another story.

"Not cut out for the job," was Dan's verdict, and the Maluka covered my retreat by saying that he had more than enough to do without taking part in the rounding-up of cattle. Had mustering been one of a manager's duties, I'm afraid the house would have "come in handy" to pack the dog away in with its chain.

As the yard of the Springs came into view, we were making plans for the morrow, and admiring the fine mattress swinging before us on the tails of the cattle; but there were cattle buyers at the Springs who upset all our plans, and left no time for the bang-tailing of the mob in hand.

The buyers were Chinese drovers, authorized by their Chinese masters to buy a mob of bullocks. "Want big mob," they said. "Cash! Got money here," producing a signed cheque ready for filling in.

A Chinese buyer always pays "cash" for a mob—by cheque —generally taking care to withdraw all cash from the bank before the cheque can be presented, and, as a result, a dishonoured cheque is returned to the station, reaching the seller some six or eight weeks after the sale. Six or eight weeks more then pass in demanding explanations, and six or eight more obtaining them, and after that just as many more as Chinese slimness can arrange for before a settlement is finally made. "Cash," the drover repeated insinuatingly at the Maluka's unfathomable "Yes?" Then, certain that he was inspired, added, "Spot Cash!"

But already the Maluka had decided on a plan of campaign, and echoing the drover's "Spot Cash", began negotiations for a sale; and within ten minutes the drivers retired to their camp, bound to take the mob when delivered, and inwardly marvelling at the Maluka's simple trust.

Dan was appalled at it; but, always deferential where the Maluka's business insight was concerned, only "hoped he knew that them chaps needed a bit of watching".

"Their cash does," the Maluka corrected, to Dan's huge delight; and, leaving the musterers to go on with their branding work, culling each mob of its prime bullocks as they mustered, he set about finding someone to "watch the cash", and four days later rode into the Katherine Settlement, with Brown and the missus, as usual, at his heels.

We spent one week out-bush, visiting the four points of the compass; half a day at the homestead packing a fresh swag; three days riding into the Katherine, having found incidental entertainment on the road; but on the fourth day were entering into an argument by wire with Chinese slimness. "The monotony would kill me," declared the townsfolk.

On the road in we had met the Village Settlement homeward bound—the bonnie baby still riding on its mother's knee, and smiling out of the depths of its sun-bonnet; but everyone else was longing for the bush. Darwin had proved all unsatisfying bustle and fluster, and the trackless sea, a wonder that inspired strange sickness when travelled over.

For four days the Maluka argued with Chinese slimness before he felt satisfied that his cash was in safe keeping, while the Wag and others did as they wished with their spare time. Then, four days later, again Cheon and Tiddle'ums were hailing us in welcome at the homestead.

But their joy was short-lived, for as soon as the homestead affairs had been seen to, and a fresh swag packed, we started out-bush again to look for Dan and his bullocks, and, coming on their tracks at our first night camp, by following them up next morning we rode into the Dandy's camp at the Yellow Hole well after midday, to find ourselves surrounded by the stir and bustle of a cattle camp.

"Whatever do you do with your time?" asked the townsfolk, sure that life out-bush is stagnation, but forgetting that life is life wherever it may be lived.

18

Only three weeks before, as we hunted for it through scrub and bush and creek-bed, the Yellow Hole had been one of our Unknown Waters, tucked snugly away in an out-of-the-way elbow of creek country, and now we found it transformed into the life-giving heart of a bustling world of men and cattle and commerce. Beside it stood the simple camp of the stockman —a litter of pack-bags, mosquito-nets, and swags; here and there were scattered the even more simple camps of the black boys; and in the background, the cumbrous camp of the Chinese drovers reared itself up in strong contrast to the camps of the bush-folk—two fully equipped tents for the drovers themselves and a simpler one for their black boys. West of the Yellow Hole boys were tailing a fine mob of bullocks, and to the east other "boys" were "holding" a rumbling mob of mixed cattle, and while Jack and Dan rode here and there shouting orders for the "cutting out" of the cattle, the Dandy busied himself at the fire, making tea as a refresher, before getting going in earnest, the only restful, placid, unoccupied beings in the whole camp being the Chinese drovers. Not made of the stuff that "lends a hand" in other people's affairs, they sat in the shade of their tents and looked on, well pleased that men should bustle for their advantage. As we rode past the drovers they favoured us with a sweet smile of welcome, while Dan met us with a chuckle of delight at the sweetness of their smile, and as Jack took our horses—amused both at the drovers' sweetness and Dan's appreciation of it—the Dandy greeted us with the news that we had "struck it lucky, as usual", and that a cup of tea would be ready in "half a shake".

Dan also considered we had "struck it lucky", but from a different point of view; for he had only just come into camp with the mixed cattle; and as the bullocks among them more than completed the number required, he suggested the drovers should take delivery at once, assuring us, as we drank the tea, that he was just about dead sick of them "little Chinese darlings".

The "little Chinese darlings", inwardly delighted that the Maluka's simple trust seemed as guileless as ever, smugly professed themselves willing to fall in with any arrangement that was pleasing to the white folk, and as they mounted their horses Dan heaved a sigh of satisfaction.

But Dan's satisfaction was premature, for it took time and much galloping before the "little Chinese darlings" could satisfy themselves and each other that they had the very finest bullocks procurable in their mob. A hundred times they changed their minds; rejecting chosen bullocks, recalling rejected bullocks, and comparing every bullock accepted with every bullock rejected. Bulk was what they searched for—plenty for their money, as they judged it, and finally gathered together a mob of coarse, wide-horned, great-framed beasts rolling in fat that would drip off on the road as they travelled in.

"You'd think they'd got 'em together for a boiling-down establishment, with a bone factory for a side-line," Dan chuckled, secretly pleased that our best bullocks were left on the run, and, disbanding the rejected bullocks before "they" could "change their minds again", he gathered together the mixed cattle and shut them in the Dandy's new yard, to keep them in hand for later branding.

But the "little Chinese darlings" had counted on the use of that yard for themselves, and finding that their bullocks would have to be "watched" on camp that night, they stolidly refused to take delivery before morning, pointing out that should the cattle stampede during the night, the loss would be ours, not theirs.

"Well, I'm blowed!" Dan chuckled, but the Maluka cared

little whether the papers were signed then or at sun-up; and the
drovers, pleased with getting their way so easily, magnanimously offered to take charge of the first "watch"—the evening
watch—provided that only our horses should be used, and that
Big Jack and Jackeroo and others should lend a hand.

Dan wouldn't hear of refusing the offer. "Bit of exercise'll
do 'em good," he said; and deciding the bullocks would be safe
enough with Jack and Jackeroo, we white folk stretched ourselves in the warm firelight after supper, and, resting, watched
the shadowy mob beyond the camp, listening to the shoutings
and gallopings of the watchers as we chatted.

When a white man watches cattle, if he knows his business
he quiets his mob down and then opens them out gradually,
to give them room to lie down, or ruminate standing without
rubbing shoulders with a restless neighbour, which leaves him
little to do beyond riding round occasionally, to keep his "boys"
at their posts, and himself alert and ready for emergencies.
But a Chinaman's idea of watching cattle is to wedge them into
a solid body, and hold them huddled together like a mob of
frightened sheep, riding incessantly round them and forcing
back every beast that looks as though it might extricate itself
from the tangle, and galloping after any that do escape with
screams of anxiety and impotency.

"Beck ! beck!" (back), screamed our drovers, as they
galloped after escaped beasts, flopping and wobbling and
gurgling in their saddles like half-filled water-bags; galloping
invariably after the beasts, and thereby inciting them to further
galloping. And "Beck! beck!" shouted our boys on duty with
perfect mimicry of tone, and yells of delight at the impotency
of the drovers, galloping always *outside* the runaways and
bending them back into the mob, flopping and wobbling and
gurgling in *their* saddles, until, in the half-light, it was difficult
to tell drover from "boy". Not detecting the mimicry, the
drovers in no way resented it; the more the boys screamed
and galloped in their service the better pleased they were; while
the "boys" were more than satisfied with their part of the
entertainment, Jackeroo and Big Jack particularly enjoying
themselves.

"They'll have 'em stampeding yet," Dan said at last, growing uneasy, as more and more cattle escaped, and the mob shifted ground with a rumbling rattle of hooves every few minutes. Finally, as the rumbling rattle threatened to become permanent, a long-drawn-out cry of "Ring-ing" from Big Jack sent Dan and the Quiet Stockman to their saddles. In ten minutes the hubbub had ceased. Dan's master-hand having opened them out he returned to the camp-fire alone. Jack had gone on duty before this time and sent the "little Chinese darlings" to bed.

Naturally Dan's cattle-tussle reminded him of other tussles with ringing cattle; then the cattle camp suggesting other cattle-camp yarns, he settled down to reminiscences, until he had us all cold thrills and skin-creeps, although we were gathered around a blazing fire.

Tale after tale he told of stampedes and of weaners piling up against fences. Then followed a tale or two of cattle lying quiet as mice one minute, and up on their feet crashing over camps the next, then tales of men being "treed" or "skied", and tales of scrub-bulls, maddened cow-mothers, and "pokers".

"Pokers", it appears, have a habit of poking out of mobs, grazing quietly as they edge off until "they're gone before you miss 'em". Camps seem to have some special attraction for pokers, but we learned they object to interference. "Poke round peaceful as cats until you rile them," Dan told us, and then glided into a tale of how a poker "had us all treed once".

"Poked in a bit too close for our fancy while we were at supper," he explained, "so we slung sticks at him to turn him back to the mob, and the next minute was making for trees, but as there was only saplings handy, it would have been a bit awkward for the heavy-weights if there hadn't have been enough of us to divide his attentions up a bit." (Dan was a good six feet, and well set up at that.) "Climbing saplings to get away from a stag ain't much of a game," he added, with a reminiscent chuckle; "they're too good at the bending trick. The farther up the sapling you climb, the nearer you get to the ground."

Then he favoured us with one of his word-pictures: "There was the sapling bending like a weeping willow," he said, "and there was the stag underneath it, looking up at me and asking if he could do anything for me, taking a poke at me boot now and then, just to show nothing would be no bother; and there was me, hanging on to the sapling, and leaning lovingly over him, telling him not to go hanging round, tiring himself out on my account; and there was the other chaps—all light-weights—laughing fit to split, safe in their saplings. 'Twasn't as funny as it looked, though," he assured us, finding us unsympathetic, "and nobody was exactly sorry when one of the lads on duty came along to hear the fun, and stockwhipped the old poker back to the mob."

The Maluka and the Dandy soon proved it was nothing to be "treed". "Happens every time a beast's hauled out of a bog, from all accounts, that being the only thanks you get for hauling 'em out of the mess." Then Dan varied the recital with an account of a chap getting skied once who forgot to choose a tree before beginning the hauling business, and immediately after froze us into horror again with the details of two chaps "lying against an old rotten log with a mob of a thousand going over 'em"; and we were not surprised to hear that when they felt well enough to sit up they hadn't enough arithmetic left between 'em to count their bruises.

After an evening of ghost stories, a creaking door is enough to set teeth chattering; and after an evening of cattle-yarns, told in a cattle camp, a snapping twig is enough to set hair lifting; and just as the most fitting place for ghost stories is an old ruined castle, full of eerie noises, so there is no place more suited to cattle-camp yarns than a cattle camp. They need the reality of the camp-fire, the litter of camp baggage, the rumbling mob of shadowy cattle near at hand, and the possibilities of the near future—possibilities brought home by the sight of tethered horses standing saddled and bridled ready "in case of accidents".

Fit surroundings add intensity to all tales, just as it added intensity to my feelings when Dan advised the Maluka to swing our net near a low-branched tree, pointing out that it would "come in handy for the missus if she needed it in a hurry".

I favoured climbing the tree at once, and spending the night in it, but the men-folk assuring me that I would be "bound to hear them coming", I turned in, sure only of one thing, that death may come to the bush-folk in any form but ennui. Yet so adaptable are we bush-folk to circumstances that most of that night was oblivion.

At sun-up, the drovers, still sweetly smiling, announced that two bullocks had strayed during someone's watch. Not in theirs, they hastened to assure us, when Dan sniffed scornfully in the background.

But Dan's scorn turned to blazing wrath when—the drovers refusing to replace the "strays" with cows from the mixed cattle in hand, and refusing also to take delivery of the bullocks two beasts short—the musterers had to turn out to gather in a fresh mob of cattle for the sake of two bullocks. "Just as I was settling down to celebrate Sunday, too," Dan growled, as he and Jack rode out of camp.

Forty years out-bush had not been enough to stamp generations of Sabbath-keeping out of Dan's blood, although he was not particular which day of the week was set apart for his Sabbath. "Two in a fortnight" was all he worried about.

Fortune favouring the musterers, by midday all was peace and order; the drovers, placid and contented, had retired to their tents once more, reprieved from taking delivery for another day and night, and after dinner, as the "boys" tailed the bullocks and mixed cattle on the outskirts of the camp, to graze them, we settled down to "celebrate our Sabbath" by resting in the warm, dry shade.

Here and there upon the grassy incline that stretched between the camp and the Yellow Hole, we settled down each according to his taste: Dan with his back against a tree-trunk and far-reaching legs spread out before him; the Maluka, Jack, and the Dandy flat upon their backs, with bent-back folded arms for pillows, and hats drawn over eyes to shade them from the too-dazzling sunlight; dogs, relaxed and spread out, as near to their master as permitted, and the missus "fixed up" in an opened-out, bent-back grassy tussock, which had thus been formed into a luxurious arm-chair. At the foot of the incline lay the Yellow Hole, gleaming and glancing in the sunshine;

all around and about us were the bush creatures, rustling in the scrub and grasses—flies were conspicuous by their absence; here and there shafts of sunlight lay across the grey-brown shade; in the distance the grazing cattle moved among the timber; away out in the glorious sunshine, beyond and above the tree-tops, brown-winged, slender Bromli kites wheeled and circled and hovered and swooped; and lounging in the sun-flecked shade, well satisfied with our lot, we looked out into the blue, sunny depths, each one of us the embodiment of lazy contentment, and agreeing with Dan that "Sunday wasn't a bad institution for them as had no objection to doing a loaf now and then".

That suggesting an appropriate topic of conversation to Dan, for a little while we spoke of the Sabbath-keeping of our Scottish forefathers; as we spoke, idly watching the circling, wheeling Bromli kites, that seemed then, as at all times, an essential part of the sunshine. To the bush-folk of the Never-Never, sunshine without Bromli kites would be as a summer's day without the sun. All day and every day they hover throughout it, as they search and wait and watch for carrion, throwing dim, gliding shadows as they wheel and circle, or flashing sunshine from brown wings by quick, sudden swoops, hovering and swooping throughout the sunshine, or rising to melt into blue depths of the heavens, where other arching, floating specks tell of myriads there, ready to swoop, and fall and gather the feast wherever their lowest ranks drop earthwards with the crows.

Lazily we watched the floating movement, and as we watched, conversation became spasmodic—not worth the energy required to sustain it—until gradually we slipped into one of those sociable silences of the bush-folk—silences that draw away all active thought from the mind, leaving it a sensitive plate ready to absorb impressions and thoughts as they flit about it; silences where everyone is so in harmony with his comrades and surroundings that the breaking of them rarely jars—spoken words so often defining the half-absorbed thoughts.

Dimly conscious of each other, of the grazing cattle, the Bromli kites, the sweet scents and rustling sounds of the bush, of each other's thoughts and that the last spoken thought among us had been Sabbath-keeping, we rested, idly, *not* thinking, until Dan's voice crept into the silence.

"Never was much at religion myself," he said, lazily altering his position, "but Mrs Bob was the one to make you see things right off." Lazily and without stirring, we gave our awakened attention, and after a quiet pause the droning Scotch voice went on, too contented to raise itself above a drone: "Can't exactly remember how she put it; seemed as though you'd only got to hoe your own row the best you can, and lend others a hand with theirs, and just let God see after the rest."

Quietly, as the droning voice died away, we slipped back into our silence, lazily dreaming on, with Dan's words lingering in our minds, until, in a little while, it seemed as though the dancing tree-tops, the circling Bromli kites, every rustling sound and movement about us, had taken them up and were shouting them to the echo. "How much you will be able to teach the poor, dark souls of the stockmen," a well-meaning South-erner had said, with self-righteous arrogance; and in the brilliant glory of that bush Sabbath, one of the "poor, dark souls" had set the air vibrating with the grandest, noblest principles of Christianity, summed up into one brief sen-tence resonant with its ringing commands: *Hoe your own row the best you can. Lend others a hand with theirs. Let God see to the rest.*

Men there are in plenty out-bush, "not much at religion", as they and the world judge it, who have solved the great problem of "hoeing their own rows" by the simple process of leaving them to give others a hand with theirs; men loving their neighbours as themselves, and with whom God does the rest, as of old. "Be still, and know that I am God" is still whispered out of the heart of Nature, and those bush-men, unconsciously obeying, as unconsciously belong to that great simple-hearted band of worshippers, the Quakers; men who, in the hoeing of their own rows, have ever lived their lives in the ungrudging giving of a helping hand to all in need, content that God will see to the rest.

Surely the most scrupulous Quaker could find no fault with

the "Divine Meeting" that God was holding that day: the long, restful preparation of silence; that emptying of all active thought from the mind; that droning Scotch voice, so perfectly tuned to our mood, delivering its message in a language that could pierce to the depths of a bushman's heart; and then silence again—a silence now vibrating with thought. As gradually and naturally as it had crept upon us, that silence slipped away, and we spoke of the multitude of sounds and creatures about us, until, seeing deeper and deeper into Dan's message every moment, we learned that each sound and creature was hoeing its own row as it alone knew how, and, in the hoeing, was lending all others a hand with theirs, as they toiled in the Mighty Row of the Universe, each obedient to the great law of the Creator that all else shall be left to Him, as through them He taught the world that no man liveth to himself alone.

"You will find that a woman alone in a camp of men is decidedly out of place," the Darwin ladies had said; and yet that day, as at all times, the woman felt strangely and sweetly *in* place in the bushmen's camp. "A godforsaken country" others of the town have called the Never-Never, because the works of men have not yet penetrated into it. Let them look for their own dark alleys and hideous midnights into some or all of the cattle camps out-bush, or, better still, right into the "poor, dark souls" of the bush-folk themselves—if their vision is clear enough—before they judge.

Long before our midnight had come, the camp was sleeping a deep, sound sleep—those who were not on watch—a dreamless sleep, for the bullocks were peaceful and ruminating, the Chinese drovers having been "excused" from duty lest other beasts should stray during "someone's" watch.

Soon after sun-up the head drover formally accepted the mob, and, still inwardly marvelling at the Maluka's trust, filled in his cheque, and, blandly smiling, watched while the Maluka made out receipts and cancelled the agreement. Then, to show that *he* dealt little in simple trust, he carried the receipts and agreement, in private and in turn, to Dan and Jack, and the Dandy, asking each if all were honestly made out.

Dan looked at the papers critically ("Might have been holding 'em upside down for all I knew," he said later), and assured the drover that all was right. "Which was true," he added, also later, "seeing the boss made 'em out." Dan dealt largely in simple trust where the boss was concerned. Jack, having heard Dan's report, took his cue from it and passed the papers as "just the thing"; but the Dandy read out every word in them in a loud, clear voice, to his own amusement and the drover's discomfiture.

The papers having been thus proved satisfactory, the drovers started their boys with the bullocks, before giving their attention to the packing up of their camp baggage, and we turned to our own affairs.

As the Dandy's new yard was not furnished yet with a drafting lane and branding-pens, the mixed cattle were to be taken to the Bitter Springs yard; and by the time Jack had been seen off with them and our camp packed up, the drovers had become so involved in baggage that Dan and the Dandy felt obliged to offer assistance. Finally, everyone was ready to mount, and then we and the drovers exchanged polite farewells and parted, seller and buyer each confident that he knew more about the cash for that cheque than the other. No doubt the day came when those drovers ceased to marvel at the Maluka's simple trust.

The drovers rode away to the north-west, and as we set out to the south-east, Dan turned his back on "them little darlings" with a sigh of relief. "Reckon that money's been earned, anyway," he said. Then, as Jackeroo was the only available "boy", the others all being on before with the cattle, we gathered together our immense team of horses and drove them out of camp. In open order we jogged along across country, with Jackeroo riding ahead as pilot, followed by the jangling, straggling team of pack and loose horses, while behind the team rode the white folk all abreast with six or eight dogs trotting along behind again. For a couple of hours we jogged along in the tracks of Jack's cattle, without coming up with them, then, just as we sighted the great rumbling mob, a smaller mob appeared on our right.

"Run 'em into the mob," Dan shouted; and at his shout every man and horse leapt forward—pack-horses and all—and went after them in pell-mell disorder.

"Scrub bulls! Keep behind them!" Dan yelled, giving directions as we stampeded at his heels (it is not all advantage for musterers to ride with the pack-team), then as we and they galloped straight for Jack's mob, everyone yelled in warning, "Hi! Look out there! Bulls! Look out!" until Dan's revolver rang out above the din.

Jack turned at the shot and saw the bulls, but too late. Right through his mob they galloped, splitting it up into fragments, and in a moment pack-horses, cattle, riders, bulls, were part of a surging, galloping mass—boys galloping after bulls, and bulls after boys, and the white folk after anything and everything, peppering bulls with revolver-shots (stockwhip having no effect), shouting orders, and striving their utmost to hold the mob; pack-and loose horses galloping and kicking as they freed themselves from the hubbub; and the missus scurrying here and there on the outskirts of the *mêlée*, dodging behind bushes and scrub in her anxiety to avoid both bulls and revolver-shots. Ennui forsooth! Never was a woman farther from death by ennui.

Finally the horses gathered themselves together in the friendly shelter of some scrub, and as the woman sought safety among them, the Maluka's rifle rang out, and a charging bull went down before it. Then out of the thick of the uproar Sambo came full gallop, with a bull at his horse's heels, and Dan full gallop behind the bull, bringing his rifle to his shoulder as he galloped; and as all three galloped madly on Dan fired, and the bull pitching blindly forward, Sambo wheeled, and he and Dan galloped back to the mob to meet another charging outlaw and deal with it.

Then in quick succession from all sides of the mob bulls darted out with riders at their heels, or riders shot forward with bulls at *their* heels, until the mob looked like a great spoked wheel revolving on its own axis. Bull after bull went down before the rifles, old Roper, with the Maluka riding him, standing like a rock under fire; and then, just as the mob was quietening down, a wild scrub cow with a half-grown calf at her heels shot out of the mob and headed straight for the pack-team, Dan galloping beside her and cracking thunder-claps out of a stock-whip. Flash and I scuttled to shelter, and Dan, bending the cow back to the mob, shouted as he passed by, at full gallop, "Here you are, missus; thought you might like a drop of milk."

For another five minutes the mob was "held" to steady them a bit before starting, and then, just as all seemed in order, one of the prostrate bulls staggered to its feet—anything but dead; and as a yell went up, "Look out, boss! Look out!" Roper sprang forward in obedience to the spurs, just too late to miss a sudden, mad lunge from the wounded outlaw, and the next moment the bull was down with a few more shots in him, and Roper was receiving a tribute that only he could command.

With that surging mob of cattle beside them, the Maluka and Dan had dismounted, and were trying to staunch the flow of blood, while black boys gathered round, and Jack and the Dandy, satisfied that the injuries were not "too serious", were leaning over from their saddles congratulating the old horse on having "got off so easy". The wound, fortunately, was in the thigh, and just a clean deep punch, for, as by a miracle, the bull's horn had missed all tendons; and as the old campaigner was led away for treatment he disdained even to limp, and was well within a fortnight.

"Passing the time of day with Jack," Dan called the scrim-mage; as we left the field of battle and looking back, we found that already the Bromli kites were closing in and sinking and settling earthwards towards the crows, who were impatiently waiting our departure—waiting to convert the erst raging scrub bulls into white, bleaching bones.

Travelling quicker than the cattle, we were camped and at dinner at "Abraham's"—another lily-strewn billabong— when the mob came in, the thirsty brutes travelling with down-drooping heads and lowing deeply and incessantly. Their direction showing that they would pass within a few yards of our camp-fire, on their way to the water, as a matter of course I stood up, and Dan, with a chuckle, assured me that they had "something else more important on than chivvying the missus".

But the recollection of that raging mob was too vividly in mind, and the cattle beginning to trot at the sight of the water, decided against them, and the next moment I was three feet from the ground, among the low-spreading branches of a giant Paper-bark. Jackeroo was riding ahead, and flashed one swift, sidelong glance after me, but as the mob trotted by he trotted with them as impassive as a statue.

But we had by no means done with Jackeroo; for as we sat in camp that night at the Springs, with the cattle safe in the yard, shouts of laughter from the "boys'" camp attracted our attention, and we found Jackeroo the centre-piece of the camp, preparing to repeat some performance. For a second or so he stood irresolute; then, clutching wildly at an imaginary something that appeared to encumber his feet, with a swift, darting run and a scrambling clamber, he was into the midst of a sapling; then, our silence attracting attention, the black world collapsed in speechless convulsions.

"How the missus climbed a tree, little 'un," the Maluka chuckled; and the mimicry of action had been so perfect that we knew it could only be that. Every detail was there: the moment of indecision, the wild clutch at the habit, the quick, feminine lift of the running feet, and the indescribably feminine scrambling climb at the finish.

In that one swift, sidelong glance every movement had been photographed on Jackeroo's mind, to be reproduced later on for the entertainment of the camp with that perfect mimicry characteristic of the black folk.

And it was always so. Just as they had "beck-becked" and bumped in their saddles with the Chinese drovers, so they imitated every action that caught their fancy, and almost every human being that crossed their path—riding with feet outspread after meeting one traveller; with toes turned in in imitation of another; flopping, or sitting rigidly in their saddles; imitating actions of hand and turns of the head; anything to amuse themselves, from riding side-saddle to climbing trees.

Jackeroo, being "funny man" in the tribe, was first favourite in exhibitions; but we could get no further pantomime from him that night, although we heard later from Bett-Bett that "How the missus climbed a tree" had a long run.

The next day passed branding the cattle, and the following, as we arrived within sight of the homestead, Dan was congratulating the Maluka on the "missus being educated up to do without a house", and then he suddenly interrupted himself. "Well, I'm blest!" he said. "If we didn't forget all about bang-tailing that mob for her mattress."

We undoubtedly had, but thirty-three nights or thereabouts, with the warm, bare ground for a bed, had made me indifferent to mattresses, and hearing that, Dan became most hopeful of "getting her properly educated yet".

Cheon greeted us with his usual enthusiasm, and handed the Maluka a letter containing a request for a small mob of bullocks within three weeks.

"Nothing like keeping the ball rolling," Dan said, also waxing enthusiastic, while the South-folk remained convinced that life out-bush is stagnation.

19

Dan and the Quiet Stockman went out to the north-west immediately, to "clean up there" before getting the bullocks together, but the Maluka, settling down to arrears of book-keeping, with the Dandy at his right hand, Cheon once more took the missus under his wing, feeding her up and scorning her gardening efforts.

"The idea of a white woman thinking she could grow water-melons," he scoffed, when I planted seeds, having decided on a carpet of luxuriant green to fill up the garden beds until the shrubs grew. The Maluka advised "waiting", and the seeds coming up within a few days, Cheon, after expressing surprise, prophesied an early death or a fruitless life.

Billy Muck, however, took a practical interest in the water-melons, and to incite him to water them in our absence, he was made a shareholder in the venture. As a natural result, the Staff, the Rejected, and the Shadows immediately applied for shares—pointing out that they too carried water to the plants—and the water-melon beds became the property of a Working Liability Company with the missus as Chairman of Directors.

The Shadows were as numerous as ever, the Rejected on the increase, but the Staff was, fortunately, reduced to three for the time being; or, rather, reduced to two, and increased again to three: Judy had been called "bush" on business, and the Macs having got out in good time, Bertie's Nellie and Biddy had been obliged to resign and go with the waggons, under protest, of course, leaving Rosy and Jimmy's Nellie augmented by one of the most persistent of all the shadows—a tiny child lubra, Bett-Bett.

Most of us still considered Bett-Bett one of the Shadows, but she persisted that she was the mainstay of the Staff. "Me all day dust 'im paper, me round 'im up goat," she would say. "Me sit down all right."

She certainly excelled in "rounding-up goat", riding the old Billy like a race-horse; and with Rosy filling the position of housemaid to perfection, Jimmy's Nellie proving invaluable in her vigorous treatment of the Rejected, and the wood-heap gossip filling in odd times, life—so far as it was dependent on black folk—was running on oiled wheels: the house was clean and orderly; the garden flourished; and as the melons grew apace, throwing out secondary leaves in defiance of Cheon's prophecies, Billy Muck grew more and more enthusiastic, and, usurping the position of Chairman of the Directors, he inspired the shareholders with so much zeal that the prophecies were almost fulfilled through a surfeit of watering. But Cheon's attitude towards the water-melons did not change, although he had begun to look with favour upon mail-matter and station books, finding in them a power that could keep the Maluka at the homestead.

For two full weeks after our return from the drovers' camp our life was exactly as Cheon would have it—peaceful and regular, with an occasional single day "out-bush"; and when the Maluka in his leisure began to fulfil his long-standing promise of a fence round my garden, Cheon expressed himself well-pleased with his reform.

But even the demands of station books and accumulated mail-matter can be satisfied in time, and Dan reporting that he was "getting going with the bullocks", Cheon found his approval had been premature; for, to his dismay, the Maluka abandoned the fence, and began preparations for a trip "bush". "Surely the missus is not going?" he said; and next day, we left him at the homestead, a lonely figure, seated on an overturned bucket, disconsolate and fearing the worst.

Cheon often favoured an upside-down bucket for a seat. Nothing more uncomfortable for a fat man can be imagined, yet Cheon sat on his rickety perch, for the most part chuckling and happy. Perhaps, like Mark Tapley, he felt it a "credit being jolly" under such circumstances.

By way of contrast, we found Dan and Jack optimistic and happy, with some good bullocks in hand, a record branding to report for the fortnight's work, and a drover in camp of such a delightful turn of mind that he was inclined to look upon every bullock mustered as "just the thing". He was easily disposed of, and within a week we were back at the homestead.

We had left Cheon sad and disconsolate, but he met us, filled with fury, and holding a sack of something soft in his arms. "What's 'er matter?" he spluttered, almost choking with rage. "Me savey grow cabbage"; and he flung the sack at our feet as we stood in the homestead thoroughfare staring at him in wonder. "Paper yabber!" he added curtly, passing a letter to the Maluka.

It was a kindly, courteous letter from our Eastern neighbour, who had "ventured to send a cabbage, remembering the homestead garden did not get on too well". (His visits had been in Sam's day.) "How kind!" we said, and not understanding Cheon's wrath, the Maluka opened the bag, and passed two fine cabbages to him, after duly admiring them.

They acted on Cheon like a red rag on a bull. Flinging them from him, he sent them spinning across the stony ground with two furious kicks, following them up with further furious kicks as we looked on in speechless amazement. "What's 'er matter?" he growled, as, abandoning the chase with a final lunge, he stalked indignantly back to us, and as the unfortunate cabbages turned over and lay still on their tattered backs, he began to explain his wrath. Was he not paid to grow cabbages, he asked, and where had he failed that we should accept cabbages from neighbours? Cabbages for ourselves, but insults for him! Then, the comical side of his nature coming to the surface as unexpectedly as his wrath, he was overcome with laughter, and clung to a verandah post for support, while, still speechless, we looked on in consternation, for laughing was a serious matter with Cheon.

"My word, me plenty cross fellow," he gasped at intervals,

and finally led the way to the vegetable garden, where he cut an enormous cabbage and carried it to the store to weigh it. The scale turned at twelve pounds, and, sure of our ground now, we compared its mighty heart to the stout heart of Cheon—a compliment fully appreciated by his Chinese mind; then, having disparaged the tattered insults to his satisfaction, we went to the house and wrote a letter of thanks to our neighbour, giving him so vivid a word picture of the reception of his cabbages that he felt inspired to play a practical joke on Cheon later on. One thing is very certain—everyone enjoyed those cabbages, including even Cheon and the goats.

Of course, we had cabbage for dinner that day, and the day following, and the next day again, and were just fearing that cabbage was becoming a confirmed habit when, Dan coming in with reports, we all went bush again, and the spell was broken. "A pity the man from Beyanst wasn't about," Dan said when he heard of the daily menu.

It was late in September when Dan came in, and four weeks slipped away with the concerns of cattle and cattle-buyers and cattle-duffers, and as we moved hither and thither the water-melons leafed and blossomed and fruited, to Billy's delight, and Cheon's undisguised amazement, and the Line Party, creeping on, crept first into our borders and then into camp at the Warlochs, and Happy Dick's visits, dog-fights, and cribbage became part of the station routine. Now and then a traveller from Inside passed out, but as the roads Inside were rapidly closing in, none came from the Outside going in, and because of that there were no extra mails, and towards the end of October we were wondering how we were "going to get through the days until the Fizzer was due again", when Dan and Jack came in unexpectedly for a consultation.

"Run clean out of flour," Dan announced, with a wink and a mysterious look towards the black world, as he dismounted at the head of the homestead thoroughfare; then, after inquiring for the "education of the missus", he added, with further winks and mystery, that it only needed a nigger-hunt to round off her education properly, but it was after supper before he found a fitting opportunity to explain his winks and mystery. Then, joining us as we lounged in the open starry space between the billabong and the house, he chuckled, "Yes, it just needs a nigger-hunt to make her education a credit to us."

Dan never joined us in the evenings without an invitation, although he was not above putting himself in the way of one. Whenever he felt inclined for what he called "a pitch with the boss and missus" he would saunter past at a little distance, apparently bound for the billabong, but in reality ready to respond to the Maluka's "Is that you, Dan?" although just as ready to saunter on if that invitation was not forthcoming—a happy little arrangement born of that tact and delicacy of the bush-folk that never intrudes on another man's privacy.

Dan being just Dan rarely had need to saunter on; and as he settled down on the grass in acceptance of this usual form of invitation, he wagged his head wisely, declaring "she had got on so well with her education that it 'ud be a pity not to finish her off properly". Then, dropping his bantering tone, he reported a scatter-on among the river cattle.

"I wasn't going to say anything about it before the 'boys'," he said, "but it's time someone gave a surprise party down the river' ; and a "scatter-on" meaning "niggers in", Maluka readily agreed to a surprise patrol of the river country, that being forbidden ground for blacks' camps.

"It's no good going unless it's going to be a surprise party," Dan reiterated; and when the Quiet Stockman was called across from the Quarters, he was told that "there wasn't going to be no talking before the boys".

Further consultations being necessary, Dan feared arousing suspicion, and to ensure his surprise party, and to guard against any word of the coming patrol being sent out-bush by the station "boys", he indulged in a little dust-throwing; and there was much talking in public about going "out to the north-west for the boss to have another look round there", and much laying of deep plans in private.

Finally, it was decided that the Quiet Stockman and his "boys" were to patrol the country north from the river while we were to keep to the south banks and follow the river down to the boundaries in all its windings, each party appointed to camp at the Red Lily lagoons second night out, each, of course, on its own side of the river. It being necessary for Jack to cross the river beyond the Springs, he left the homestead half a day before us—public gossip reporting that he was "going beyond the Waterhouse horse-mustering", and Dan, finding dust-throwing highly diverting, shouted after him that he "might as well bring some fresh relays to the Yellow Hole in a day or two", and then giving his attention to the packing of swags and pack-bags, "reckoned things were just about fixed up for a surprise party".

20

At our appointed time we left the homestead, taking the north-west track for over a mile to continue the dust-throwing; and for the whole length of that mile Dan reiterated the "advantages of surprise parties", and his opinion that "things were just about properly fixed up for one"; and when we left the track abruptly and set off across country at right angles to it, Sambo's quick, questioning, suspicious glance made it very evident that he, for one, had gleaned no inkling of the patrol, which naturally filled Dan with delight.

"River tonight, Sambo," he said airily; but after that one swift glance Sambo rode after us as stolid as ever—Sambo was always difficult to fathom—while Dan spent the afternoon congratulating himself on the success of his dust-throwing, proving with many illustrations that "it's the hardest thing to spring a surprise on niggers. Something seems to tell 'em you're coming," he explained. "Some chaps put it down to second-sight or thought-reading."

When we turned in, Dan was still chuckling over his cute handling of the trip. "Bluffed 'em this time all right," he assured us, little guessing that the blacks at the Red Lilies, thirty miles away, and other little groups of blacks travelling down the river towards the lagoons were conjecturing on the object of the Maluka's visit—"something having told them we were coming".

The "something", however, was neither second-sight nor thought-reading, but a very simple, tangible "something".

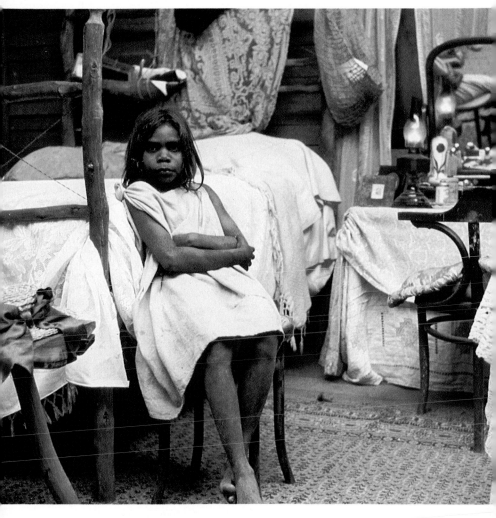

A reflective Bett Bett in her room at the Elsey
Homestead.

Tommy Lewis (Jackaroo), an Aboriginal stockman,
in the bush.

Sambo had gone for a stroll from our camp about sun-down, and one of Jack's boys had gone for a stroll from Jack's camp, and soon afterwards two tell-tale telegraphic columns of smoke, worked on some black-fellow dot-dash system, had risen above the timber, and their messages had also been duly noted down at the Red Lilies and elsewhere, and acted upon. The Maluka was on the river, and when the Maluka was about, it was considered wisdom to be off forbidden ground; not that the blacks feared the Maluka, but no one cares about vexing the goose that lays the golden eggs.

On stations in the Never-Never the blacks are supposed to camp either in the homesteads, where no man need go hungry, or right outside the boundaries on waters beyond the cattle, travelling in or out as desired, on condition that they keep to the main traveller's tracks—blacks among the cattle have a scattering effect on the herd, apart from the fact that "niggers in" generally means cattle-killing.

Of course no man ever hopes to keep his blacks absolutely obedient to this rule; but the judicious giving of an odd bullock at not too rare intervals, and always at corroboree times, the more judicious winking at cattle killing on the boundaries, where cattle scaring is not all disadvantage, and the even more judicious giving of a hint, when a hint is necessary, will do much to keep them fairly well in hand, anyway from openly harrying and defiant killing, which in humanity is surely all any man should ask.

The white man has taken the country from the black fellow, and with it his right to travel where he will for pleasure or food, and until he is willing to make recompense by granting fair liberty of travel, and a fair percentage of cattle or their equivalent in fair payment—openly and fairly giving them, and seeing that no man is unjustly treated or hungry within his borders—cattle killing, and at times even man killing, by blacks will not be an offence against the white folk.

A black fellow kills cattle because he is hungry and must be fed with food, having been trained in a school that for generations has acknowledged "catch who catch can" among its commandments; and until the long arm of the law interfered,

white men killed the black fellow, because they were hungry
with a hunger that must be fed with gold, having been trained
in a school that for generations has acknowledged "Thou shalt
not kill" among its commandments; and yet men speak of the
"superiority" of the white race, and, speaking, forget to ask who
of us would go hungry if the situation were reversed, but
condemn the black fellow as a vile thief, piously quoting—now
it suits them—from those same commandments, that men
"must not steal", in the same breath referring to the "white
man's crime" (when it finds them out) as "getting into trouble
over some shooting affair with blacks". Truly we British-born
have reason to brag of our "inborn sense of justice".

The Maluka being more than willing to give his fair percentage, a judicious hint from him was generally taken quietly and
for the time discreetly obeyed, and it was a foregone conclusion
that our "nigger hunt" would only involve the captured with
general discomfiture; but the Red Lilies being a stronghold of
the tribe, and a favourite hiding-place for "outsiders", emergencies were apt to occur "down the river", and we rode out
of camp with rifles unslung and revolvers at hand.

Dan's sleep had in no wise lessened his faith in the efficiency
of dust-throwing, and as we set out he "reckoned" the missus
would "learn a thing or two about surprise parties this trip".
We all did, but the black fellows gave the instruction.

All morning we rode in single file, following the river through
miles of deep gorges, crossing here and there stretches of grassy
country that ran in valleys between gorge and gorge, passing
through deep Ti Tree forests at times, and now and then
clambering over towering limestone ridges that blocked the
way, with, all the while, the majestic Roper River flowing deep
and wide and silent on our left, between its water-lily fringed
margins. It would take a mighty drought to dry up the waters
of the Territory—permanent, we call them, sure of our rivers
and our rains. Almost fifty miles of these deep-flowing waterways fell to our share; thirty-five miles of the Roper, twelve in
the Long Reach, besides great holes scattered here and there
along the beds of creeks that are mighty rivers in themselves
"during the Wet". Too much water, if anything, was the com-

plaint of the Elsey, for water everywhere meant cattle everywhere.

For over two hours we rode, prying into and probing all sorts of odd nooks and crannies before we found any sign of blacks, and then, Roper giving the alarm, everyone sat to attention. Roper had many ways of amusing himself when travelling through bush, but one of his greatest delights was nosing out hidden black fellows. At the first scent of "niggers" his ears would prick forward, and if left to himself, he would carry his rider into an unsuspected nigger camp, or stand peering into the bushes at a discomfited black fellow, who was busy trying to think of some excuse to explain his presence and why he had hidden.

As Roper's ears shot forward and he turned aside towards a clump of thick-set bushes, Dan chuckled in expectation, but all Roper found was a newly deserted gundi camp, and fresh tracks travelling eastwards—tracks left during the night—after our arrival at the river, of course.

Dan surveyed the tracks, and his chuckles died out, and growing sceptical of the success of his surprise party, he followed them for a while in silence, Sambo riding behind, outwardly stolid, but no doubt inwardly chuckling.

Other eastward-going tracks a mile or so farther on made Dan even more sceptical, and further tracks again set him harking back to his theory of "something always telling 'em somehow", and, losing interest in nigger-hunts, he became showman of the Roper River scenery.

Down into the depths of gorges he led us, through ferny nooks, and over the sandy stretches at the base of the mighty clefts through which the river flows; and as we rode, he had us leaning back in our saddles, in danger of cricking our necks, to look up at lofty heights above us, then a rocky peninsula running right into the river, after we had clambered up its sides like squirrels, he led the way across its spiky surfaced summit, and soon we were leaning forward over our horses' necks in danger of taking somersaults into space, as we peered over the sides of a precipice at the river away down beneath us. "Nothing like variety," Dan chuckled; and a few minutes later again we were leaning well back in our saddles as the horses picked their way down the far side of the ridge, old Roper letting himself down in his most approved style; dropping from ledge to ledge as he went; stepping carefully along their length, he would pause for a moment on their edges to judge distance, then, gathering his feet together, he would sway out and drop a foot or more to the next ledge. Riding Roper was never more than sitting in the saddle and leaving all else to him. Wherever he went there was safety, both for himself and his rider, whether galloping between trees or beneath overhanging branches, whether dropping down ridges with the sure-footedness of a mountain pony, or picking his way across the treacherous "springy country". No one knew better than he his own limits, and none better understood "springy country". Carefully he would test suspicious-looking turf with a cautious fore-hoof, and when all roads proved risky, in his own unmistakable language he would advise his rider to dismount and walk over, having shown plainly that the dangerous bit was not equal to the combined weight of horse and man. When Roper advised, wise men obeyed.

But gorges and ridges were not all Dan had to show us. Twice in our thirty-five miles of the Roper—about ten miles apart—wide-spreading rocky arches completely span the river a foot or so beneath its surface, forming natural crossing-places; for at them the full volume of water takes what Dan called a "duck-under", leaving only smoothly flowing shallow streams, a couple of hundred yards wide, running over the rocky bridgeways. The first "duck-under" occurs in a Ti Tree valley, and, marvelling at the wonder of the rippling streamlet —so many yards wide and so few in length, with that deep silent river for its source and estuary—we loitered in the pleasant forest glen, until Dan, coming on further proofs of a black fellow's "second sight" along the margins of the "duck-under", he turned away in disgust, and as we followed him through the great forest he treated us to a lengthy discourse on thought-reading.

The Salt Creek, coming into the Roper with its deep, wide estuary, interrupted both Dan's lecture and our course, and following along the creek to find the crossing, we left the river, and before we saw it again a mob of "brumbies" had lured us into a "drouth" that even Dan declared was the "dead finish".

Brumby horses being one of the problems of the run, and the destruction of brumby stallions imperative, as the nigger-hunt was apparently off, the brumby mob proved too enticing to be passed by, and for an hour and more it kept us busy, the Maluka and Dan being equally "set on getting a stallion or two".

As galloping after brumbies when there is no trap to run them into is about as wise as galloping after a flight of swallows, we followed at a distance when they galloped, and stalked them against the wind when they drew up to reconnoitre; beautiful, clean-limbed, graceful creatures, with long flowing manes and tails floating about them, galloping freely and swiftly as they drove the mares before them, or stepping with light, dancing tread as they drew up and faced about, with the mares now huddled together behind them. Three times they drew up and faced about, and each time a stallion fell before the rifles, then, becoming more wary, they led us farther and farther back, evading the rifles at every halt, until finally they galloped out of sight, and beyond all chance of pursuit. Then, Dan discovering he had acquired the "drouth", advised "giving it best" and making for the Spring Hole in Duck Creek.

"Could do with a drop of spring water," he said; but Dan's luck was out this trip, and the Spring Hole proved a slimy bog "alive with dead cattle", as he himself phrased it. Three dead beasts lay bogged on its margin, and held as in a vice, up to their necks in slime and awfulness, stood two poor living brutes. They turned piteous, terrified eyes on us as we rode up, and then Dan and the Maluka firing in mercy, the poor heads drooped and fell; and the bog with a sickening sigh sucked them under.

As we watched, horribly fascinated, Dan indulged in a soliloquy—a habit with him when ordinary conversation seemed out of place. " 'Awful dry Wet we're having,' sez he," he murmured; " 'the place is alive with dead cattle. Fact,' sez he, 'cattle's dying this year that never died before.' " Then, remarking that "this sort of thing" wasn't "exactly a thirst quencher", he followed up the creek bank into a forest of cabbage-tree palms—tall, feathery-crested palms everywhere, taller even than the forest trees; but never a sign of water.

It was then two o'clock, and our last drink had been at breakfast—soon after sun-up; and for another hour we pegged wearily on, with that seven hours' drouth, done horses, the beating sun of a Territory October overhead, Brown stretched across the Maluka's knees on the verge of apoplexy, and Sool'em panting wearily on. With the breaking of her leg, little Tiddle'ums had ended her bush days, but as she lost in bushcraft she gained in excellency as a fence personifier.

By three o'clock we struck water in the Punch Bowl—a deep, volcanic hole, bottomless, the blacks say, but apparently fed beneath by the river; but long before then Dan's chuckle had died out, and soliloquies had ceased to amuse him.

At the first sight of the water we revived, and as Brown and Sool'em lay down and revelled on its margin, Dan "took a pull as an introduction", and then, after unpacking the team and getting the fire going for the billy, he opened out the tucker-bags, having decided on a "fizz" as a "good quencher".

"Nothing like a fizz when you've got a drouth on," he said, mixing soda and cream-of-tartar into a cup of water, and drinking deeply. As he drank, the "fizz" spattered its foam all over his face and beard, and after putting down the empty cup with a satisfied sigh, he joined us as we sat on the pebbly incline, waiting for the billy to boil, and with the tucker-bags dumped down around and about us. "Real refreshing that!" he said, drawing a red handkerchief from his belt and mopping his spattered face and beard, adding, as he passed the damp handkerchief over his ears and neck with chuckling exaggeration: "Tell you what! A fizz'd be a great thing if you were short of water. You could get a drink and have a good wash-up with the one cupful."

With the "fizz", Dan's interest in education revived, and after dinner he took up the role of showman of the Roper scenery once more, and had us scrambling over boulders and cliffs along the dry bed of the creek that runs back from the Punch Bowl, until, having clambered over its left bank into a shady glen, we found ourselves beneath the gem of the Roper

—a wide-spreading banyan tree, with its propped-up branches turning and twisting in long winding leafy passages and balconies, over a feathery grove of young palm trees that had crept into its generous shade.

Here and there the passages and balconies graded one to another's level, all being held together by innumerable stays and props, sent down from branch to branch, and from branches to the grassy turf beneath; and one sweeping limb, coming almost to the ground in a gentle incline before twisting away and up again, made ascent so simple that the men-folk sent the missus for a "stroll in mid-air", sure that no white woman's feet had yet trodden those winding ways. And as she strolled about the tree—not climbed—hindered only by her holland riding-skirt, Brown followed, anxiously but cautiously. Then, the spirit of vandalism taking hold of the Maluka, he cut the name of the missus deep into the yielding bark.

There are some wonderful trees on the Elsey, but not one of them will compare with the majesty and grandeur of that old banyan. Away from the world it stands, beyond those rocky ways and boulders, with its soft shade, sweeping curves, and feathery undergrowths, making a beautiful world of its own. For years upon years it has stood there—maybe for centuries—sending down from its branches those props for its old age, bountiful with its shade, and indifferent whether its pathways be trodden by white feet or black.

After the heat and "drouth" we could have loitered in that pleasant shade; but we were due at the Red Lilies "second night out"; and it being one of the unwritten laws of a "nigger-hunt" to keep appointments—"the other chaps worrying a bit if you don't turn up"—soon after four o'clock we were out in the blazing heat again, following the river now along its higher flood-bank, through grassy plains and open forest land.

By five o'clock Dan was prophesying that "it 'ud take us all we knew to do the trick in daylight", but at six o'clock, when we were still eight miles from the Red Lilies, the Maluka settled the question by calling for a camp there and then. "The missus had had enough," the Maluka decided, and Dan became anxious. "It's that drouth that's done it," he lamented; and although agreeing with the Maluka that Jack would survive a few hours' anxiety, regretted we had "no way of letting him know". (We were not aware of the efficiency of smoke signalling.)

We turned back a short distance for better watering for horses, settling down for the night at the second "duck-under" —McGinn's bar—within sound of the rushing of many waters; for here the river comes back to the surface with a mighty roar and swirling currents. "Knock-up camp," Dan christened it in his pleasant way, and Sambo became unexpectedly curious. "Missus knock up?" he asked; the Maluka nodded. Sambo's question was forgotten until the next midday.

By then we had passed the Red Lily lagoons, and ridden across the salt-bush plain, and through a deep belt of tall, newly sprung green grass, that hugged the river there just then, and having been greeted by smug, smiling old black fellows, were saluting Jack across two or three hundred feet of water, as we stood among our horses.

"Slewed!" Jack called in answer, through hollowed hands. "Didn't worry. Heard—the—missus—had—knocked—up", and Dan leaned against his horse, limp with amazement.

"Heard the missus had knocked up?" he gasped. "Well, I'm blowed! Talk of surprise parties!" and the old black fellows looked on enjoying the effect.

"Black fellow plenty savey," they said loftily, and Dan was almost persuaded to a belief in debbil-debbils, until our return to the homestead, when Jimmy's Nellie divulged the Court secret; then Dan ejaculated another "Well, I'm blowed!" with the theory of second-sight and thought-reading falling about his ears.

After a consultation across the river in long-drawn-out syllables, Jack decided on a horse muster for the return trip— genuine this time—and went on his way, after appointing to meet us at Knock-up camp next evening. But our horses refusing to leave the deep green feed, we settled down just where we were, beside the river, and formed a curious camping-ground for ourselves, a small space hacked out and trampled down, out of the dense rank grass that towered above and around us.

But this was to be a record trip for discomfort. Dan, on opening out the tucker-bags, announced ruefully that our supply of meat had "turned on us"; and as our jamtin had "blown", we feared we were reduced to damper only, until the Maluka unearthed a bottle of anchovy paste, falsely labelled "Chicken and Ham". "Lot's Wife", Dan called it, after "tackling some as a relish".

Birds were everywhere about the lagoon—ducks, shags, great geese, and pigmy geese, hovering and settling about them in screaming clouds; and after dinner, deciding we "might as well have a bit of game for supper", we walked across the open salt-bush plain to the Big Red Lily. But revolvers are hardly the thing for duck shooting, and the soft-nosed bullets of the Maluka's rifle reducing an unfortunate duck to a tangled mass of blood and feathers, we were obliged to accept, willy-nilly, the prospect of damper and "Lot's wife" for supper. But our hopes died hard, and we sneaked about the gorgeous lagoons, revolvers in hand, for a good hour, "learning a thing or two about the lagoons" from Dan as we sneaked.

The Red Lily lagoons lie away from the Roper, on either side of it, wide-spreading and shallow—great sheets of water with tall reeds and rushes about them, and glorious in flowering time with their immense cup-shaped crimson blossoms clustering on long stalks above great floating leaves—leaves nearly approaching three feet in diameter, I think; and everywhere about the leaves hover birds, and along the margins of the lagoons stalk countless waders, cranes, jabiroos, and oftentimes douce native companions.

Being so shallow and wide-spreading, the lagoons would dry up early in the Dry were it not that the blacks are able to refill them at will from the river, for here the Roper indulges in a third "duck-under", so curious that with a few logs and sheets of bark the blacks can block the way of its water and overflow them into the lagoons, thereby ensuring a plentiful larder to hosts of wild fowl, and, incidentally, to themselves.

As the mystery of this "duck-under" lies under water, it can only be described from hearsay. Here, so the blacks say, a solid wall of rock runs out into the river, incomplete, though, and complicated, rising and terminating before midstream into a large island, which, dividing the steam unequally, sends the main body of water swirling away along its northern borders, while the lesser current glides quietly round the southern side, slipping partly over the submerged wall, and partly through a great side-long cleft on its face—gliding so quietly that the cleft can be easily blocked and the wall heightened when the waters are needed for the lagoons. Black-fellow gossip also reports that the island can be reached by a series of sub-terranean caves that open into daylight away at the Cave Creek, miles away.

Getting nothing better than one miserable shag by our revolvers, we faced damper and "Lot's wife" about sundown, returning to camp through a dense Leichhardt pine forest, where we found myriads of bat-like creatures, inches long, perhaps a foot, hanging head downwards from almost every branch of every tree. "Flying foxes," Dan called them, and Sambo helped himself to a few, finding "Lot's wife" unsatisfying; but the white folk "drew the line at varmints".

"Had bandicoot once for me Christmas dinner," Dan informed us, making extra tea "on account of 'Lot's wife' taking a bit of washing down". Then, supper over, the problem of watering the horses had to be solved. The margins of the lagoons were too boggy for safety, and as the horses, fearing alligators apparently, refused the river, we had a great business persuading them to drink out of the camp mixing dish.

The sun was down before we began; and long before we were through with the tussle, peculiar shrilling cries caught our attention, and, turning to face down-stream, we saw a dense cloud approaching—skimming along and above the river; a shrilling, moving, cloud, keeping all the while to the river; but reaching right across it, and away beyond the tree-tops.

Swiftly it came to us and sped on, never ceasing its peculiar cry; and as it swept on, and we found it was made up of innumerable flying creatures, we remembered Dan's "flying foxes". In unbroken continuity the cloud swept out of the pine forest, along the river, and past us, resembling an elongated kaleidoscope, all dark colours in appearance; for as they swept by, the shimmering creatures constantly changed places— gliding downwards as they flew, before dipping for a drink, to rise again with swift, glancing movement, shrilling that peculiar cry all the while. Like clouds of drifting fog they swept by, and in such myriads that, even after the Maluka began to time them, full fifteen minutes passed before they began to straggle out, and twenty before the last few stragglers were gone. Then, as we turned up-stream to look after them, we found that the dense cloud was rising and fanning out over the tree-tops. The evening drink accomplished, it was time to think of food.

Dan welcomed the spectacle as an "impromptu bit of education. Learnt something meself, even," he said, with lordly superiority. "Been out-bush forty years and never struck *that* before"; and later, as we returned to camp, he declared it "just knocked spots off De Rougemont".

But it had taken so long to persuade the horses that a drink could proceed out of a mixing dish, that it was time to turn in by then; and Dan proceeded to clear a space for a sleeping-ground with a tomahawk. "Seems no end to education once you start," he chuckled, hacking at a stubborn tussock. "Reckon no other woman ever learned to make a bed with a tomahawk." Then Sambo created a diversion by asking for the loan of a revolver before taking a message to the blacks' camp.

"Big mob bad fellow black fellow sit down longa island," he explained; and Dan, whimsical under all circumstances, "noticed the surprise party wasn't exactly going off without a hitch". "Couldn't have fixed up better for them if they've got a surprise party of their own up their sleeves," he added ruefully, looking round at the dense wall of grass about us; and as he and the Maluka swung the two nets not six feet apart, we were all of one mind that "getting murdered was an experience we could nicely do without". Then Sambo, returning and swinging his net in the narrow space between the two others, set Dan chuckling again. "Doesn't mean to make a target of himself," he said; but his chuckle died out when Sambo, preparing to curl up in the safest place in the camp, explained his presumption tersely by announcing that

"Monkey sit down longa camp." Monkey was a law unto himself, and a very unpleasant law, being a reputed murderer several times over; and when he and his followers were about, white men saw to their rifles; and as we turned in we also agreed "that this wasn't exactly the kind of nigger hunt we had set out for. It makes a difference when the other chap's doing the hunting. Sool'em, old girl," Dan added, cautioning her to keep her "weather eye open", as he saw to his rifle and laid it, muzzle outwards, in his net. Then, as we settled down for the night with revolvers and rifle at hand, and Brown at the head of our net, he "hoped" the missus would not "go getting night-mare, and make things unpleasant by shooting round pro-miscuous like", and having by this tucked himself in to his satisfaction, he lay down, "reckoning this ought to just about finish off her education, if she doesn't get finished off herself by niggers before morning".

A cheerful nightcap; but such was our faith in Sool'em and Brown as danger signals, that the camp was asleep in a few minutes. Perhaps also because nigger alarms were by no means the exception: the bush-folk would get little sleep if they lay awake whenever they were camped near doubtful company. We sleep wherever we are, for it is easy to grow accustomed even to nigger alarms; and besides, the bush-folk know that when a man has clean hands and heart he has little to fear from even his "bad fellow black fellows". But the Red Lilies were beyond our boundaries, and Monkey was a notorious exception, and shrill cries approaching the camp at dawn brought us all to our elbows, to find only the flying foxes returning to the pine forest, fanning inwards this time.

After giving the horses another drink and breakfasting on damper and "Lot's wife", we moved on again, past the glory of the lagoons, to further brumby encounters, carrying a water-bag on a pack-horse by way of precaution against further "drouths". But such was the influence of "Lot's wife" that long before midday the bag was empty, and Dan was recommending bloater-paste as a "grand thing for breakfast during the Wet, seeing it keeps you dry all day long".

Further damper and "Lot's wife" for dinner, and an afternoon of thirst, set us all dreading supper, and about sun-down, three very thirsty, forlorn white folk were standing by the "duck-under" below "Knock-up camp", waiting for the Quiet Stockman, and hoping against hope that his meat had not "turned on him"; and when he and his "boys" came jangling down the opposite bank, and splashing and plunging over the "duck-under" below, driving a great mob of horses before them, we assailed him with questions.

But although Jack's meat was "chucked out days ago" he was merciful to us and shouted out: "Will a dozen boiled duck do instead? Got fourteen at one shot this morning, and boiled 'em right off," he explained, as we seized upon his tucker-bags. "Kept a dozen of 'em in case of accidents." Besides a shot-gun, Jack had much sense.

A dozen cold boiled duck "did" very nicely after four meals of damper and bloater-paste; and a goodly show they made set out in our mixing dish.

Dan, gloating over them, offered to "do the carving". "I'm real good at the poultry-carving trick, when there's a bird apiece", he chuckled, spearing bird after bird with a two-pronged fork, and passing round one apiece as we sat expectantly around the mixing dish, all among the tucker-bags and camp baggage. And so excellent a sauce is hunger that we received and enjoyed our "bird apiece" unabashed and unblushingly—the menfolk returning for further helpings, and the "boys" managing all that were left.

All agreed that "you couldn't beat cold boiled duck by much"; but in the morning grilled fish was accepted as "just the thing for breakfast"; then finding ourselves face to face with "Lot's wife", and not too much of that, we beat a hasty retreat to the homestead; a further opportune "catch" of duck giving us heart for further brumby encounters and another night's camp out-bush. Then the following morning as we rode towards the homestead Dan "reckoned" that from an educational point of view the trip had been a pronounced success.

21

Just before midday—five days after we had left the homestead
—we rode through the Southern slip rails to find the Dandy
at work "cleaning out a soakage" on the brink of the billabong,
with Cheon enthusiastically encouraging him. The billabong,
we heard, had threatened to "peter out" in our absence, and
riding across the now dusty wind-swept enclosure we realized
that November was with us, and that the Dry was preparing for
its final fling—"just showing what it could do when it tried".

With the South-east Trades to back it up it was fighting
desperately against the steadily advancing North-west monsoon, drying up, as it fought, every drop of moisture left from
last Wet. There was not a blade of green grass within sight of
the homestead, and everywhere dust whirled, and eddied, and
danced, hurled all ways at once in the fight, or gathered itself
into towering centrifugal columns, to speed hither and thither,
obedient to the will of the elements.

Half the heavens seemed part of the Dry, and half part of the
Wet; dusty blue to the south-east, and dark banks of clouds to
the north-west, with a fierce beating sun at the zenith. Already
the air was oppressive with electric disturbances, and Dan,
fearing he would not get finished unless things were kept
humming, went out-bush next morning, and the homestead
became once more the hub of our universe—the south-east
being branded from that centre. Every few days a mob was
brought in, and branded, and disbanded; hours were spent on
the stockyard fence; pack-teams were packed, unpacked, and

repacked; and every day grew hotter and hotter, and every night more and more electric, and as the days went by we waited for the Fizzer, hungry for mail-matter, with a six weeks' hunger.

When the Fizzer came in he came with his usual lusty shouting, but varied his greeting into a triumphant: "Broken the record this time, missus. Two bags as big as a house and a few et-cet-eras!" And presently he staggered towards us bent with the weight of a mighty mail. But a Fizzer without news would not have been our Fizzer, and as he staggered along we learned that Mac was coming out to clear the run of brumbies. "Be along in no time now," the Fizzer shouted. "Fallen clean out with bullock-punching. Wouldn't put his worst enemy to it. Going to tackle something that'll take a bit of jumping down." Then the mail-bags and et-cet-eras came down in successive thuds, and no one was better pleased with its detail than our Fizzer; fifty letters, sixty-nine papers, dozen of books and magazines, and parcels of garden cuttings.

"Last you for the rest of the year by the look of it," the Fizzer declared later, finding us at the house walled in with a litter of mail-matter. Then he explained his interruption. "I'm going straight on at once," he said, "for me horses are none too good as it is, and the lads say there's a bit of good grass at the Nine Mile"; and, going out, we watched him set off.

"So long!" he shouted, as cheerily as ever as he gathered his team together. "Half past eleven four weeks."

But already the Fizzer's shoulders were setting square, for the last trip of the Dry was before him—the trip that perished the last mailman—and his horses were none too good.

"Good luck!" we called after him. "Early showers!" and there was a note in our voices brought there by the thought of that gaunt figure at the well—rattling its dice-box as it waited for one more round with our Fizzer: a note that brought a bright look into the Fizzer's face, as with an answering shout of farewell he rode on into the forest. And watching the sturdy figure, and knowing the luck of our Fizzer—that luck that had given him his fearless judgment and steadfast, courageous spirit—we felt his cheery "Half past eleven four weeks" must be prophetic, in spite of those long dry stages, with their beating heat and parching dust eddies—stages eked out now at each end with other stages of bad going.

"Half past eleven four weeks," the Fizzer had said; and as we returned to our mail-matter, knowing what it meant to our Fizzer, we looked anxiously to the north-west, and "hoped the showers" would come before the "return trip of the Downs".

In addition to the fifty letters for the house, the Fizzer had left two others at the homestead to be called for—one being addressed to Victoria Downs (over two hundred miles to our west), and the other to:

F. BROWN, Esq.,
IN CHARGE OF STUD BULLS GOING WEST
via NORTHERN TERRITORY

The uninitiated may think that the first was sent out by mistake, and that the second was too vaguely addressed; but both letters went into the rack to await delivery, for our faith in the wisdom of our Postal Department was great; it makes no mistakes and to it—in a land where everybody knows everybody else, and all his business, and where it has taken him—an address could never be too vague. The bush-folk love to say that when it opened out its swag in the Territory it found red tape had been forgotten, but having a surplus supply of common sense on hand, it decided to use that in its place.

And so it would seem. "Down South" envelopes are labori-ously addressed with the names of stations, and vias here and vias there; and throughout the Territory, men move hither and thither by compulsion or free-will, giving never a thought to an address; while the Department, knowing the ways of its people, delivers its letters in spite of, not because of, these addresses. It reads only the name of the man that heads the address of his letters, and sends the letters to where that man happens to be. Provided it has been clearly stated which Jones is meant, the Department will see to the rest, although it is wise to add Northern Territory for the guidance of Post Offices "Down South". "Jones travelling with cattle for Wave Hill", reads the Department; and the gossiping, friendly wire reporting Jones as "just leaving the Powell", the letter lies in the Fizzer's loose-bag until he runs into Jones's mob; or a mail coming in for Jones, Victoria River, when this Jones is on the point of sailing for a trip south, *his* mail is delivered on ship-board; and as the Department goes on with its work, letters for east go west, and for west go south—in mail-bags, loose-bags, travellers' pockets, or per black boy—each one direct to the bush-folk as a migrating bird to its destination.

But, painstaking as our Department is with our mail-matter, it excels itself in its handling of telegrams. Southern red tape has decreed—no doubt wisely as far as it goes—that telegrams shall travel by official persons only; but out-bush official persons are few, and apt to be on duty elsewhere when important telegrams arrive; and it is then that our Department draws largely on that surplus supply of common sense.

Always deferential to the South, it obediently pigeon-holes the telegram, to await some official person, then, knowing that a delay of weeks will probably convert it into so much waste paper, it writes a "duplicate", and goes outside to send it "bush" by the first traveller it can find. If no traveller is at hand, the "Line" is "called up" and asked if anyone is going in the desired direction from elsewhere; if so, the "duplicate" is repeated "down the line", but if not, a traveller is created in the person of a black boy by means of a bribing stick of tobacco. No extra charge, of course. Nothing *is* an extra in the Territory. "Nothing to do with the Department," says the chief; "merely the personal courtesy of our officers." May it be many a long day before the forgotten shipment of red tape finds its way to the Territory to strangle this courtesy of our officers!

Nothing finds itself outside this courtesy. The Fizzer brings in great piles of mail-matter, unweighed and unstamped, with many of the envelopes bursting, or, at times, in place of an envelope, a request for one; and "our officers", getting to work with their "courtesy", soon put all in order, not disdaining even the licking of stamps or the patching or renewing of envelopes. Letters and packets are weighed, stamped and repaired—often readdressed where addresses for South are blurred; stamps are supplied for outgoing mail-matter and telegrams; postage-dues and duties paid on all incoming letters and parcels—in fact, nothing is left for us to do but to pay expenses incurred when the account is rendered at the end of each six months. No doubt our Department would also read and write our letters for us if we wished it, as it does, at times, for the untutored.

Wherever it can, it helps the bush-folk, and they, in turn, doing what they can to help it in its self-imposed task, are ever ready to "find room somewhere" in packbags or swags for mail-matter in need of transport assistance—the general opinion being that "a man that refuses to carry a man's mail to him 'ud be mean enough to steal bread out of a bird-cage"

In all the knowledge of the bush-folk, only one man had proved "mean enough". A man who shall be known as the Outsider, for he was one of a type who could never be one of the bush-folk, even though he lived out-bush for generations: a man so walled in with self and selfishness that, look where he would, he could see nothing grander or better than his own miserable self, and knowing all a mail means to a bushman, he could refuse to carry a neighbour's mail—even though his road lay through that neighbour's run—because he had had a difference with him.

"Stealing bread from a caged bird wasn't in it!" the homestead agreed, with unspeakable scorn; but the man was so reconciled to himself that the scorn passed over him unnoticed. He even missed the contempt in the Maluka's cutting "Perfectly!" when he hoped we understood him. (The Outsider, by the way, spoke of the Never-Never as a land where you can Never-Never get a bally thing you want! the Outsider's wants being of the flesh-pots of Egypt.) It goes without saying that the Maluka sent that neighbour's mail to him without delay, even though it meant a four-days' journey for a "boy" and station horses; for the bush-folk do what they can to help each other and the Department in the matter of mails, as in all else.

Fortunately, the Outsider always remained the only exception, and within a day or two of the Fizzer's visit a traveller passed through going east who happened to know that the "chap from Victoria Downs was just about due at Hodgson going back west", and one letter went forward in his pocket

en route to its owner. But before the other could be claimed,
Cheon had opened the last eighty-pound chest of tea, and the
homestead fearing the supply might not be equal to the
demands of the Wet, the Dandy was dispatched in all haste for
an extra loading of stores. And all through his absence, as before
it, and before the Fizzer's visit, Dan and the elements "kept
things humming".

Daily the soakage yielded less and less water, and daily
Billy Muck and Cheon scrimmaged over its yield; for Billy's
melons were promising to pay a liberal dividend, and Cheon's
garden was crying aloud for water. Every day was filled with
flies, and dust and prickly heat, and daily and hourly our hands
waved unceasingly, as they beat back the multitude of flies that
daily and hourly assailed us—the flies and dust treated all alike,
but the prickly heat was more chivalrous, and refrained from
annoying a woman. "Her usual luck!" the men-folk said,
utilizing verandah-posts or tree-trunks for scratching-posts
when not otherwise engaged. Daily "things" and the elements
hummed, and as they hummed Dan and Jack came and went
like will-o'-the-wisps—sometimes from the south-east and
sometimes from the north-east; and as they came and went,
the Maluka kept his hand on the helm; Happy Dick filled in
odd times as he alone knew how; a belated traveller or two
passing out came in, and went on, or remained; Brown of Bulls
sent on a drover ahead of the mob to spy out the land, and the
second letter left the rack, while all who came in, or went on,
or remained, during their stay at the homestead, stood about
the posts and uprights waving off flies, and rubbing and
wriggling against the posts like so many Uriah Heeps, as they
laid plans, gossiped; gave in reports, or "swopped yarns". The
Territory is hardly an earthly paradise just before the showers.
Still, Cheon did all he could to make things pleasanter, regaling
all daily on hop-beer, and all who came in were sure of a welcome from him—Dan invariably inspiring him with that ever-
fresh little joke of his when announcing afternoon tea to the
Quarters. "Cognac!" he would call, and also, invariably, Dan
made a great show of expectant haste, and a corresponding show
of disappointment, when the teapot only was forthcoming.

But Cheon's little joke and the afternoon tea were only interludes in the heat and thirst and dust. Daily things hummed faster and faster, and the South-east Trades skirmished and fought with the North-west monsoon, until the Willy-Willys, towering higher and higher, sped across the plain incessantly, and whirled, and spun, and danced like storm witches, in, and out, and about the homestead enclosure, leaving its acres all dust, and only dust, with the house, lightly festooned in creepers now, and set in its deep-green luxuriant garden of melons, as a pleasant oasis in a desert of glare and dust.

Daily and hourly men waved and perspired and rubbed against scratching-posts, and daily and hourly the Willy-Willys whirled and spun and danced, and daily and hourly as they threatened to dance, and spin, and whirl through the house, the homestead sped across the enclosure to slam doors and windows in their faces, thus saving our belongings from their whirling, dusty ravages; and when nimbler feet were absent, it was no uncommon sight to see Cheon, perspiring and dishevelled, speeding towards the house like a huge humming-top, with speeding Willy-Willys speeding after him, each bent on reaching the goal before the other. Oftentimes, Cheon outraced the Willy-Willys, and a very chuckling, triumphant Cheon slammed-to doors and windows; but at other times the Willy-Willys outraced Cheon, and, having soundly buffeted him with dust and debris, sped on triumphant in their turn, and then a very wrathful, spluttering, dusty Cheon sped after them. Also after a buffeting Cheon was generally persuaded an evil spirit dwelt within certain Willy-Willys.

But there is even a limit to keeping things humming during a Territory November; and things coming to a climax in a succession of dry thunderstorms, two cows died in the yards from exhaustion, and Dan was obliged to "chuck it".

"Not too bad, though," he said, reviewing the year's work, after fixing up a sleeping-camp for the Wet.

The camp consisted of a tent-fly, extended verandah-like behind the Quarters, open on three sides to the air, and furnished completely with a movable four-legged wooden bunk; and surveying it with satisfaction, as the Willy-Willys

danced about it, Dan reckoned it looked pretty comfortable.
"No fear of catching cold, anyway," he said, and meant it;
having got down to the root of hygiene; for among Dan's pet
theories was the theory that "houses are fine things to catch
cold in", backing up the theory by adding, "Never slept in
one yet without getting a cold."

The camp fixed up, Dan found himself among the un-
employed, and finding the Maluka had returned to station
books and the building of that garden fence, and that Jack had
begun anew his horse-breaking with a small mob of colts,
he envied them their occupation.

"Doing nothing's the hardest job I ever struck," he growled,
shifting impatiently from shade to shade, and dratting the
flies and dust; and even sank so low as to envy the missus
her house.

"Gives her something to do cleaning up after Willy-Willys,"
he growled further, and in desperation took to out-racing
Willy-Willys—"so the missus 'ull have a bit of time for pitching", and was drawn into the wood-heap gossip, until Jack
provided a little incidental entertainment in the handling of
a "kicker".

But Jack and the missus had found occupation of greater
interest than horse-breaking, gossiping, or spring cleaning—an
occupation that was also affording Dan a certain amount of
entertainment, for Jack was "wrestling with book-learning",
which Dan gave us to understand was a very different thing
from "education".

"Still, it takes a bit of time to get the whole mob properly
broken in," he said, giving Jack a preliminary caution. Then,
the first lesson over, he became interested in the methods of
handling the mob.

"That's the trick, is it? You just put the yearlings through
the yard, and then tackle the two-year-olds," he commented,
finding that after a run through the Alphabet we had settled
down to the first pages of Bett-Bett's discarded Primer.

Jack, having "roped all the two-year-olds" in that first lesson,
spent all evening handling them, and the Quarters looked on
as he tested their tempers, for although most proved willing,

yet a few were tricky or obstinate. All evening he sat, poring over the tiny Primer, amid a buzzing swarm of mosquitoes, with the doggedness all gone from his face, and in its place the light of a fair fight, and, to no one's surprise, in the morning we heard that "all the two-year-olds came at his call".

Another lesson at the midday spell roped most of the three-year-olds, and another evening brought them under the Quiet Stockman's will, and then in a few more days the four-year-olds and upwards had been dealt with, and the Primer was exhausted.

"Got through with the first draft, anyway," Dan commented, and, no Second Book being at our service, we settled down to Kipling's *Just-So Stories*. Then the billabong "petering out" altogether, and the soakage threatening to follow suit, its yield was kept strictly for personal needs, and Dan and the Maluka gave their attention to the elements.

"Something's got to happen soon," they declared, as we gasped in the stifling calm that had now settled down upon the Territory; for gradually the skirmishings had ceased, and the two great giants of the Territory element met in the centre of the arena for their last desperate struggle. Knee to knee they were standing, marvellously well matched this year, each striving his utmost, and yet neither giving nor taking an inch, and as they strove their satellites watched breathlessly.

Even the Willy-Willys had lain down to watch the silent struggle, and Dan, finding himself left entirely without occupation, "feared he would be taking to book-learning soon if something didn't happen"! "Never knew the showers so late," he growled; and the homestead was inclined to agree that it was the "dead-finish"; but remembering that even then our Fizzer was battling through that last stage of the Dry, we were silent, and Dan, remembering also, devoted himself to the missus, she being also a person of leisure now the Willy-Willys were at rest.

For hours we pitched near the restful green of the melon-beds, and as we pitched the Maluka ran fencing wires through two sides of the garden fence, while Tiddle'ums and Bett-Bett, hovering about him, adapted themselves to the new order of things, finding the line the goats had to stop at no longer imaginary. And as the fence grew, Dan lent a hand here and there; the Rejected and the Staff indulged in glorious washing-days among the lilies of the Reach; Cheon haunted the vegetable patch like a disconsolate ghost; while Billy Muck, the rainmaker, hovered batlike over his melons, lending a hand also with the fence when called upon. As Cheon mourned, his garden also mourned, but when the melons began to mourn, at the Maluka's suggestion, Billy visited the Reach with two buckets, and his usual following of dogs, and after a two-mile walk gave the melons a drink.

Next day Billy Muck pressed old Jimmy into the service and, the Reach being visited twice, the melons received eight buckets of water. Then Cheon tried every wile he knew to secure four buckets for his garden. "Only four," he pleaded, lavish in his bribes. But Billy and Jimmy had "knocked up longa a carry water", and Cheon watched them settle down to smoke on the verge of tears. Then a traveller coming in with the news that heavy rain had fallen in Darwin—news gleaned from the gossiping wire—Cheon was filled with jealous fury at the good fortune of Darwin, and taunted Billy with rain-making taunts. "If he were a rain-maker," he taunted, "he would make a little when he wanted it, instead of walking miles with buckets," and the taunts rankling in Billy's royal soul, he retired to the camp to see about it.

"Hope he does the trick," the traveller said, busy unpacking his team. "Could do with a good bath fairly soon." But Dan cautioned him to "have a care", settling down in the shade to watch proceedings. "These early showers are a bit tricky," he explained; "can't tell how long they'll last. Heard of a chap once who reckoned it was good enough for a bath, but by the time he'd got himself nicely soaped the shower was travelling on ten miles a minute, and there wasn't another drop of rain for a fortnight, which wasn't too pleasant for the prickly heat."

The homestead rubbed its back in sympathy against the nearest upright, and Dan added that "of course, the soap kept the mosquitoes dodged a bit, which was something to be thankful for. There generally is something to be thankful for, if you only reckon it out," he assured all. But the traveller, reduced to a sweltering prickliness by his exertions, wasn't "noticing much at present", as he rubbed his back in his misery against the saddle of the horse he was unpacking. Then his horse, shifting his position, trod on his foot; and as he hopped round, nursing his stinging toes, Dan found an illustration for his argument. "Some chaps," he said, "'ud be thankful to have toes to be trod on"; and ducking to avoid a coming missile, he added cheerfully: "But there's even an advantage about having wooden legs at times. Heard once of a chap that reckoned 'em just the thing. Trod on a death-adder unexpected-like in his camp, and when the death-adder whizzed round to strike, it just struck wood, and the chap enjoyed his supper as usual that night. That chap had a wooden leg," he added, unnecessarily explicit; and then, his argument being nicely rounded off, he lent a hand with the pack-bags.

The traveller filled in Dan's evening, and Neaves's mate coming through next day gave the Quarters a fresh start, and then just before that sun-down we felt the first breath of victory from the monsoon—just a few cool, gusty puffs of wind, that was all, and we ran out to enjoy them, only to scurry back into shelter, for our first shower was with us. In pelting fury it rushed upon us out of the north-west, and rushing upon us, swept over us and away from us into the south-east, leaping from horizon to horizon in the triumph of victory.

As a matter of course, it left a sweltering awfulness behind it, but it was a promise of better things; and even as Dan was inquiring with a chuckle "whether that chap in the Quarters had got a bath out of it", a second pelting fury rushed over us, filling Cheon's heart with joy, and Billy with importance. Unfortunately it did not fill the water-butts with water, but already the garden was holding up its head, and Billy was claiming that he had scored a win.

"Well?" he said, waylaying Cheon in the garden. "Well, me rain-maker? Eh?" and Cheon's superstitious heart bowed down before such evidence.

A ten-minutes' deluge half an hour later licked up every grain of dust, filled the water-butts to overflowing, brought the insect

pest to life as by magic, left a shallow pool in the heart of the
billabong, and added considerably to Billy's importance.
Had not Brown of the Bulls come in during that ten-minutes'
deluge, Cheon would probably have fallen to offering sacrifices
to Billy. As it was, he could only load him with plum-cake,
before turning his attention to the welcoming of Brown of
the Bulls.

"What was the boss drover's fancy in the way of cooking?"
he inquired of the missus, bent on his usual form of welcome,
and the boss drover, a great burly Queenslander, with a voice
as burly as his frame, answered for himself with a laughing,
"Vegetables; and as many as you think I've room for." Then, as
Cheon gravely measured his inches with his eye, a burly
chuckle shook the boss drover's great frame as he repeated,
"Just as many as you think I can hold," adding in half-apology,
"Been away from women and vegetables for fifteen months."

"That's nothing," we told him, quoting the man from
Beyanst, but hopeful to find the woman placed first. Then,
acting on a hint from Cheon, we took him to the banana clump.

During the evening another five-minutes' deluge gladdened
our hearts, as the "lavender" bugs and other sweet pests of the
Territory insect pest saddened our bodies.

Soon after breakfast-time Happy Dick was across. "To see
how you've fared," he said; and then, to the diversion of Brown
of the Bulls, Cheon and Happy Dick rejoiced together over
the brimming water-butts, and mourned because the billabong
had not done better, regretting the while that the showers were
so "patchy".

Then while Happy Dick was assuring us that "both Warlochs
were bankers", the Sanguine Scot rode in through the slip-rails
at the North track, waving his hat in greeting, and with Bertie
and Bertie's Nellie tailing along behind him.

"Back again!" Mac called, light-hearted as a schoolboy just
escaped from drudgery, while Bertie's Nellie, as a matter of
course, was overcome with ecstatic giggles.

With Mac and the showers with us, we felt there was little
left to wish for, and told Brown of the Bulls that he might now
prepare to enjoy himself, and with a chuckle of anticipation,

Brown "hoped" the entertainment would prove "up to samples already met with", as he could "do with a little enjoyment for a change".

22

As a matter of course, Bertie's Nellie quietly gathered the reins of management into her own hands, and, as a matter of course, Jimmy's Nellie indulged in ear-splitting continuous protest, and Brown of the Bulls expressed himself as satisfied, so far, with the entertaining powers of the homestead.

As a matter of course, we left the servant problem to work out its own solution, and, also as a matter of course, the Sanguine Scot was full of plans for the future, but particularly bubbling over with the news that he had secured Tam-o'-Shanter for a partner in the brumby venture.

"He'll be along in a few days," he explained, confident that he was "in luck this time all right", and remembering Tam among the horses at the Katherine, we congratulated him.

As a matter of course, our conversation was all of brumbies, and Mac was also convinced that "when you reckoned everything up, there was a good thing in it".

"Of course, it'll take a bit of jumping round," he agreed. But the Wet was to be devoted to the building of a strong holding-yard, a "trap", and a "wing", so as to be able to get going directly the Wet lifted; and knowing the run well, and the extent of the brumby mobs on it, Mac then and there set to work to calculate the "sized mob" that could be "got together after the Wet", listening with interest to the account of our brumby encounters out east.

But long before we had done with brumbies Cheon was announcing dinner in his own peculiar way.

"Din-ner! Mis-sus! Boss! All about!" he chanted, standing in the open doorway nearest to us; and as we responded to his call, he held open the door of the dining-net and glided into the details of his menu: "Veg-e-table Soooup!" he sang. "Ro-oast Bee-ef! Pee-es! Bee-ens! Too-martoos! Mar-row!" and listening, we felt Brown of the Bulls was being right royally welcomed with as many vegetables as were good for him. But the sweets shrank into a simple "bakee custard".

"This is what you might call style!" Mac and Brown of the Bulls declared, as Cheon waved them to seats with the air of an Emperor, and for two courses the dinner went forward according to its menu, but at the third course tinned peaches had usurped the place of the "bakee custard".

Everyone looked surprised, but, being of the bush-folk, accepted peaches and cream without comment, until Cheon, seeing the surprise, and feeling an explanation was due—anyway, to the missus—bent over her and whispered in a hoarse aside, "Pussy-cat been tuck-out custard."

For a moment the bushmen bent over their plates, intent on peaches and cream; but there was a limit to even a bushman's dignity, and with a choking gulp Mac exploded, and Brown of the Bulls, joining in with a roar, dragged down the Maluka's self-control; and as Cheon reiterated, "What name all about laugh, missus," chuckled in sympathy himself. Brown of the Bulls pulled himself together for a moment, once more to assure us that he was "satisfied so far".

But the day's entertainment was only just beginning, for after comparing weights and heights, Mac, Jack, Dan, and Brown of the Bulls entered into a trial of strength, and a heavy rail having been brought down from the stock-yard, the "caber" was tossed before an enthusiastic company. The homestead thoroughfare was the arena, and around it stood or sat the onlookers: the Quarters, travellers, Happy Dick, some of the Line Party, the Maluka, the missus, and others, and as the caber pitched and tossed, Cheon came and went, cheering every throw lustily with charming impartiality, beating up a frothy cake mixture the while, until, finally, the cakes being in the oven, he was drawn, with others, into the competition.

A very jaunty, confident Cheon entered the lists, but a very surprised, chagrined Cheon retired in high dudgeon. "What's 'er matter!" he said indignantly. "Him too muchee heavy fellow. S'pose him little fellow, me chuck him all right," explaining a comical failure with even more comical explanations. Soon after the retirement of our crestfallen Cheon, hot cakes were served by a Cheon all rotundity and chuckles once more, but immediately afterwards a snort of indignation riveted our attention on an exceedingly bristling, dignified Cheon, who was glaring across the enclosure at two of our neighbour's black boys, one of whom was the bearer of a letter, and the other, of a long yellow vegetable marrow.

Right up to the house verandah they came, and the letter was presented to the Maluka, and the marrow to the missus in the presence of Cheon's glare and an intense silence; for most of the bush-folk had heard of the cabbage insult. Cheon had seen to that.

"Hope you will wish me luck while enjoying my little gift," said the letter, and mistaking its double meaning, I felt really vexed with our neighbour, and passing the marrow to Cheon reflected a little on his bristling dignity as I said, "This is of no use to anyone here, Cheon; you had better take it away"; and as Cheon accepted it with a grateful look, those about the verandah, and those without the garden, waited expectantly.

But there was to be no unseemly rage this time. In dignified silence Cheon received the marrow—a sinuous yellow insult; and as the homestead waited he raised it above his head, and stalking majestically from us towards the finished part of the fence flung it from him in contemptuous scorn, adding a satisfied snort as the marrow, striking the base of a fence-post, burst asunder, and the next moment, after a flashing swoop, he was grovelling under the wires, making frantic efforts to reach a baby bottle of whisky that had rolled from within the marrow away beyond the fence. "Cognac!" he gasped, as he struggled, and then, as shouts greeted his speedy success, he sat up, adding comically: "My word! Me close up smash him Cognac." At the thought came his inevitable laughter; and as he leant against the fence-post, surrounded by the shattered marrow, he sat hopelessly gurgling, and choking, and shaking, and hugging his bottle, the very picture of a dissolute old Bacchanalian. (Cheon would have excelled as a rapid change artist.) And as Cheon gurgled, and spluttered, and shook, the homestead rocked with yells of delight, while Brown of the Bulls rolled and writhed in a canvas lounge, gasping between his shouts: "Oh, chase him away, somebody; cover him up. Where *did* you catch him?"

Finally Cheon scrambled to his feet, and, perspiring and exhausted, presented the bottle to the Maluka. "My word, me cross fellow!" he said weakly, and then, bubbling over again at the recollection, he chuckled, "Close up smash him Cognac all right." And at the sound of the chuckle, Brown of the Bulls broke out afresh.

"Chase him away!" he yelled. "You'll kill me between you! I never struck such a place! Is it a circus or a Wild West Show?"

Gravely the Maluka accepted the bottle, and with the same mock gravity answered Brown of the Bulls. "It is neither, my man," he said; "neither a circus, nor a Wild West Show. This is the land the poets sing about, the land where dull despair is king."

Brown of the Bulls naturally wished "some of the poets were about now", and Dan, having joined the house-party, found a fitting opportunity to air one of his pet grievances.

"I've never *done* wishing some of them town chaps that write bush yarns 'ud come along and learn a thing or two," he said. "Most of 'em seem to think that when we're not on the drink we're whipping the cat or committing suicide." Rarely had Dan any excuse to offer for those "town chaps", who, without troubling to learn "a thing or two" first, depict the bush as a pandemonium of drunken orgies, painted women, low revenge, remorse, and suicide; but being in a more magnanimous mood than usual, as the men-folk flocked towards the Quarters he waited behind to add, unconscious of any irony, "Of course, seeing it's what they're used to in town, you can't expect 'em to know any better."

Then in the Quarters "Luck to our neighbour" was the

toast—"luck", and the hope that all his ventures might be as successfully carried through as his practical joke. After that the Maluka gravely proposed "Cheon", and Cheon instantly became statuesque and dignified, accepting a thimbleful for himself, and, as gravely, drinking his own health, the Maluka just as gravely "clinking glasses" with him. And from that day to this when Cheon wishes to place the Maluka on a fitting pedestal, he ends his long, long tale with a triumphant, "Boss bin knock glass longa me one time."

Happy Dick and Peter filled in time for the Quarters until sun-down, when Cheon announced supper there with an inspired call of "Cognac!" And then, as if to prove that we are not always on the drink, or "whipping the cat, or committing suicide", that we can love and live for others besides self, Neaves's mate came down from the little rise beyond the slip-rails, where he had spent his day carving a headstone out of a rough slab of wood that now stood at the head of our sick traveller's grave.

Not always on the drink, or whipping the cat, or committing suicide, but too often at the Parting of the Ways, for within another twelve hours the travellers, Happy Dick, the Line Party, Neaves's mate, Brown of the Bulls, and Mac had all gone or were going their ways, leaving us to go ours—Brown back to hold his bulls at the Red Lilies until further showers should open up all roads, and Mac to "pick up Tam". But in the meantime, Dan had become Showman of the Showers.

"See anything?" he asked, soon after sun-up, waving his hands towards the northern slip-rails, as we stood at the head of the thoroughfare speeding our parting guests; and then he drew attention to the faintest greenish tinge throughout the homestead enclosure—such a clean-washed-looking enclosure now.

"That's going to be grass soon," he said, and, the sun coming out with renewed vigour after another shower, by midday he had gathered a handful of tiny blades half an inch in length with a chuckling, "What did I tell you?"

By the next midday, grass, inches tall, was rippling all around the homestead in the now prevalent north-west breeze, and

Dan was preparing for a trip out-bush to see where the showers had fallen, and Mac and Tam coming in as he went out, Mac greeted us with a jocular, "The flats get greener every year about the Elsey."

"Indeed!" we said, and Mac, overcome with confusion, spluttered an apology: "Oh, I say! Look here! I didn't mean to hit off at the missus, you know!" and then, catching the twinkle in Tam's eyes, stopped short, and with a characteristic shrug "reckoned he was making a fair mess of things".

Mac would never be other than our impetuous Brither Scot, distinct from all other men, for the bush never robs her children of their individuality. In some mysterious way, she clean-cuts out the personality of each of them, and keeps it sharply clean-cut; and just as Mac stood apart from all men, so Tam also stood apart, the quiet, self-reliant man, though, we had seen among the horses, for that was the real man; and as Mac built castles, and made calculations, Tam put his shoulder to the drudgery, and before Mac quite knew what had happened, he was hauling logs and laying foundations for a brumby trap in the south-east country, while Bertie's Nellie found herself obliged to divide her attention between the homestead and the brumby camp.

As Mac hauled and drudged, the melons paid their first dividend; half past eleven four weeks drew near; *Just-So Stories* did all they could, and Dan coming in found the Quiet Stockman away back in the days of old, deep in a simply written volume of Scottish history.

Dan had great news of the showers, but had to find other audience than Jack; for he was away in a world all his own and, bent over the little volume, was standing shoulder to shoulder with his Scottish fathers, fighting with them for his nation. All evening, he followed where they led, enduring and suffering, and mourning with them, and rejoicing over their final victory with a ringing "You can't beat the Scots," as the little volume, coming to with a bang, roused the Quarters at midnight.

"You can't beat the Scots, missus!" he repeated, coming over in the morning for "more of that sort", all unconscious how true he was to type, as he stood there, flushed with the victories of his forefathers, a strong, young Scot, with a newly conquered world of his own at his feet.

As we hunted for "more of that sort", through a medley of odds and ends, the Quiet Stockman scanned titles, and dipped here and there into unknown worlds, and Dan, coming by, stared open-eyed.

"You don't say he's got the whole mob mouthed and reined and schooled in all the paces?" he gasped; but Jack put aside the word of praise. "There's writing and spelling yet," he said, and Dan, with his interest in book-learning reviving, watched the square chin setting squarer, and was bewildered. "Seems to have struck a mob of brumbies," he commented.

But before Jack could "get properly going" with the brumbies, two travellers rode into the homestead, supporting between them a third rider, a man picked up off the track delirious with fever, and foodless; and at the sight of his ghastly face our hearts stood still with fear. But the man was one of the Scots—another Mac—of the race that loves a good fight, and his plucky heart stood by him so well that within twenty-four hours he was lying contentedly in the shade of the Quarters, looking on, while the homestead shared the Fizzer's welcome with Mac and Tam and a traveller or two.

Out of the south came the Fizzer, lopping once more in his saddle, with the year's dry stages behind him, and the set lines all gone from his shoulders, shouting as he came: "Hullo! What-ho! Here's a crowd of us!" But on his return trip the Fizzer was a man of leisure, and we had to wait for news until his camp was fixed up.

"Now for it!" he shouted, at last joining the company, and Mac felt the time was ripe for his jocular greeting and, ogling the Fizzer, noticed that "the flats get greener every year about the Elsey".

But the Fizzer was a dangerous subject to joke with. "So I've noticed," he shouted as, improving on Mac's ogle, he singled him out from the company, then, dropping his voice to an insinuating drawl, he challenged him to have a deal.

Instantly the Sanguine Scot became a Canny Scot, for Mac

prided himself on a horse-deal. And as no one had yet got the better of the Fizzer, the company gathered round to enjoy itself.

"A swop," suggested the Fizzer, and Mac agreeing with a "Right-ho!" a preliminary handshake was exchanged before "getting to business"; and then, as each made a great pretence of mentally reviewing his team, each eyed the other with the shrewdness of a fighting cock.

"My brown mare," Mac offered at last; and knowing the staunch little beast, the homestead wondered what Mac had up his sleeve.

We explained our suspicions in asides to the travellers, but the Fizzer seemed taken by surprise. "By George!" he said. "She's a stunner! I've nothing fit to put near her excepting that upstanding chestnut down there."

The chestnut was standing near the creek-crossing, and everyone knowing him well, and sure that "something" was up Mac's sleeve, feared for the Fizzer as Mac's hand came out with a "Done!" and the Fizzer gripped it with a clinching "Right-ho!"

Naturally we waited for the *dénouement*, and the Fizzer appearing unsuspicious and well-pleased with the deal, we turned our attention to the Sanguine Scot.

Mac felt the unspoken flattery, and with an introductory cough, and a great show of indifference, said: "By the way! Perhaps I should have mentioned it, but the brown mare's down with the puffs since the showers," and looked around the company for approval.

But the Fizzer was filling the homestead with shoutings. "Don't apologize," he yelled. "That's nothing! The chestnut's just broken his leg; can't think how he got here. This'll save me the trouble of shooting him." Then dropping back to that chuckling drawl, and reassuming the ogle, he added, "The— flats—get—greener—every—year—about—the Elsey," and with a good-humoured laugh Mac asked if "any other gentleman felt on for a swop".

Naturally, for a while the conversation was all of horse deals, until, Happy Dick coming in, it turned as naturally to dog-fights, as Peter and Brown stalked aggressively about the thoroughfare.

Daily we hinted to Happy Dick that Peter's welcome was wearing out, and daily Happy Dick assured us that he "couldn't keep him away nohow". But then Happy Dick's efforts to keep him away were peculiar, taking the form of monologues as Peter trotted beside him towards the homestead—reiterations of:

"We're not the sort to say nuff, are we, Peter? We'll never say die, will we, Peter? We'll win if we don't lose, won't we, Peter?" Adding, after his arrival at the homestead, a subdued "S—s—ss, go it, Peter!" whenever Brown appeared in the thoroughfare.

But the homestead's hour of triumph was at hand, for as the afternoon wore on, Happy Dick found the best told recital a poor substitute for the real thing, and thirsting for a further "Peter's latest", hissed "S—ss—s, go it, Peter!" once too often. For, well, soon afterwards—figuratively speaking—Peter was carried off the field on a stretcher.

True, Brown had only one sound leg left to stand on, but by propping the other three carefully against it, he managed to cut a fairly triumphant figure. But Brown's victory was not to be all advantage to the homestead, for never again were we to hear "Peter's latest".

"Can't beat the Elsey for a good dog-fight! Can you, Peter!" the Fizzer chuckled, as Peter lay licking his wounds at Happy Dick's feet; but the Quarters, feeling the pleasantry ill-timed, delicately led the conversation to cribbage, and at sun-up next morning Happy Dick "did a get" to his work, with bulging pockets, leaving the Fizzer packing up and declaring that "half a day at the Elsey gave a man a fresh start".

But Dan also was packing up—a "duplicate" brought in by the Fizzer having necessitated his presence in Darwin, and as he packed up he assured us he would be back in time for the Christmas celebrations, even if he had to swim for it; but before he left he paid a farewell visit to the Christmas dinner. "In case of accidents," he explained, "mightn't see it again. Looks like another case of one apiece," he added, surveying with interest the plumpness of six young pullets Cheon was cherishing under a coop.

"Must have pullet longa Clisymus," Cheon had said, and all readily agreeing, "Of course!" he added, "Must have really good Clisymus"; and another hearty "Of course" convincing him we were at one with him in the matter of Christmas, he entered into details.

"Must have big poodinn, and almond, and Clisymus cake, and mince pie," he chuckled, and then, after confiding to us that he had heard of the prospective glories of a Christmas dinner at the Pine Creek "Pub", the heathen among us urged us to do honour to the Christian festival.

"Must have top-fellow Clisymus longa Elsey," he said, and even more heartily we agreed, "Of course," giving Cheon *carte blanche* to order everything as he wished us to have it. "We are there to command," we assured him; and accepting our service, Cheon opened the ball by sending the Dandy in to the Katherine on a flying visit to do a little shopping, and, pending the Dandy's return, we sat down and made plans.

The House and the Quarters should join forces that day, Cheon suggested, and dine under the eastern verandah. "No good two-fellow dinner longa Clisymus," he said. And the blacks, too, must be regaled in their humpy. "Must have Vealer longa black fellow Clisymus," Cheon ordered, and Jack's services being bespoken for Christmas Eve, to "round up a Vealer", it was decided to add a haunch of "Vealer" to our menu as a trump card—Vealers being rarities at Pine Creek. Our only regret was that we lived too far from civilization to secure a ham. Pine Creek would certainly have a ham; but we had a Vealer and faith in Cheon, and waited expectantly for the Dandy, sure the Elsey would "come out top-fellow".

And as we waited for the Dandy, the Line Party moved on to our northern boundary, taking with it possible Christmas guests; the Fizzer came in and went on, to face a "merry Christmas with damper and beef served in style on a pack-bag", also regretting empty mail-bags—the Southern mail having been delayed *en route*. Tam and the Sanguine Scot accepted invitations to the Christmas dinner; and the Wet broke in one terrific thunder-clap, as the heavens, opening, emptied a deluge over us.

In that mighty thunderclap the Wet rushed upon us with a roar of falling waters, and with them Billy Muck appeared at the house verandah dripping like a beaver, to claim further credit.

"Well?" he said again. "Me rainmaker, eh?" and the Maluka shouted above the roar and din:

"You're the boy for my money, Billy! Keep her going!" and Billy kept her going to such purpose that by sun-up the billabong was a banker, Cheon was moving over the face of the earth with the buoyancy of a child's balloon, and Billy had five inches of rain to his credit. (So far, eleven inches was the Territory record for one night.) Also the fringe of birds was back at the billabong, having returned with as little warning as it had left, and once more its ceaseless chatter became the undertone of the homestead.

At sun-up Cheon had us in his garden, sure now that Pine Creek could not possibly outdo us in vegetables, and the Dandy coming in with every commission fulfilled, we felt ham was a mere detail.

But Cheon's cup of happiness was to brim over that day, for after answering every question hurled at him, the Dandy sang cheerfully, "He put in his thumb and pulled out a plum", and dragged forth a ham from its hiding-place, with a laughing, "What a good boy am I!"

With a swoop Cheon was on it, and the Dandy, trying to regain it, said: "Here, hold hard! I've to present it to the missus with a bow and the compliments of Mine Host." But Cheon would not part with it, and so the missus had the bow and the compliments, and Cheon the ham.

Lovingly he patted it and asked us if there ever was such a ham, or ever such a wonderful man as Mine Host, or ever such a fortunate woman as the missus. Had any other woman such a ham or such a friend in need? And bubbling over with affection for the whole world, he sent Jackeroo off for mistletoe, and presently the ham, all brave in Christmas finery, was hanging like a gay wedding-bell in the kitchen doorway.

Then the kitchen had to be decorated, also in mistletoe, to make a fitting setting for the ham, and after that the fiat went forth. No one need expect either eggs or cream before "Clisymus"—excepting, of course, the sick Mac—he must be kept in condition to do justice to our "Clisymus" fare.

What a week it was—all festivities, and meagre fare, and whirring egg-beaters, and thunderstorms, and downpours, and water-melon dividends, and daily visits to the vegetable patch; where Happy Dick was assured, during a flying visit, that we were sure of seven varieties of vegetables for "Clisymus".

But alas for human certainty! Even then swarms of grasshoppers were speeding towards us, and by sun-down were with us.

In vain Cheon and the Staff, the Rejected, Bett-Bett, every shadow and the missus, danced war-dances in the vegetable patch, and chivvied and chased, and flew all ways at once; the grasshoppers had found greenstuff exactly to their liking, and coming in clouds, settled, and feasted, and flew upwards, and settled back, and feasted, and swept on, leaving poor Cheon's heart as barren of hope as the garden was of vegetables. Nothing remained but pumpkins, sweet potatoes, and Cheon's tardy water-melons, and the sight of the glaring blotches of pumpkins filled Cheon with fury.

"Pumpee-kin for Clisymus!" he raved, kicking furiously at the hideous wens. Not if he knew it! and going to some stores left in our care by the Line Party, he openly stole several tins of preserved vegetables. "Must have vegetable longa Clisymus," he said, feeling his theft amply justified by circumstances, but salved his conscience by sending a gift of eggs to the Line Party as a donation towards its "Clisymus".

Then finding everyone sympathetic, he broached a delicate subject. By some freak of chance, he said, the missus was the only person who had succeeded in growing good melons this year, and taking her to the melon beds, which the grasshoppers had also passed by, he looked longingly at three great fruits that lay like mossy green boulders among the rich foliage. "Just chance," he reiterated, and surely the missus would see that

chance also favoured our "Clisymus". "A Clisymus without
dessert would be no Clisymus at all," he continued, pressing
each fruit in turn between loving hands until it squeaked in
response. "Him close up ripe, missus. Him sing out!" he said,
translating the squeak.

But the missus appeared strangely inattentive, and in
desperation Cheon humbled himself and apologized handsomely for former scoffings. Not chance, he said, but genius!
Never was there white woman like the missus. "Him savey
all about," he assured the Maluka. "Him plenty savey gardin."
Further, she was a woman in a thousand! A woman all China
would bow down to! Worth ninety-one hundred pounds in any
Chinese matrimonial market. "A valuable asset," the Maluka
murmured.

It was impossible to stand against such flattery. Billy Muck
was hastily consulted, and out of his generous heart voted two of
the mossy bounders to the white folk, keeping only one for
"black fellow all about". Poor old Billy! He was to pay dearly
for his leaning to the white folk.

Nothing was amiss now but Dan's non-appearance; and the
egg-beater whirring merrily on, by Christmas Eve the Dandy
and Jack, coming in with wild duck for breakfast and the
Vealer, found the kitchen full of triumphs and Cheon wrestling
with an immense pudding. "Four dozen egg sit down," he
chuckled, beating at the mixture. "One bottle port wine,
almond, raisin, all about, more better'n Pine Creek all right";
and the homestead, taking a turn at the beating "for luck",
assured him that it "knocked spots off Pine Creek".

"Must have money longa poodin'!" Cheon added, and our
wealth lying also in a cheque-book, it was not until after a
careful hunt that two threepenny bits were produced, when
one, with a hole in it, went in "for luck", and the other followed
as an omen for wealth.

The threepenny bits safely in, it took the united efforts of
the homestead to get the pudding into a cloth and thence into
a boiler, while Cheon explained that it would have been larger
if only we had had a larger boiler to hold it. As it was, it had to
be boiled out in the open, away from the buildings, where

Cheon had constructed an ingenious trench to protect the fire from rain and wind.

Four dozen eggs in a pudding necessitates an all-night boiling, and because of this we offered to share "watches" with Cheon, but were routed in a body. We were "better in bed", he said. What would happen to his dinner if anyone's appetite failed for want of rest? There were too few of us as it was, and, besides, he would have to stay up all night in any case, for the mince pies were yet to be made, in addition to brownie and another plum pudding for the "boys", to say nothing of the hop beer, which if made too soon would turn with the thunder and if made too late would not "jump up" in time. He did not add that he would have trusted no mortal with the care of the fires that night.

He did add, however, that it would be as well to dispatch the Vealer overnight, and that an early move (about fowl-sing-out) would not be amiss; and, always obedient to Cheon's will, we all turned in, in good time, and becoming drowsy, dreamed of "watching" great mobs of Vealers, with each Vealer endowed with a plum pudding for a head.

23

At earliest dawn we were awakened by wild, despairing shrieks, and were instinctively groping for our revolvers when we remembered the fatted fowls and Cheon's lonely vigil, and turning out, dressed hastily, realizing that Christmas had come, and the pullets had sung their last "sing-out".

When we appeared the stars were still dimly shining, but Cheon's face was as luminous as a full moon, as, greeting each and all of us with a "Melly Clisymus", he suggested a task for each and all. Some could see about taking the Vealer down from the gallows; six lubras were "rounded up" for the plucking of the pullets, while the rest of us were sent out, through wet grass and thicket, into the cold, grey dawn, to gather in "big, big-mob bough and mistletoe", for the beautifying of all things.

How we worked! With Cheon at the helm, everyone was of necessity enthusiastic. The Vealer was quartered in double-quick time, and the first fitful rays of sunlight found their way to the Creek crossing to light up an advancing forest of boughs and mistletoe clumps that moved forward on nimble black legs.

In a gleaming, rustling procession the forest of green boughs advanced, all crimson-flecked with mistletoe and sunlight, and prostrated itself around us in mighty heaps at the head of the homestead thoroughfare. Then the nimble black legs becoming miraculously endowed with nimble black bodies and arms, soon the gleaming boughs were piled high upon the iron roof of the Eastern verandah to keep our impromptu dining-hall cool and fresh. High above the roof rose the greenery, and over the edge of the verandah, throughout its length, hung a deep fringe of green, reaching right down to the ground at the posts; everywhere among the boughs trailed long strands of bright red mistletoe, while within the leafy bower itself, hanging four feet deep from the centre of the high roof, one dense elongated mass of mistletoe swayed gently in the breeze, its heaped-up scarlet blossoms clustering about it like a swarm of glorious bees.

Cheon interrupted the decorations with a call to "Bress-fass! Duck cully and lice," he sang boldly, and then followed in a doubtful, hesitating quaver: "I think—sausage. Must have sausage for Clisymus bress-fass," he said emphatically, as he ushered us to seats, and we agreed with our usual "Of course!" But we found fried balls of minced collops, which Cheon hastened to explain *would* have been sausages if only he had had skins to pack them into.

"Him close up sausage!" he assured us, but that anxious quaver was back in his voice, and to banish all clouds from his loyal old heart, we ate heartily of the collops, declaring they were sausages in all *but* skins. Skins, we persuaded him, were merely appendages to sausages, barriers, in fact, between men and delectable feasts; and satisfied that we were satisfied, he became all beams once more, and called our attention to the curried duck.

The duck discussed, he hinted that dinner was the be-all and end-all of "Clisymus", and, taking the hint, we sent the preparations merrily forward.

Every chair and stool on the run was mustered; two tables were placed end to end beneath that clustering mistletoe and covered with clean white tablecloths—remembering the story of the rags and hobble rings we refrained from serviettes—the hop beer was set in canvas water-bags to keep it cool; and Cheon pointing out that the approach from the kitchens was not all that could be desired, an enormous tent-fly was stretched away from the roof of the verandah, extending it half-way to the kitchen, and further greenery was used, decorating it within and without to make it a fitting passage-way for the transport of Cheon's triumphs. Then Cheon's kitchen decorations were renewed and added to; and after that further suggestions suggested and attended to. Everything that could be done was done, and by eight o'clock all was ready for Cheon's triumphs, all but our appetites and time of day.

· By nine o'clock Mac and Tam had arrived, and after every-thing had been sufficiently admired, we trooped in a body to the kitchen, obedient to a call from Cheon.

Triumph after triumph was displayed, and after listening gravely and graciously to our assurances that already every-thing was "more better'n Pine Creek last year", Cheon allowed us a glimpse of the pudding through a cloud of steam, the company standing reverently around the fire trench in a circle as it bent over the bubbling boiler; then scuttling away before us like an old hen with a following of chickens, he led the way to the water-bags, and asked our opinion on the hop-beer. "You think him jump-up longa dinner-time, eh, boss?" he said anxiously, as the Maluka, holding a bottle between us and the light, examined it critically. "Me make him three o'clock longa night-time."

It looked remarkably still and tranquil, but we hoped for the best, and half an hour later were back at the water-bags, called thither to decide whether certain little globules were sediments or air-bubbles. Being sanguine, we decided in favour of bubbles, and in another half-hour were called back again to the bags to see that the bubbles were bubbles indeed, having dropped in at the kitchens on our way to give an opinion on veal stuffing and bread sauce; and within another half-hour were peering into the oven to inspect further triumphs of cooking.

Altogether the morning passed quickly and merrily, any time Cheon left us being spent in making our personal appear-ance worthy of the feast.

Scissors and hand-glasses were borrowed, and hair cut, and chins shaved, until we feared our Christmas guests would look like convicts. Then the Dandy producing blacking brushes, boots that had never seen blacking before, shone like ebony. After that a mighty washing of hands took place, to remove the blacking stain; and then the Quarters settled down to a general "titivation", Tam "cleaning his nails for Christmas", amid great applause.

By eleven o'clock the Dandy was immaculate, the guests satisfied that they "weren't too dusty", while the Maluka in spotless white relieved with a silk cummerbund and tie, bid fair to outdo the Dandy. Even the Quiet Stockman had succeeded in making a soft white shirt "look as though it had been ironed once". And then every lubra being radiant with soap, new dresses, and ribbons, the missus, determined not to be outdone in the matter of Christmas finery, burrowed into trunks and boxes, and appeared in cream washing silk, lace fichu, ribbons, rings, and frivolities—finery, by the way, packed down South for that "commodious station home".

Cheon was enraptured with the appearance of his company, and worked, and slaved, and chuckled in the kitchen as only Cheon could, until at last the critical moment had arrived. Dinner was ready: but an unforeseen difficulty had presented itself. How was it to be announced, Cheon queried, having called the missus to the kitchen for a hasty consultation, for was it wise to puff up the Quarters with a chanted summons?

A compromise being decided on as the only possible course, after the booming teamster's bell had summoned the Quarters, Cheon, all in white himself, bustled across to the verandah to call the gentry to the dinner by word of mouth. "Dinner! Boss! Missus!" he sang—careful to specify his gentry, for not even reflected glory was to be shed over the Quarters. Then, moving in and out among the greenery as he put finishing touches to the table here and there, he glided into the wonders of his Christmas menu: "Soo-oup! Chuckie! Ha-am! Roo-oast Veal-er!" he chanted. "Cauli-flower! Pee-es! Bee-ens! Toe-ma-toes! (with a regretful "tinned" in parenthesis)—"Shweet Poo-tay-toes! Bread Sau-ce!" On and on through mince pies, sweets, cakes, and fruits, went the monotonous chant, the Maluka and the missus standing gravely at attention, until a triumphant paean of "Plum-m Poodinn!" soared upwards as Cheon waddled off through the decorated verandah extension for his soup tureen.

But a sudden, unaccountable shyness had come over the

Quarters, and as Cheon trundled away, a hurried argument reached our ears of "Go on! You go first!" "No, you. Here, none of that!"; and then, after a short subdued scuffle, the Dandy, looking slightly dishevelled, came through the doorway with just the suspicion of assistance from within; and the ice being thus broken, the rest of the company came forward in a body and slipped into whichever seat came handiest.

As all of us, with the exception of the Dandy, were Scots, four of us being Macs, the Maluka chose our Christmas grace from Bobby Burns; and quietly and reverently our Scotch hearts listened to those homely words:

> *Some ha'e meat, and canna eat.*
> *And some wad eat that want it;*
> *But we ha'e meat, and we can eat,*
> *And sae the Lord be thankit.*

Then came Cheon's turn, and gradually and cleverly his triumphs were displayed.

To begin with, we were served clear soup—"just to tickle your palates," the Maluka announced, as Cheon in a hoarse whisper instructed him to serve "little-fellow-helps", anxious that none of the keenness should be taken from our appetites. All served, the tureen was whisked away to ensure against further inroads, and then Cheon trundled around the table, removing the soup plates, inquiring of each guest in turn if he found the soup to his liking, and informing all that lubras were on guard in the kitchen, lest the station cats should so far forget themselves as to take an unlawful interest in our dinner.

The soup finished with, Cheon disappeared into the kitchen regions, to reappear almost immediately at the head of a procession of lubras, each of whom carried a *pièce de résistance* to the feast; Jimmy's Nellie leading with the six pullets on one great dish, while Bett-Bett brought up the rear with the bread sauce. On through a vista of boughs and mistletoe came the triumphs—how glad we were the way had been made more worthy of their progress—the lubras, of course, were with them, but we had eyes only for the triumphs. Those pullets all a-row with plump brown breasts bursting with impatience to reveal the snowy flesh within; marching behind them that great sizzling "haunch" of veal, taxing Rosy's strength to the utmost; then Mine Host's crisply crumbled ham trudging along, and filling Bertie's Nellie with delight, with its tightly bunched little wreath of mistletoe usurping the place of the orthodox paper frill; behind again vegetable dishes two abreast, borne by the lesser lights of the Staff (lids off, of course; none of our glory was to be hidden under cover); tailing along with the rejected and gravy boats came laden soup-plates to eke out the supply of vegetable dishes; and, last of all, that creamy delight of bread sauce, borne sedately and demurely by Bett-Bett.

As the triumphs ranged themselves into a semi-circle at the head of the table, our first impulse was to cheer, but obeying a second impulse we did something infinitely better, for, as Cheon relieved his grinning waitresses, we assured him collectively, and individually, and repeatedly that never had anyone seen anything in Pine Creek so glorious as even the dimmest shadow of this feast; and as we reiterated our assurance, I doubt if any man in all the British Empire was prouder or more justified in his pride than our Cheon. Cook and gardener forsooth! Cheon was Cheon, and only Cheon; and there is no word in the English language to define Cheon or the position he filled, simply because there was never another like Cheon.

"Chuckie!" he sang, placing the pullets before the Maluka, and dispatching Jimmy's Nellie for hot plates; "Roast Vealer for Mac," and as Mac smiled and acknowledged the honour, Rosy was dismissed. "Boilee Ham" was allotted to the Dandy, and as Bertie's Nellie scampered away, Cheon announced other triumphs in turn and in order of merit, each of the company receiving a dish also in order of merit: Tam-o'-Shanter contenting himself with the gravy boat, while, from the beginning, the Quiet Stockman had been honoured with the hop-beer.

Long before the last waitress was relieved, the carvers were at work, and the company was bubbling over with merriment.

"Have some veal, chaps?" the Sanguine Scot said, opening the ball by sticking a carving fork into the great joint, and waving the knife in a general way round the company; then as the gravy sizzled out in a steaming gurgle he added invitingly: "Come on, chaps! This is *Veal* prime stuff! None of your staggering Bob tack"; and the Maluka and the Dandy bidding against him, to Cheon's delight, everyone "came on" for some of everything; for veal and ham and chicken and several vegetables and sauces blend wonderfully together when a Cheon's hand has been at the helm.

The higher the plates were piled the more infectious Cheon's chuckle became, until nothing short of a national calamity could have checked our flow of spirits. Mishaps only added to our enjoyment, and when a bottle of hop-beer went off unexpectedly as the Quiet Stockman was preparing to open it, and he, with the best intentions in the world, planted his thumb over the mouth of the bottle, and directed two frothing streams over himself and the company in general, the delight of every-one was unbounded—a delight intensified a hundredfold by Cheon, who, with his last doubt removed, danced and gurgled in the background, chuckling in an ecstasy of joy. "My word, missus! That one beer *plenty* jump up!" As there were no carpets to spoil, and everyone's clothes had been washed again and again, no one's temper was spoiled, and a clean towel quickly repairing all damages, our only regret was that a bottle of beer had been lost.

But the plum-pudding was yet to come, and only Cheon was worthy to carry it to the feast; and as he came through the leafy way, bearing the huge mottled ball, as big as a bullock's head—all ablaze with spirits and dancing light and crowned with mistletoe—it would have been difficult to say which looked most pleased with itself, Cheon or the pudding; for each seemed wreathed in triumphant smiles.

We held our breaths in astonishment, each feeling like the entire Cratchit family rolled into one, and by the time we had recovered speech, Cheon was soberly carrying one third of the pudding to the missus. The Maluka had put it aside on a plate to simplify the serving of the pudding, and Cheon, sure that the Maluka could mean such a goodly slice for no one but the missus, had carried it off.

There were to be no "little-fellow helps" this time. Cheon saw to that, returning the goodly slice to the Maluka under protest, and urging all to return again and again for more. How he chuckled as we hunted for the "luck" and the "wealth", like a parcel of children, passing round bushman jokes as we hunted.

"Too much country to work," said one of the Macs, when after a second helping they were both still "missing". "Covered their tracks all right," said another. The Quiet Stockman "reckoned they were bushed all right". "Going in a circle," the sick Mac suggested, and then a shout went up as the Dandy found the "luck" in his last mouthful.

"Perhaps someone's given the 'wealth' to his dog," Tam suggested, to our consternation; for that was more than possible, as the dogs from time to time had received tit-bits from their masters as a matter of course.

But the man who deserved it most was to find it. As we sat sipping tea, after doing our best with the cakes and water-melons, we heard strange gurgles in the kitchen, and then Cheon appeared choking and coughing, but triumphantly announcing that *he* had found the wealth in his first mouthful. "My word! Me close up gobble him," he chuckled, exhibiting the pudding-coated threepence, and not one of us grudged him his good omens. May they have been fulfilled a thousandfold!

Undoubtedly our Christmas dinner was a huge success— from a black fellow's point of view it was the most sensible thing we Whites had ever organized; for half the Vealer, another huge pudding, several yards of sweet currant "brownie", a new pipe apiece, and a few pounds of tobacco had found their way to the "humpy"; and although headaches may have been in the near future, there was never a heartache among them.

All afternoon we sat and chatted as only the bush-folk can (the bush-folk are only silent when in uncongenial society), "putting in" a fair amount of time writing our names on one page of an autograph album; and as strong, brown hands tried their utmost to honour Christmas Day with "something decent in the way of writing", each man declared that he had never written so badly before, while the company murmured: "Oh, *yours* is all right. Look at mine!"

Jack, however, was the exception; for when his turn came, with quiet humour he "thought that on the whole his was a bit better'n last Christmas", which naturally set us discussing the advantages of "learning"; but when we all agreed "it would be a bit off having to employ a private secretary when you were doing a bit of courting", Jack hastened to assure us that "courting" would never be in *his* line—coming events do not always throw shadows before them. Thus from "learning" we slipped into "courtship" and marriage, and on into life—life and its problems—and, chatting, agreeing that, in spite of, or perhaps *because* of, its many acknowledged disadvantages, the simple, primitive bush-life is the sweetest and best of all—sure that although there may have been more imposing or less unconventional feasts elsewhere that Christmas Day, yet nowhere in all this old round world of ours could there have been a happier, merrier, healthier-hearted gathering. No one was bored. No one wished himself elsewhere. All were sure of their welcome. All were light-hearted and at ease; although no one so far forgot himself as to pour his hop-beer into the saucer in a lady's presence, for, low be it spoken, although the missus had a glass tumbler, there were only two on the run, and the men-folk drank the Christmas healths from cups, and enamel at that; for a Willy-Willy had taken Cheon unaware when he was laden with a tray containing every glass and china cup fate had left us, and, as by a miracle, those two glasses had been saved from the wreckage.

But enamel cups were no hardships to the bush-folk, and besides, nothing inconvenienced us that day—excepting perhaps doing justice to further triumphs at afternoon tea; and all we had to wish for was the company of Dan and the Fizzer.

To add to the general comfort, a gentle north-west breeze blew all through the day, besides being what Bett-Bett called a "shady day", cloudy and cool; and to add to the general rejoicing, before we had quite done with "Clisymus" an extra mail came in per black boy—a mail sent out to us by the "courtesy of our officers" at the Katherine, "seeing some of the packages felt like Christmas".

It came to us on the verandah. Two very full mail-bags borne by two very empty black boys; and in an incredibly short space of time there were two very full black boys, and two very empty mail-bags; for the mail was our delayed mail, and exactly what we wanted, and the boys had found all they wanted at Cheon's hospitable hands.

But even Christmas Days must come to an end; and as the sun slipped down to the west, Mac and Tam "reckoned it was time to be getting a move on"; and as they mounted amid further Christmas wishes, with saddle-pouches bursting with offerings from Cheon for "Clisymus supper", a strange feeling of sadness crept in among us, and we wondered where "we would all be next Christmas". Then our Christmas guests rode out into the forest, taking with them the sick Mac, and as they faded from our sight we knew that the memory of that Christmas Day would never fade out of our lives; for we bush-folk have long memories and love to rest now and then beside the milestones of the past.

24

A day or two after Christmas, Dan came in full of regrets because he had "missed the celebrations", and gratified Cheon's heart with a minute and detailed account of the "Clisymus" at Pine Creek. Then the homestead settled down to the stagnation of the Wet, and as the days and weeks slipped by, travellers came in and went on, and Mac and Tam paid us many visits, as with the weeks we slipped through a succession of anniversaries.

"A year today, Mac, since you sent those telegrams!" we said, near the beginning of those weeks; and, all mock gravity, Mac answered: "Yes! And blocked that Goer! ...Often wondered what happened to her!"

"A year today, gentlemen," I added a few days later, "since you flung that woman across the Fergusson"; and as Mac enjoyed the reminiscence, the Maluka said, "And forgot to fling the false veneer of civilization after her."

A few days later again we were greeting Tam at the homestead. "Just a year ago, Tam," we said, "you were..." but Tam's horse was young and untutored, and getting out of hand, carried Tam away beyond the buildings. "A Tam-o'-Shanter fleeing," the Maluka once more murmured.

Then Dan filled in the days, until one evening just at sundown, when we said:

"A year this sun-down, Dan, since we first sampled one of your dampers," and, chuckling, Dan reviewed the details of that camp, and slipped thence into reviewing education.

235

"Somebody's learned a thing or two since then," he chuckled: "don't notice people catching cows and milking'em round these parts quite so often."

In the morning came the Quiet Stockman's turn. "There's a little brown filly in the mob I'm just beginning on, cut out for the missus," he said, coming to the house on his way to the stockyard, and we went with him to see the bonnie creature.

"She's the sort that'll learn anything," Jack said, his voice full of admiration. "If the missus'll handle her a bit, I'll learn her everything a horse can learn."

"Gipsy," he had named her, and in a little while the pretty creature was "roped" and standing quietly beneath Jack's caressing hand. "Now, missus," he said—and then followed my first lesson in "handling", until the soft brown muzzle was resting contentedly in my hand. "She'll soon follow you," Jack said eagerly; "you ought to come up every day"; and looking up at the glowing, boyish face, I said quietly:

"Just a year today, Jack, since you met us by the roadside," and the strong young giant looked down with an amused light in his eyes. "Just a year", he said, with that quiet smile of his; and that quiet smile, and that amused "Just a year," were more eloquent than volumes of words, and set Dan "reckoning" that "somebody else's been learning a thing or two besides book learning".

But the Dandy was waiting for some tools from the office, and as we went with him he, too, spoke of the anniversaries. "Just a year since you first put foot on this verandah," he said; and that reminiscence brought into the Maluka's eyes that deep look of bush comradeship, as he added, "And became just One of Us."

Before long Mac was reminding us that "a year ago she was wrestling with the servant question", and Cheon coming by, we indulged in a negative anniversary. "A year ago, Cheon," we said, "there was no Cheon in our lives," and Cheon pitied our former forlorn condition as only Cheon could, at the same time asking us what could be expected of one of Sam's ways and caste.

Then other anniversaries crowded on us thick and fast,

and with them there crept into the Territory that scourge of the wet season—malarial dysentery, and travellers coming in stricken-down with it rested a little while before going on again.

But two of these sick travellers went down to the very gates of death, where one, a little Chinaman, slipped through, blessing the "good boss", who treated all men alike, and leaving an echo of the blessing in old Cheon's loyal heart. But the other sick traveller turned back from those open gates, although bowed with the weight of seventy years, and faced life anew, blessing in his turn "the whitest man" those seventy years had known.

Bravely the worn, bowed shoulders took up the burden of life again, and, as they squared to their load, we slipped back to our anniversaries—once more Jack went bush for the schooling of his colts, once more Mac and Dan went into the Katherine to "see about the ordering of stores", Tam going with them; and as they rode out of the homestead, once more we slipped, with the Dandy, into the Land of Wait-a-while—waiting once more for the Wet to lift, for the waggons to come, and for the Territory to rouse itself for another year's work.

Full of bright hopes, we rested in that Land of Wait-a-while, speaking of the years to come, when the bush-folk will have conquered the Never-Never and lain it at the feet of great cities; and, waiting and resting, made merry and planned plans, all unconscious of the great shadow that was even then hovering over us.

25

There is little more to tell. Just that old, old story—that sad refrain of the Kaffir woman that we British-born can conquer anything but Death.

All unaware, that scourge of the Wet crept back to the homestead, and the great Shadow, closing in on us, flung wide those gates of Death once more, and turning, before passing through, beckoned to our Maluka to follow. But at those open gates the Maluka lingered a little while with those who were fighting so fiercely and impotently to close them—lingering to teach us out of his own great faith that "Behind all Shadows standeth God". And then the gates gently closing, a woman stood alone in that little home that had been wrested, so merrily, out of the very heart of Nature.

That is all the world need know. All else lies deep in the silent hearts of the men of the Never-Never—in those great, silent hearts that came in to the woman at her need; came in at the Dandy's call, and went out to her, and shut her in from all the dangers and terrors that beset her, quietly mourning their own loss the while. And as those great hearts mourned ever and anon a long-drawn-out, sobbing cry went up from the camp, as the tribe mourned for their beloved dead—their dead and ours—our Maluka, "the best Boss that ever a man struck"

FINIS